# WAITING
## *Together*

Hope and Healing for Families of Prisoners

# CAROL KENT

## Discovery House
### from Our Daily Bread Ministries

*To family members and friends of the incarcerated.*
*Let's wait together as we choose fresh hope,*
*renewed courage, and an enduring faith.*

Discovery House is affiliated with Our Daily Bread Ministries,
Grand Rapids, Michigan.

Requests for permission to quote from this book should be directed to:
Permissions Department, Discovery House, P.O. Box 3566, Grand Rapids,
MI 49501, or contact us by e-mail at permissionsdept@dhp.org.

All Scripture quotations, unless otherwise indicated, are taken from the Holy
Bible, New International Version®, NIV®. Copyright © 1973, 1978, 1984, 2011 by
Biblica, Inc.™ Used by permission of Zondervan. All rights reserved worldwide.
www.zondervan.com. The "NIV" and "New International Version" are trademarks
registered in the United States Patent and Trademark Office by Biblica, Inc.™

Scripture quotations marked ESV are from The Holy Bible, English Standard Version® (ESV®), copyright © 2001 by Crossway, a publishing ministry
of Good News Publishers. Used by permission. All rights reserved.

Scripture quotations marked KJV are from the King James Version.

Scripture quotations marked MSG are from *The Message.* Copyright
© by Eugene H. Peterson 1993, 1994, 1995, 1996, 2000, 2001,
2002. Used by permission of Tyndale House Publishers, Inc.

Scripture quotations marked NASB are from the New American Standard
Bible®, copyright © 1960, 1962, 1963, 1968, 1971, 1972, 1973, 1975, 1977, 1995
by The Lockman Foundation. Used by permission. (www.Lockman.org)

Scripture quotations marked NLT are taken from the *Holy Bible,*
New Living Translation, copyright © 1996, 2004, 2007, 2013 by
Tyndale House Foundation. Used by permission of Tyndale House
Publishers, Inc., Carol Stream, Illinois 60188. All rights reserved.

Scripture quotations marked TLB are taken from *The Living Bible*
copyright © 1971. Used by permission of Tyndale House Publishers,
Inc., Carol Stream, Illinois 60188. All rights reserved.

Library of Congress Cataloging-in-Publication Data

Kent, Carol, 1947- author.
Waiting together : hope and healing for families of prisoners / Carol Kent.
Description: Grand Rapids : Discovery House, 2016.
Identifiers: LCCN 2015045929 | ISBN 9781627074124
Subjects: LCSH: Imprisonment--Religious aspects--Christianity. | Prisoners
    families--Prayers and devotions. | Prisoners families--Religious life.
Classification: LCC HV8687 .K46 2016 | DDC 248.8/6--dc23
LC record available at http://lccn.loc.gov/201504592

Interior designed by Sherri L. Hoffman

Printed in the United States of America
First printing in 2016

# CONTENTS

## PART 4: HOLDING ON TO HOPE

## PART 5: IMPORTANT QUESTIONS

## PART 6: DEALING WITH THE NEGATIVES

## PART 7: MAKING GOOD CHOICES

## PART 8: UNEXPECTED SURPRISES

## PART 9: WAITING IS HARD

## PART 10: NEW OPPORTUNITIES

## PART 11: SURVIVAL TOOL BOX

## PART 12: FIND GOD IN THE MESS

## PART 13: WHERE DO WE GO FROM HERE?

# INTRODUCTION

We were in shock. Our only child had been arrested and my husband and I didn't know what to think, who to call, or what practical steps to take. We didn't know anyone in our circle of friends who had experienced what we were going through. We had no idea where to turn for helpful advice or how we could pay for legal fees. We were paralyzed with fear over what might happen to our son. It was the most shocking, confusing, and hurtful experience we'd ever faced—and initially, even with the support of our immediate family members, we felt so very alone.

Our emotions were intense. We were embarrassed and ashamed, and we didn't know who we could trust or who might have already heard rumors about our story. We felt like hiding, but we still needed to make a living—and that meant facing the public. At times we felt incapable of making the simplest decisions. At other times we put on plastic smiles and did "the next thing" with determination amid the anguish. Our emotions were unpredictable: sometimes I wanted to cry but no tears would come, and sometimes tears plummeted down my cheeks at embarrassing and unexpected moments. There were moments when my husband, Gene, and I would just hold each other and sob.

Who could we talk to who would really "get" what we were experiencing? We didn't know of any resources, written by family members of inmates, that would give us practical advice and encouragement for our journey—a journey we never wanted and certainly didn't expect. But somehow we kept moving forward, trying to learn what we could from Internet articles, jail and prison ministries, and individuals we met as we visited our son.

We often felt overwhelmed. When we called the jail (and eventually the prison), we sometimes received conflicting answers to our questions depending on who was on duty. We met some friendly, compassionate employees who were extremely helpful, and we dealt with others who were just putting in their time. They would provide the least amount of information possible.

Our frustrations grew, but we slowly learned how to make it one day at a time. We met more people who had family members who were prisoners. As we waited in long lines to be processed into the visitation room, we shared stories with other families, learning important information on how to advocate for our incarcerated love ones. We started a journal about our emotions and experiences, and we began typing up helpful tips, placing them in a file on our computer. I called it "The Fire File," because the emotional pain we were going through made me feel like I was walking on hot coals in the middle of a raging fire of negative experiences.

Gene and I are people of faith, so we also made a record of lessons God was teaching us as we lived our "new kind of normal," one we never would have picked, but prayed we wouldn't waste. We learned two important things. First, when you have an incarcerated loved one, you do a lot of waiting—waiting for a trial, waiting for a plea bargain or a jury to make a decision, waiting for a sentence, waiting for a sentence to end, waiting in visitation lines, waiting for resolution in your life. The second and most important thing we learned is that it's a lot easier to wait with someone else—waiting *together*, rather than waiting alone.

In this book you'll learn about my journey as I became the mother of an inmate. I'll share honest stories of our struggle—from the unexpected shock of the news of the arrest, through our long journey with the legal process, all the way to a sentence that left us in emotional shambles. I'll try to be as vulnerable as possible, and I invite you to read these articles as if they come from a friend who understands the tough experience you're going through.

Each article begins with a story—sometimes my own and occasionally that of other family members of inmates or even prisoners themselves. The next section will give some application and advice for the topic being discussed that I hope you'll find practical, helpful, and uplifting. In some of the articles you'll find tips about what you can specifically *do* to be an advocate for your loved one.

You'll discover I don't always have answers for the questions I ask, but I promise you'll find hope and helpful advice for the situation you're facing. Most importantly, I hope this book will be an encouragement to embrace the spiritual part of this journey.

At the end of each entry you'll find a section called "His Words over You." One of the most helpful things I've found to keep myself moving forward is to read the Bible and then write down what I believe God wants me to understand as a result of what I'm experiencing and learning. My words aren't inspired, but what I write in that section is based on Scripture—and I hope the personalization will help you to know you're not alone and that you *will* get through this!

How should you use this book? Read it in the way that will be most helpful to you. Of course, it can be read straight through as you would normally read any book. But some may want to read it one day at a time for ninety days. This may be helpful if you're early in your own process, as the first part of the book details the chronology of our own experience. Or you may want to look at the table of contents and go directly to a topic you're dealing with right now. Perhaps your family can read one article at the end of a meal, like a daily devotional, and then discuss your own experiences and what you're learning.

However you choose to go through this book, my prayer is that you'll know you're not alone. There are many people who have experienced what you're going through—and we're still alive. You'll live through this too. Be encouraged! We're always *better together!*

# 1. The Call that Changed Everything

*God has mercifully ordered that the human brain works*
*slowly; first the blow, hours afterwards the bruise.*

WALTER DE LA MARE

The sound was loud. Disruptive. Piercing. Waking from a sound sleep, I realized it was the phone in our bedroom. The clock said 12:35 a.m. As my husband, Gene, answered the call, he turned on the light. Something was wrong. His face was ashen and his eyes filled with tears. Pulling the receiver away from his ear, he spoke shocking words: "Jason has just been arrested for the murder of his wife's first husband. He's in the jail in Orlando."

How could this be happening? Our only child had always been a good kid. In high school, he was president of the National Honor Society. He was now a U.S. Naval Academy graduate with an exciting military career ahead. Jason had a beautiful wife and two adorable stepdaughters—a charming, six-year-old princess-in-training and a precocious, high-spirited, hilariously funny three-year-old. Could this be a mistake? Could it be a horrific nightmare?

I sat up as waves of nausea swept over me. Getting out of bed, I discovered my legs could not hold the weight of my body and I slumped to the floor. Crawling to my office, thoughts swirled: *Carol, this is a dream—a very bad dream. You will soon wake up and everything will be okay.* But everything was far from okay.

Still on the floor, I pulled the phone off my desk and dialed information to get the number for the Orlando jail. I chose the "immediate connection" option, and following a long wait, the phone was answered. I asked about my son and the voice on the other end of the line said, "Lady, we ain't got nobody by the name of Jason Kent in here. Your son ain't here."

Hope struggled to crush the fear in my racing heart. Perhaps it was a dream after all! But we soon discovered that the first time I called, Jason had not yet been processed into the Orlando jail's computer system. This was reality.

Our son, fresh from military training, had discovered that the biological father of his two stepdaughters was about to get unsupervised visitation of the girls. There had been multiple allegations of abuse against the man and Jason unraveled—mentally, emotionally, and spiritually. Then Jason did the unthinkable—he shot and killed a person he believed was a threat to the girls. Now Jason was facing first-degree murder charges in the state of Florida.

It was the middle of the night, and Gene and I intermittently sobbed and held each other for hours. But in the midst of the shock, we began making a list of calls we needed to make. There were grandparents, aunts, uncles, cousins, and friends to contact. Jason needed an attorney . . . and we had little experience with the legal system.

Thoughts swirled:

*What is the jail like where Jason is being held? Is he safe?*

*We need money for Jason's defense—lots of money. Where will get it?*

*Is there enough in our retirement account to pay a deposit for an attorney?*

*When will this hit the local newspaper?*

*What do we do now?*

———

When someone you love is arrested, there is an agony of the soul that defies explanation. If you are the parent, spouse, or close friend of that person, the pain is multiplied. The shock can feel like an earthquake inside as we slowly assimilate the truth about our loved one's bad choice. We feel helpless. Afraid. Sometimes we feel responsible.

Perhaps you, like me, can identify with this prayer from the Bible: "My heart is in anguish within me; the terrors of death have fallen on me. Fear and trembling have beset me; horror has overwhelmed me. I said, 'Oh, that I had the wings of a dove! I would fly away and be at rest. I would flee far away and stay in the desert; I would hurry to my place of shelter, far from the tempest and storm'" (Psalm 55:4–8). We want to help our loved one, but we feel like running away to hide. We don't want to face our coworkers, friends, and relatives. Our pain is piercing. Harsh. Unrelenting. Where can we go for help?

### HIS WORDS OVER YOU

"I am close to the brokenhearted and I will save you when you are crushed in spirit. I know your pain, and I will not leave you comfortless because I am the God of all comfort. You are mine."

*Based on Psalm 34:18 and 2 Corinthians 1:3*

# 2. Keep Breathing

*I have this strange feeling none of this is really happening.*
*Like I'm standing far away from myself. Like nothing's*
*quite real. Have you ever had a feeling like that?*

A. MANETTE ANSAY

In the first few days following our son's arrest, my body and mind felt disjointed. I was used to multitasking, but suddenly I could do only one thing at a time. I would walk into a room and forget why I was there. Everything and everyone around me seemed to be moving in slow motion—like I was watching life on a video without being part of the picture.

My mind flashed to the invisible, spiritual world, where I could envision Satan with a cadre of his demons. He was pointing at me, saying, "Hey, let's wipe her out mentally, emotionally, and spiritually. Let's make her feel so guilty and responsible for the choices of her son that she cracks under the pressure and gives up on her faith. She's already a mess, so this should be an easy job."

The enemy taunted me with lies:

- You are a terrible parent.
- If you had prayed harder and read your Bible more fervently, this would not have happened.
- If you had been less busy, you would have known what might take place—and you could have stopped it.
- Your child is in terrible danger in a place where you can't protect him.
- You will lose your livelihood because no one wants to hear a speaker who can't even raise a son to be law-abiding.
- God must not love you.

As I struggled to make it through the next several days, the lies from the enemy circled over my head like vultures. I wrestled with panic, shame, shock, and guilt. I wrote in my journal:

> When your only offspring commits a murder, you can't think of yourself as "a good parent." Will Gene and I ever stop wondering what we could have done differently in our parenting that would have prohibited our son from taking the life of another human being? We did our best, but obviously that wasn't good enough.

Gene found solace in reading through his Bible. One day he rushed into the room and said, "Carol, I'm in Genesis 28—it's that passage where Jacob is in a dream. He sees a ladder that stretches from earth to heaven and there are angels going up and down on that ladder. Suddenly, Jacob awakens more alert than he has ever been before—because he realizes there is so much more going on in the visible and in the invisible worlds than he's ever been aware of." Then my husband read Genesis 28:16 to me: "Surely the LORD is in this place, and I was not aware of it."

———

You may be in a place where it feels like you can hardly hold on, where God seems far away. I understand. After Gene read that Scripture to me, we held each other and wept. It felt like we were going through a personal earthquake, but that didn't mean that God had left us on our own. We came to understand that when God seems the most absent, He is indeed the most present. It was a reminder to believe that the truth of God's Word, the Bible, does not change because of a personal crisis.

## HIS WORDS OVER YOU

"You feel poor and needy, like someone searching for water who finds only dry land. But I am the God of Israel and I will not leave you helpless. I will not turn my back on you. I am already making rivers flow in unexpected places. I am here to be found. I will turn your parched ground into springs. I formed man out of the dust of the earth and breathed into him the breath of life. You will breathe again."

*Based on Isaiah 41:17–18 and Genesis 2:7*

# 3. Consolation and Coping

*How one handles grief is a personal matter. Let the one who has
suffered the loss take the lead. If he feels like talking, encourage him
to talk. If he prefers to sit in silence, don't intrude on his silence.*

ABIGAIL VAN BUREN

It was hard to see the grief on my husband's face. Gene is by nature
optimistic, energetic, humorous, and excited about life. But I suddenly
saw a man who was hurt, discouraged, withdrawn, and sick at heart.
He and Jason had always been very close. They both loved adventure,
like hiking the beautiful provincial parks in Canada and completing
a half marathon together. They would often read the same books and
discuss them at length. The loss of the physical presence of his son for
the foreseeable future was an unspeakable grief for Gene.

Walking into my husband's home office, I would sometimes find
him with his head in his hands. At other times I saw a faraway look on
his face, as if he were trying to create a different reality than the one
we were experiencing. Gene had always enjoyed running, biking, and
walking outdoors, but now I saw him withdrawing inside the walls of
our home, safe from the eyes and curious questions of neighbors and
acquaintances.

I tried to console Gene by talking about day-to-day matters in our
work and ministry lives—but there was a dark cloud hanging over
him. That cloud was enveloping me in its shadow too. Sometimes we
rehearsed the past, trying to figure out what we had done wrong. We
couldn't think of anything about our parenting, or his response to it,
that would indicate Jason might commit a dreadful crime. We were
baffled.

My way of coping was to work harder, more intensely, with the goal
of being so tired by day's end I would fall into bed and actually sleep.
Gene, who'd been an English major, found the best way to move toward
survival was through journaling. He began to chronicle the harsh truth
of what we were experiencing:

> October 25: We received the news that J. P. (Jason Paul) was arrested.
> Cried. Found an attorney.
> October 26: Coped poorly. Cried. I am so afraid for my son.
> October 27: Carol and I go through the motions of being alive, but
> inside we are dying.

Sometimes we talked. More often we sat in silence. At other times we held each other and quietly wept. We both had a hard time focusing. Our minds wandered and our fears consumed us. I recalled a verse from the book of James: "If you don't know what you're doing, pray to the Father. He loves to help. You'll get his help, and won't be condescended to when you ask for it. Ask boldly, believingly, without a second thought. People who 'worry their prayers' are like wind-whipped waves" (James 1:5–6 MSG). We didn't do formal prayers. We did begging, wailing, moaning prayers. *Please protect and comfort our son. God, please console the family of the deceased during this agonizing time. Put your arms around our daughter-in-law and our two step-granddaughters. Give us wisdom. We don't know what to do. Dear God, help us!*

---

When you are in the first stages of grief regarding the unexpected arrest of a loved one, allow yourself to express your sorrow—either alone or in the presence of someone you feel comfortable talking to. You may feel a need for solitude, but remember that God created us to live in community. Having even one person to talk to can be a first step toward finding your way on this unexpected journey.

### HIS WORDS OVER YOU

"You're blessed when you feel you've lost what is most precious to you. Then you can be embraced by the One most dear to you. Talk to me about your concerns. I am close to the brokenhearted and I save those who are crushed in spirit. "

*Based on Matthew 5:4 and Psalm 34:18*

# 4. Going Out in Public

*If God is everywhere present, He saw what happened. . . .*
*If God is all powerful, He could have stopped it. That*
*He saw it and did nothing to stop it is the darkest*
*and most unsettling mystery in the universe.*

KEN GIRE

The day after we received the news of our son's arrest I had an appointment for an annual physical exam, scheduled months earlier. I was tempted to cancel this trip that would take me out in public, but I was getting nothing done at home and I needed to get a prescription renewed. I reasoned that very few people in our hometown would have heard what happened, so I decided to go.

Stepping into the doctor's office, I noticed the waiting room was filled with women and children who were talking, laughing, and energetically interacting with each other. A pregnant woman, trying to balance a two-year-old on her lap, caught my gaze and smiled. With fear in my heart, I thought: *My child used to be as innocent as that one.* Another woman was paying her bill at the counter, while two others watched a soap opera on the waiting area's television. My mind swirled: *They act like everything is normal, and my whole world just fell apart. How is it possible that life can go on for everyone else when the lives of my family members and those of the deceased will never be the same again?*

It was a surreal feeling, like I was sitting on the edge of the world, observing all that was going on but not really being *in* that world. I wondered if people could see the agony on my face. Then panic struck as I glanced at the front door of the office: *If anyone I know comes through that door, I will fall apart. I shouldn't be here. This was a very bad idea. I am not capable of facing anyone, much less people I know personally, after receiving such shocking news.*

Just as I was ready to make a run for the door, a nurse called my name. I blindly followed her back to the examination room where she handed me the paper gown women wear once a year. With my head still reeling from my panic attack, I slipped out of my clothes and into the examination gown. Within a few minutes the nurse came in and took my blood pressure. "My, we're a little high today," she said with concern.

*Lady,* I thought, *if you only knew what was happening, you'd know I have every right to have high blood pressure today.* She patted my arm with compassion, and I burst into totally unexpected, torrential tears.

The nurse softly touched my arm again as she spoke quietly, "Honey, the exam won't be that painful."

At that point, I heard myself laugh out loud. It startled me, because I had wondered if I would ever be able to laugh again. The moment suddenly felt even more bizarre and out of place. For the first time in two days I laughed! The nurse thought I was afraid of the exam, and had no idea that my true distress was the sadness I felt for my son and the family of the deceased. I discovered over time that a kind of "black humor" would strike me at inappropriate moments like this. But it was a reminder that I was still alive.[1]

---

After someone we love is arrested, facing people feels overwhelming. There is a combined feeling of sorrow, humiliation, and fear as we wonder if others have heard about what has taken place. Our emotions are raw, and we sometimes respond awkwardly or inappropriately. In our feelings of being alone in our misery, not really connecting with people in the usual way, we wonder if even God cares about what has happened. It's easy to identify with this prayer from the Bible: "How long, LORD? Will you forget me forever? How long will you hide your face from me? How long must I wrestle with my thoughts and day after day have sorrow in my heart?" (Psalm 13:1–2).

## HIS WORDS OVER YOU

"I see your grief and pain. Look to me. I will give you joy instead of mourning, and praise instead of despair. One day you will be glad again, and the purpose of your life will be for the display of my splendor. I will walk with you through this trial and you will become an oak of righteousness. I take great delight in bringing you comfort and joy instead of sorrow."

*Based on Isaiah 61:3 and Jeremiah 31:13*

---

1. Some content taken from *When I Lay My Isaac Down*, by Carol Kent. Copyright © 2004, 2013. Used by permission of NavPress. All rights reserved. Represented by Tyndale House Publishers, Inc.

# 5. Headlines that Hurt

*When you go through a traumatic event, there's a
lot of shame that comes with that. A lot of loss of
self-esteem. That can become debilitating.*

WILLIE AAMES

It took over two weeks for the news of Jason's arrest to reach our local paper in Port Huron, Michigan. The story had already appeared in the *Orlando Sentinel,* and we knew it was only a matter of time before our local news organizations caught on. During those fourteen days we shared what had happened with our pastor, our relatives, and our closest friends. However, most local people did not have any idea of the crisis shaking our lives to the core.

Then it happened. An editor from the Port Huron paper called three times asking for comments from the parents of the accused. We refused to respond to the calls, but the voice mail messages gave us a day's notice that Jason's arrest would be known all over the city. The knot in my stomach grew tighter. The following day's headline took my breath away.

### FORMER PORT HURON MAN
### FACES MURDER CHARGE

A Port Huron native and Naval Academy graduate could face up to life in prison and possibly the death penalty in the shooting death of his wife's ex-husband outside a busy Orlando, Florida, restaurant last month.

Jason Paul Kent, 25, is expected to be charged Tuesday at an Orange County Jail with . . . murder.[2]

Embarrassment, shame, and guilt hit us between the eyes. From that point on, the whole community knew the details of what had taken place. Though much of our guilt and shame was false (I'll explain that idea later in this book), I still wrestled with a choice: would I hide in my home or face life by going out in public? Right then, I had an appointment to get my hair colored and cut at a large, busy salon. I decided if I was ever going to face people after J. P.'s arrest, it had better be that day—or I might never have the courage again.

---

2. Syeda Ferguson, "Former Port Huron Man Faces Murder Charge," *Times Herald* (Port Huron, MI), November 24, 1999.

I walked in the front door of the salon, and in my highly emotional state, it seemed like all of the conversation ceased—that all of the patrons were looking at me while their hairdressers worked on them. I thought I could read the minds of the women:

*Oh no! There's the mother of the murderer!*
*Did you read about her son in the paper yesterday?*
*I bet she's embarrassed to be seen in public today.*
*I don't know if I should look up or down; this is really awkward.*

I was tempted to turn and leave, but out of the corner of my eye, I saw Azam, my eyebrow plucker. She saw my need and felt my pain. Making her way through that crowded workplace, she took me by the hand and led me to a private room in the back. Putting her arms around me, she wept, feeling my pain as her own.

Speaking softly with a comforting voice, she said, "I'm so sorry about what's happened to your family. I pray for you. I pray for your husband. I pray for your son." Then she pointed at the wall that separated us from the other women and spoke again. "Don't worry about them. They will find someone else to talk about next week!" And she was right![3]

———

If I had not been so upset, I might have read the faces in the salon as compassionate rather than judgmental. But my perception that day could only translate the women's eye contact as something negative. I have now been on this journey long enough to realize that no matter how intense the newspaper headlines or stories about your loved one get, very soon people get back to their own lives, their own challenges, and their own agendas. They simply don't have time to think continually about those of us with incarcerated loved ones.

So we face a choice. Will we allow the opinions and reactions of others to consume us, or will we be honest about our situation, acknowledge our pain, and begin living again? Matthew 6:34 (MSG) says, "Give your entire attention to what God is doing right now, and don't get worked up about what may or may not happen tomorrow. God will help you deal with whatever hard things come up when the time comes."

---

3. Adapted from Carol Kent, *A New Kind of Normal* (Nashville: Thomas Nelson, 2007), 43.

"Don't worry about the opinions or judgments of others. Spend time with uplifting people. Those who speak kind words heal and help. Cutting words wound and maim. Look to me for approval. I know what I'm doing and I have it all planned out. I have plans to take care of you and not to abandon you, plans to give you hope and a future."

*Based on Proverbs 15:4 and Jeremiah 29:11*

# 6. Wise Counsel

*Not till we have become humble and teachable, standing in
awe of God's holiness and sovereignty, acknowledging our own
littleness, distrusting our own thoughts, and willing to have our
minds turned upside down, can divine wisdom become ours.*

J. I. PACKER

Gene and I are both firstborns. We were used to finding solutions, giving advice to others, and being independent. But when Jason was arrested, we suddenly felt helpless and in need of counsel ourselves. We lacked any knowledge of how the jail and prison systems worked. We needed an attorney who could advise us on what legal steps to take. We needed trustworthy relatives and friends who would listen to our desperate cries without spreading gossip. Most of all, we felt we needed wisdom, as the well-ordered life we had once known was now in a disruptive, messy, senseless, and chaotic state.

Gene flew to Florida to help Jason's wife and her daughters move to Orlando, where our son was in the county jail. Gene wrote in his journal:

> The darkness of our situation hangs like a shadow over everything. I flew to Panama City with my brother to pack all of my son and his family's earthly goods into a U-Haul. The most difficult moment while packing was seeing Jason's half-eaten twenty-fifth birthday cake, with the burnt candles still on the top. I couldn't throw it out, so I stuffed it in a box with pots and pans. It was such an odd feeling—like perhaps if I kept the cake, my son would show up at the door and we'd finish eating it together. I seem unable to have the wisdom to make even small decisions.

Before Gene left, we visited our pastor and his wife. They were full of compassion and they were good listeners. Kim, who worked as a counselor, asked us what kind of support we had. We indicated that both of our families—including our parents, siblings, nieces, and nephews—as well as some close friends had already been a tremendous encouragement to us. Then Kim said something I'll never forget: "Gene and Carol, if you have even one person you can be totally honest with, someone who will give you wise advice and pray with you—that will carry you when you feel like you can't carry yourself." Her words came back to me repeatedly as days passed.

The circle of people finding out about Jason's arrest was widening. Acquaintances and friends from the past called to share advice and comfort. But one of those calls was hard to take.

"This agonizing pain will not be this acute for the rest of your life," one friend said. "One day you'll wake up and discover you can breathe again." She was trying to console me—to convey that pain has a season when it is so intense you doubt you will be able to go on living. This friend went on to explain that the mind and body eventually adjust to a new kind of normal and life becomes more tolerable. "People learn to laugh again," she added, "and they become functional, even happy."

Our long friendship had earned her the right to give me this advice. At that moment, however, I didn't want what felt like a false comfort. I just wanted to be alone with my pain.

---

Something Gene and I began to understand is that we first needed to ask God for wisdom. "If you need wisdom, ask our generous God, and he will give it to you. He will not rebuke you for asking" (James 1:5 NLT). We already knew we could gain wisdom from the Bible, but we learned that God often reveals important counsel to us through other people who are spending time with Him. In the book of Ecclesiastes it says, "Two people are better off than one, for they can help each other succeed. If one person falls, the other can reach out and help. But someone who falls alone is in real trouble" (4:9–10 NLT).

After we prayed and asked for wisdom, God used a friend to connect us to a good attorney. With the help of Jason's mother-in-law, a reasonably priced rental home was found for his family, so they could live near the jail where he was awaiting his trial. We listened to the advice of friends and began to feel much-needed support. Take some time to list the good advice you've received from others in your time of need.

### HIS WORDS OVER YOU

"If you ask me for wisdom, I will give it to you generously. Seek advice and instruction from people who know me. Even in the garden of Eden I said, 'It is not good for man to be alone.' You need support and I am eager to help you. Don't run from people. Embrace them and allow them to express my love and concern for you."

*Based on James 1:5, Genesis 2:18, and Proverbs 19:20*

# 7. Financial Realities

*The battle belongs to the Lord, and we*
*already know that He wins the war.*

JARED BROCK

We were not far into our shocking reality when a major decision had to be made. We needed money—not only for our monthly bills but also for our son's legal defense. My opportunities to speak and teach the Bible had been multiplying, and it was getting much more difficult to work with meeting planners, make all the travel arrangements, order and ship books ahead of time, and train people to work at the resource table, while also doing the keynote speaking at retreats and conferences. Gene, meanwhile, had been in the insurance business for thirty years.

A year before Jason's arrest, he had joined a Bible study which used Henry Blackaby's book *Experiencing God.* One day Gene came to me and said, "Carol, the main point of this study is to look around and see where God is at work—and join Him. I see God at work in what you're doing. You need help, and I think it's time for me to leave my business and to begin working with you in an administrative capacity." I watched my husband leave his downtown office, transfer his business to someone else, and move into a new job at a desk in our basement. We both knew that God was leading us to work together and it touched me deeply that my husband was a servant-hearted man.

The challenge now was that our only income came from ministry—from my writing of books and speaking at Christian events. A knot was forming in my stomach. I couldn't imagine stepping forward to tell women how to live by biblical principles when my own son was awaiting a trial for murder. But as Gene and I talked about our financial needs, we realized we had no choice but to keep the ministry engagements on the calendar. The following weekend we left on a four-hour drive to a women's conference.

I met the worship leader at the venue and we went to dinner together. Halfway through our meal she leaned over and said, "I almost canceled. My husband and I have been in music ministry for several years, but we're not making enough money to take care of our family. We're losing our house this week and we're going bankrupt. I can hardly look at my children and tell them God is faithful. The last thing I feel like doing is leading worship."

With tears welling up in my eyes, I took her hand and told her how sorry I was for what was happening to her family. "My husband and I are in the middle of a gigantic family crisis too," I said, choking back a sob. "It's a devastating situation that I can't even put into words yet. I don't know if I'll make it through the messages. You and I are going to be two broken people ministering out of our brokenness." We prayed together before walking to the meeting room.

As she led us in poignant worship, highlighting the love of God, I wept through every song. Then I was introduced. Standing on the platform with my Bible in my hands, I began to speak on overcoming fear. At first I felt like a fake, wondering if I even believed my own words. But the longer I spoke from God's Word, the more I sensed His empowerment. It was as if I was stomping on the enemy saying, "You loser! You meant to wipe the parents out with the kid! You thought if you could get to our child, you could totally immobilize the ministry we are doing. Satan, you were wrong."

God blessed the weekend, with many women deciding to follow Jesus. I knew it would not be easy to be in a public ministry, but I found that God gives the strength. And He would provide for our financial needs too.

———

When bad things happen, many of us feel angry with God. But as a Christian, I discovered it was important to target my anger at the real enemy. One day I screamed out loud, "Satan, you can come after me, but don't touch my child! I command you, in the name of Jesus Christ and His shed blood on the cross, to leave Jason Kent alone. Get away from him! You are wicked and disgusting! You are a loser! You have only a little while longer to leave your mark and I know the end of your story! We win! You lose!"

Allow your pain to drive you to God. The apostle Paul said: "When I think of all this, I fall to my knees and pray to the Father, the Creator of everything in heaven and on earth. I pray that from his glorious, unlimited resources he will empower you with inner strength through his Spirit" (Ephesians 3:14–16 NLT). Recognize that your real enemy is Satan, who wants to destroy your entire life—your finances, your family, and your faith—with the incarceration of your loved one. Don't let him win.

"Dear one, you are in a spiritual battle that is agonizing. The enemy goes to and fro in the earth looking for strategic ways he can defeat you. Be strong. I will meet your needs. You feel hopeless, but there's more to this story than you can see today."

*Based on 1 Peter 5:8 and Philippians 4:19*

# 8. Out of My Control

*We can hug our hurts and make a shrine out of our sorrow, or we can offer them to God as a sacrifice of praise. The choice is ours.*

RICHARD EXLEY

Six days after Jason's arrest, Gene flew to Florida to visit him at the jail, and to assist our daughter-in-law with her move. I was at home pulling together the last of the down payment for our attorney. The phone rang. Picking up the receiver, I heard a digitized message asking if I would accept the charges from an inmate. It was my son, who was weeping. He sounded very frightened.

"Mom, I've just been jumped by ten inmates here at the jail," he said. "They were kicking me repeatedly in the head. My two front teeth have been broken off. I have a cut in my ear. I'm pretty busted up."

I had trouble breathing. "Do you have any broken bones?" I asked.

"I don't think so," he said, choking back a sob.

"Why did they do this?" I stammered, trying to sound calmer than my racing heart made me feel.

"An officer was with them during my meeting with one of the psychologists," Jason answered. "He lied and told the inmates that my crime was racially motivated. He told the men that I had killed an African-American man and his little girl. Sometimes false rumors are spread at the jail, and that often results in fights—especially when an inmate first arrives." Jason's words spilled out in fast succession, through intermittent sobs. "The inmates stole all of my stuff, except for my Bible.

"But Mom," he went on, "after the beating, the corrections officers took me to the faith-based area of the jail. Those men were just like Jesus to me. They washed my wounds and they prayed over me. They brought me soap and deodorant. One by one, at least ten different guys, all ages and races, came by my rack [bed] and silently began to place items on it. I watched canteen items they'd purchased individually pile up on my bunk: a toothbrush, toothpaste, a washcloth, gym shorts, a T-shirt, paper, a pen. I knew it was a real sacrifice for them to give to me out of what little they had."

I fought back tears. "Dad is already in Orlando, and he has permission to have a brief visit with you tomorrow. I wish I could hold you in my arms right now." We cried together that day, a mom and her boy, eleven hundred miles apart and embarking on a journey neither one of us understood or wanted.

Suddenly the digitized voice returned, stating that we had only fifteen seconds before the call would end. "I'm praying for you, Son," I said. "I'll see you in a couple of days."

"I love you, Mom." *Click.*

I heard a guttural wail come up from the depths of my being. Sitting at my desk, I turned my head upward and with my eyes wide open, I spoke: "God, I cannot handle this journey. I cannot watch my son suffer like this. Why didn't you protect him? Why did you let him get kicked in the head and face by agitated inmates? I feel completely powerless to help him. How much more pain do you think I can take? I don't know how to help my boy. Please take care of him!"

And then the mama part of me kicked in as I realized our son needed his parents now more than he had ever needed us before.

———

One of the hardest things about having an incarcerated loved one is the loss of control over what may happen to them behind bars. Even when there are many professional corrections officers, injustices abound among prisoners, and dangers are abundant. Our temptation is to live every day in the fear of what *might* happen to our loved ones. I know how you feel. I know it's hard.

In this section, we'll explore the story of a Bible character named Abraham, who had to relinquish his beloved son Isaac. It's a powerful story of a father who gave up his "right" to protect his son from what appeared to be a disastrous outcome. Ultimately, Abraham learned that God loved Isaac even more than he did.

On the day of Jason's beating, I took my first step in letting go of control over his situation. It was one of the most difficult things I've ever done, but it is possible. Something *you* can do right now is to start practicing the discipline of living one day at a time. Jesus said, "Do not worry about tomorrow, for tomorrow will worry about itself. Each day has enough trouble of its own" (Matthew 6:34).

### HIS WORDS OVER YOU

"My child, when anxiety is great within you, my consolation will bring you joy. My unfailing love will support you. Trust in me with all your heart and don't lean on your own perceptions of what is taking place. Listen to my voice in everything you do, and I will keep you on track."

*Based on Psalm 94:18–19 and Proverbs 3:5–6*

# 9. The Power of Relinquishment

*Surrender isn't a one-time event but a moment-by-moment choice.*

PAULA HENDRICKS

I flew alone to Florida, since Gene was already there. He'd had his fifteen-minute visit with our son the day before, so he was not allowed to join me on this day.

Walking into the large compound called the 33rd Street Facility, I waited in a long line to request a visit with Jason. I am not proud to admit that I had never been inside a jail or a prison before. It wasn't that I didn't care about inmates and their families, it's just that no one in my extended family or circle of friends had ever had a loved one who was arrested. (Actually, I later found out that wasn't true. Incarceration is often the secret no one talks about.)

The woman at the front desk seemed disorganized and irritated. When I made my request for the fifteen-minute visit with my son, she said, "That will only happen if there is an officer available who can bring Jason down to the visitation area." I told her I was willing to wait as long as necessary, but I needed to see my son before I returned to Michigan.

An hour later, I was ushered into a room filled with cubicles. There was a chair in front of a Plexiglas window, and that's where I sat until I heard a shuffle on the other side. Suddenly Jason appeared. I was used to seeing my son in a Navy uniform with shiny medals attached, but now he was in jailhouse "blues" with a chain around his waist attached to his handcuffs. His ankles were in leg-irons, with a short chain between them.

Our eyes were brimming with tears as they met. It had only been three days since the beating. Scabs covered much of Jason's face; both of his eyes were completely bloodshot; there was a cut in his ear that still oozed blood. Then I saw the jagged, broken edges of what was left of his front teeth. He glanced down and simultaneously both of us experienced the weight of confusion, suffering, and hurt—for our own family and for the family of the deceased. The fact of what had taken place could not be undone.

We grabbed the old-fashioned black telephone receivers that hung along each side of the thick window. "Son, I love you," I stammered. "There is nothing you could ever do that would stop my unconditional love for you." An armed guard stood nearby, listening to every word. Through his sobs, he said, "Thank you, Mom. I love you so much."

He was beaten, broken, humbled, hurt, and sad. There was nothing I could do to change the circumstances that brought him to this place. There was no way to bring the deceased back to life. I couldn't "fix" anything. The visit ended too quickly, and I ran out to the parking lot in tears. Sitting in my car, I opened my hands palms up and prayed:

God, please help us not to waste this suffering. I could not go on living if I didn't believe I could trust you. I give up my right to control the outcome of Jason's trial. I release his future to your keeping—but God, even while I'm saying I want to relinquish my control, I want to take it back. So God, I will let go of my control for the next minute, and if I make it that far, let's try for five more minutes. Maybe there will be a time when I will come to the end of one full day without trying to regain control.

---

I thought back to my son's first day of school, that first time he rode the bus. There have been many times over the years when I've had to release my control over what happened to him. It was especially hard to let go when he graduated high school and left for the U.S. Naval Academy. But as you and I know, there's a big difference between releasing control over a loved one who moves into a new season of life and having *no* control over what happens to our family member inside a jail or prison.

*Relinquish* is a word that means "to let go of, to cease to hold in the hand."[4] When we relinquish our incarcerated loved one to God, it is an act of trust in Him—especially when we cannot envision a positive outcome. Psalm 62:7–8 (MSG) proclaims: "My help and glory are in God—granite-strength and safe-harbor-God—so trust him absolutely, people; lay your lives on the line for him. God is a safe place to be."

### HIS WORDS OVER YOU

"You can run to me for dear life and hide out under my wings. Let go and let me comfort the one you love. As you release control to me, rest in my generous love. I will make good on my Word. I've always been God and I will always be God. Relax and let me work on your behalf."

*Based on Psalm 57:1–3 and Isaiah 43:12–13*

---

4. *Webster's New World Dictionary of the American Language*, s.v. "relinquish."

# 10. Obedience Is a Choice

*God is God. Because He is God, He is worthy of my trust and obedience. I will find rest nowhere but in His holy will, a will that is unspeakably beyond my largest notions of what He is up to.*

ELISABETH ELLIOT

After my son was arrested, I did a lot of thinking about Abraham. In the book of Genesis there is a story that always gave me an unsettled feeling. God asked Abraham, a man who honored and obeyed the Lord, to go to Mount Moriah and *sacrifice* his son Isaac—on an altar, as an offering. Even though I'm a preacher's kid and I've been in the church since I was a baby, there was just something about God's request that bothered me. Why would God ask a father to lay his child on an altar, to sacrifice him as a burnt offering?

I turned to Genesis 22 and became even more mystified. "Early the next morning Abraham got up and loaded his donkey. He took with him two of his servants and his son Isaac" (verse 3). Personally, I would have waited until at least noon, hoping God would suggest a different idea.

On the surface, it seems like a horrific suggestion. But *God* is the one making the request, and we know He loves people. He always has their best interests in mind, even if the circumstances don't make it appear that way.

Remember, Abraham had history with God. They had walked together for a long time and Abraham had heard God's voice before. He knew this was not the voice of an imposter. Abraham had also failed some faith tests when he did things his own way, which meant he had already learned some lessons the hard way. There was a trust level between God and Abraham that did not require a pause. Abraham simply obeyed.

It took three days to travel from Beersheba, where Abraham and Isaac lived, to Mount Moriah. When they arrived, the man and his son built an altar. Abraham placed wood he had split on the altar, then bound his son and laid him on top. The verb form used for "*laying* him on the altar" also means "a lifting up."[5] In other words, it was a supreme act of worship for Abraham to lay his Isaac down.

At that moment, Abraham relinquished his own desires, dreams,

---

5. *Scholar's Library,* Logos Bible Software Series

plans, and hopes for his Isaac's future and made the sacrifice. This was an act of worship to the God he trusted with a supreme confidence—one so strong that even if God allowed his son to die, Abraham knew God could raise him from the dead (see Hebrews 11:17–19).

My son is not a parallel to Isaac. Because he was human, Isaac was born in sin—but there is nothing in the Bible that leads us to believe he was being sacrificed because of his own failures. But my son was guilty of taking the life of another human being. My son was not like Abraham's son, but Jason was my personal Isaac. God seemed to be asking me, with complete trust, submission, and obedience, to lay down my claim to Jason—even though everything in my heart was crying out, "There must be a way to spare my son from what lies ahead! There must be a way to protect my own heart from this crushing grief!" But it *was* happening. God was asking me to sacrifice my heart's desire in complete obedience to Him.

I had a major issue with pride—a pride that included high expectations for my only child's future. My dreams were of a "normal" family with Easter dinners, summer reunions, and grandchildren opening gifts around our Christmas tree, all complete with joy-filled conversation. But I needed to relinquish everything that represented my "Isaac." Would I honor God by continuing to love and trust and completely obey Him in the middle of these unthinkable circumstances?

———

For all of us who love someone behind bars, there is a choice—control or obedience? Will we try to orchestrate outcomes that are totally beyond our reach, or will we submit to God's authority in our lives? Abraham chose correctly, and God sent a ram as a sacrifice in place of Isaac (Genesis 22:10–14). Abraham walked away having experienced the presence of God in a way very few people do.

Are we willing to give up what we love to God? Will we open our fists and trust Him in complete obedience?

## HIS WORDS OVER YOU

"I love you even more than you love your 'Isaac.' Listen to my voice in everything you do. Hold on to me for dear life and I'll get you out of trouble. I'll give you and your loved one the best of care if you'll only trust me. Release your grip on circumstances you can't control and choose to follow my lead with an obedient heart."

*Based on Psalm 91:14 and Job 36:11*

# 11. Heart Sacrifices

*Whatever . . . sacrifice God asks you to make, the particular*
*cross He wishes you to embrace . . . rise up, and say in*
*your heart, "Yes, Lord, I accept it; I submit, I yield, I*
*pledge myself to walk in that path, and to follow that*
*Voice, and to trust [you] with the consequences."*

CATHERINE BOOTH

Not long after the news of Jason's arrest hit the local papers, an acquaintance wrote to me explaining that she had contacted every ministry where I had ever spoken, all of the television and radio stations where I had been interviewed, and each Christian leader she could think of to let them know what had happened to our family. Why? So they could pray for us. Later in the letter, she listed all of the ministries and individuals she had contacted "on our behalf." She had not checked with us to verify any of the facts, nor had she asked our permission or blessing on her plan. She simply told these people and organizations everything she read in the newspaper because she knew they would want to know.

I stopped my grieving long enough to get mad. Frustrated, I yelled to my husband, "Don't people have anything else to do? Are they experiencing a feeling of power by announcing our bad news in the name of prayer requests, when they don't even have the facts straight? This is just wrong!"

My husband, Gene, is different from me in many ways. I have highs and lows, but Gene is steady. He never gets as animated as I do and he doesn't hit bottom as severely as I do either. Most of the time, he is under control—as he was on this day. Gene took my hands in his and spoke softly. "Carol, what's happened here is way out of our control," he said. "We are proactive people who like to fix things, but we can't change anything that's happened or how this woman has responded to it. There is nothing we can do to stop the rumors, stories, or the opinions of gossiping people. Just let it go! It is far beyond us."

He was right. I clearly had a lot to learn about heart sacrifices.

The dictionary says a sacrifice is "an act of offering to a deity something precious; something offered in sacrifice; something given up."[6] Psalm 51:17 provides additional explanation: "My sacrifice, O God, is a broken spirit; a broken and contrite heart you, God, will not despise." As I meditated on this verse, I started making notes, and I discovered that true heart sacrifices involve

---

6. *Merriam-Webster's Collegiate Dictionary,* 10th ed., s.v. "sacrifice."

- identifying someone or something precious to us (our "Isaac");
- letting go of our control over the person, the situation, or even other people's gossip, as an act of worship to God;
- embracing God's love while letting go; and
- accepting the outcome, even if in this lifetime we are not allowed to know the reason for the sacrifice and pain.

A heart sacrifice isn't something that happens quickly or easily. It's an intentional, ongoing decision that is tied to the personal relationship we have with God. It is developed by spending time in His Word and by communicating with an "Abba Father" (Galatians 4:6) who loves us more than we love our Isaac.[7]

———

Heart sacrifices can involve small things—like gossip about our incarcerated loved ones. Don't allow it to immobilize you or destroy your sense of worth. *Let it go.* But more often, heart sacrifices involve the bigger issue of trying to control outcomes for the inmate we love and for our family members who deal with the embarrassment, shame, and guilt that accompany imprisonment.

God never forces us to make a heart sacrifice. He never demands our allegiance or makes us "give up" an Isaac just to play with our emotions. He always allows the choice to be ours. And that is exactly why the decision is so difficult.

Review the bullet points on heart sacrifices found earlier in this devotional. Where do you stand in this difficult process? What next step should you take to move closer to the altar and lay your Isaac down as an act of worship?

### HIS WORDS OVER YOU

"Dear friend, I am stacking up a pile of blessings for you. Your heart sacrifices are precious to me. Run to me to escape an unkind world. I will lavish my protection and blessing on you in unexpected ways. Hide in the shelter of my presence, far from people who say unkind things about you. I delight in you."

*Based on Psalm 31:19–20 and Psalm 37:23*

---

7. Some content taken from *When I Lay My Isaac Down*, by Carol Kent. Copyright © 2004, 2013. Used by permission of NavPress. All rights reserved. Represented by Tyndale House Publishers, Inc.

# 12. The Truth about Tears

*Heartache . . . forces us to embrace God out of desperate, urgent need. . . . God is never closer than when your heart is aching.*

JONI EARECKSON TADA

I once heard a health-care professional speak about tears. She claimed that tears caused by laughter are very different from tears caused by sorrow. Later I discovered that photographer Rose-Lynn Fisher put dried tears—formed from different trigger points—under a microscope, and the pictorial results were stunning. Tears that are formed due to sadness, happiness, or even by reactions to onions or tear gas contain different molecules.[8] Fisher showed that tears formed from hard laughter aren't even close to the appearance of tears formed from sorrow.

I found comfort in knowing that tears caused by sorrow matter so much to God that they have their very own molecular consistency. God created human beings who cry, and He designed us to cry in specialized ways. It's interesting that the shortest verse in the Bible is about tears: "Jesus wept" (John 11:35). We know that Jesus was very familiar with tears caused by sorrow.

When my son was young, I knew a lot about joyful tears. It was common for me to "laugh until I cried," and I enjoyed a remarkably happy life up to the time of Jason's arrest. Then came our "Isaac experience" and I understood an entirely new kind of weeping—deeply sorrowful, heartrending, unstoppable, uncontrollable tears. I cried when I woke up in the morning. I cried when I heard Jason's favorite song on the radio. I cried when I saw his dive equipment. I cried when one of his best friends stopped by the house to ask about him. I sobbed when I walked past his framed diploma from the U.S. Naval Academy, complete with a picture of the graduating midshipmen tossing their hats into the air on a sunny, joy-filled day in Annapolis, Maryland.

There was someone else I often found weeping: my husband. One day he wrote about the tears I saw so frequently:

> Growing up, I never saw my father cry. I saw him laugh at jokes, work hard on the railroad, argue with my mother—but I never, *ever*, saw him cry.

---

8. Casey Chan, "Tears of joy and tears of sadness look different under the microscope," *Sploid*, last modified November 20, 2013, http://sploid.gizmodo.com/tears-of-joy-and -tears-of-sadness-look-different-under-1468602557.

In 1974 my wife gave birth to our first and only child—a son. I cried when he was born. I cried when he walked. I even shed some tears when I heard him say, "Dada." There were joy-filled tears when he started school. Happy tears when he graduated from high school with honors. Proud tears when he was granted an appointment to the U.S. Naval Academy.

Four years later I again wept as my son received his diploma and a congratulatory handshake from then Vice President Al Gore. I had wistful and happy tears on the day of his marriage to his beautiful wife. One chapter of his life was ending and another one was beginning.

But in the early morning hours of October 25, 1999, I experienced a different kind of tears. Upon hearing that my son had just been arrested for committing first-degree murder, tears of anguish flooded over me. They didn't begin to subside until several weeks later.

———

If you are reading this book, you have no doubt experienced tears too. Our tears came from thinking about uncorrectable mistakes and the seeming absence of God. We still believed in Him, but were mystified by His choice not to intervene when He could have. But there is a hidden power in heartache. Ken Gire says, "The closest communion with God comes, I believe, through the sacrament of tears."[9]

Pour your tears out to God, and allow Him to draw you into His comforting embrace. Remember: "The LORD is close to the brokenhearted and saves those who are crushed in spirit" (Psalm 34:18).

### HIS WORDS OVER YOU

"My love for you is so great I've kept track of every time you toss and turn through sleepless nights. I've documented each of your tears in a ledger, and I see every ache in your heart. One day I'll wipe every tear from your eyes. Your pain and your tears will be gone."

*Based on Psalm 56:8 and Revelation 21:4*

---

9. Ken Gire, *Windows of the Soul* (Grand Rapids: Zondervan, 1996), 194.

# 13. A Difficult Mother's Day

*Even the saddest things can become, once we have
made peace with them, a source of wisdom and
strength for the journey that still lies ahead.*

FREDERICK BUECHNER

The spring of 2000 came slowly to Michigan. Patches of snow were still visible in April and the tulips and daffodils were having a tough time getting their blooms above ground. I found a strange comfort in the grayness of the cloudy, rainy days that finally brought us to May. The gloom of the weather perfectly matched the mood in my heart and gave me nonverbal permission to cry.

Those heavy feelings came to a head on Mother's Day. Gene and I arrived at church without considering that the ushers always passed out flowers to honor the mothers in attendance. When I received my red carnation, emotions washed over me like a wave of accusation. The brightly colored flower was a reminder that I was a failure as a mother. My son had committed a heinous crime. I would not be sharing a meal with my only child on this Mother's Day, the special day for honoring "good" mothers.

Gene instantly realized how I was feeling. "Honey," he said, "I'll take you out to our favorite restaurant for lunch."

I refused, blurting out, "That is a terrible idea! Do you think I want to go into a local restaurant today where people we know are sitting at tables surrounded by their children who are honoring their mothers? That would be the most depressing thing I could do today!" Gene got the message and quietly drove us home.

All afternoon I waited for the phone to ring. I longed to hear the digitized message asking me to accept a call from an inmate. I just needed to know that my son was okay. I wanted to hear his voice. But the call never came.

Jason's days at the jail were starting to melt into one unending day. I doubted he even remembered it was Mother's Day. My tears started slowly and soon became unstoppable.

Walking to the sofa, I picked up the afghan my mother had crocheted for me many years earlier. It had arrived with a note in Mama's distinctive handwriting: "Dear Carol, I prayed for you with every stitch. Love, Mother." I wrapped the afghan around my body from my neck to my toes. I needed my Mama that day—and she lived far away from me.

So I began to talk to God. "Father, I am so broken and hurting, unable to find peace on this day when other mothers are hugging their children and hearing words of affirmation. I am weary of this pain that never goes away. Please rescue me. And if you don't, will you please climb inside this afghan with me and hold me? What do you want me to see? To learn?"

Instinctively, I reached for my Bible and turned to a passage my mother often quoted during my growing-up years: Psalm 91. That day I read verses 1 and 2 and 14 through 16 from *The Message*:

> You who sit down in the High God's presence, spend the night in Shaddai's shadow, say this: "GOD, you're my refuge. I trust in you and I'm safe!" . . . "If you'll hold on to me for dear life," says GOD, "I'll get you out of any trouble. I'll give you the best of care if you'll only get to know and trust me. Call me and I'll answer, be at your side in bad times; I'll rescue you."[10]

---

For families of inmates, special days are hard, especially when we see people on the outside enjoying their time together. During the beginning months and years of incarceration, there are many "firsts" that bring waves of sadness and discouragement: Sometimes it's the first missed baseball game, or the first missed birthday of a child, a spouse, or a sibling; it can also be the first family reunion when your loved one is absent. It could be a teenaged child's first date or the first time your loved one misses an important funeral. During these times that are filled with emotion, I've discovered it's helpful to talk to other family members about my incarcerated son. I may tell about a recent visit or a new program he's involved with on the inside.

When a loved one is first incarcerated, it's easy to downplay the important role of celebration in the lives of your family members on the outside. We sometimes feel guilty for having fun while one of our family members is in prison. Though it may be hard, be intentional about making family weddings, holidays, birthdays, and graduations special. That will reinforce the fact that your family unit is not disintegrating because one important member is in jail or prison.

Your sadness is real and your tears are precious to God. On that Mother's Day when I felt so alone and discouraged, I was comforted by

10. Some content taken from *When I Lay My Isaac Down*, by Carol Kent. Copyright © 2004, 2013. Used by permission of NavPress. All rights reserved. Represented by Tyndale House Publishers, Inc.

Scripture and prayed, "Father, I open my hands and ask you to guide me through uncharted waters. My tears don't stop, but I am finding your presence sweeter than I've ever known before. I hate this process, but I love you in a different and deeper way."

Pour out your heart to God today. Ask Him to bring you into His comforting embrace.

### HIS WORDS OVER YOU

"I am your refuge. Trust in me and you'll be safe. My outstretched arms will protect you. Call me and I'll answer. You will find me at your side in bad times. I have ordered my angels to guard you wherever you go. If you stumble, they'll catch you. Their job is to keep you from falling."

*Based on Psalm 91:2, 4, 11, and 15*

# 14. Picking Isaac Up Again

*Suffering is unbearable if you aren't certain
that God is for you and with you.*

TIM KELLER

Soon after Jason's arrest, several large boxes of his personal items were shipped to our home. They were filled with his favorite books, handwritten journals, certificates, pictures, T-shirts, workout clothes, Naval Academy uniforms, and memorabilia from his four years in Annapolis, Maryland.

Just opening the boxes was overwhelming. I found it impossible to make decisions about where to put Jason's things—or about what to discard. A close friend told me, "Carol, don't let go of anything you can't part with yet. At a later time you will find your head is clear enough to make those decisions."

A few days later my assistant, Shirley, moved into action. She knew how hard it was for me to face those boxes. So with great compassion and kindness, Shirley emptied several of the boxes, hung up my son's clothing, and placed everything in a closet in our spare bedroom.

Time passed and one day I knew instinctively that it was time to face my private pain. Opening the closet door, my eyes immediately gravitated to Jason's dress whites—the uniform he was married in. Slowly, I ran my hands over the collar, the sleeves, the brass buttons, and the medals. I lovingly touched item after item of my son's clothing. Then I came to a dress shirt that had been worn but not laundered—there was a soiled neck ring on the collar. (Moms notice things like that.) Removing the shirt from the hanger, I held it for a long time, sniffing the collar, searching for the scent of bygone days—a happier, more peaceful, easier, and prouder time in my life.

Then I saw the box of Jason's favorite books—the ones he intended to introduce to his own children. Oh, how my boy loved books! I thought back to a statement he made while he was still a teenager. "Mom, I only need a bed and bookshelves in my room."

I refolded his old T-shirts and gym shorts. I tried on his hiking boots, thinking back to his adventures at wilderness camp and survival school in Colorado. Everything had changed—nothing would ever be the same again. I fell onto the bed and sobbed as I found myself once again picking up my Isaac and claiming a "right" to control the future.

It was hard for me to admit that a great deal of my worth stemmed from pride in my son and his achievements.

It was difficult to come to a place where I understood that "laying my Isaac down" was not a moment in time. It was going to be a process that involved daily decisions to humble myself and relinquish my son to God. But He comforted me with a powerful verse: "I learned God-worship when my pride was shattered. Heart-shattered lives ready for love don't for a moment escape God's notice" (Psalm 51:17 MSG).

———

The toughest thing for you and me is to quit picking our Isaacs up again and again. Choosing obedience and giving up our control are hard-fought battles. We often try to relive the past or to soothe our sorrows with thoughts of "what might have been."

I was surprised to find that Genesis 22 does not record anything about tears from Abraham. Could it be that Abraham's faith was at such a level that he knew God could be trusted with his child? If you find yourself continually running in circles, clutching your Isaac to your chest, make a choice. Misery or joy? Frenetic activity or relaxation? Control or release? Is the alternative to laying down our Isaacs that appealing? Not really.

The faith that carries us through unthinkable circumstances begins with being flat-out needy and allows God's love to wrap us up, hold us close, and dry our tears. One day we'll discover our cries are being transformed into renewed hope, fresh faith, and unexpected joy.

### HIS WORDS OVER YOU

"I have loved you with an everlasting love; I have drawn you with unfailing kindness. My heart toward you is good. Cast your anxiety on me. Lay it down. I am the one who sustains you. You are mine."

*Based on Jeremiah 31:3 and 1 Peter 5:7*

# 15. Yellow Roses

*A friend hears the song in my heart and*
*sings it to me when my memory fails.*

Anonymous

There seemed to be a daily rhythm in my grieving. In the morning, when the sun came up, I felt more alive and hopeful. But as the daylight faded with the late afternoon and evening, my spirits descended with the sun. The cloud of depression lurked over my head, threatening to attach itself to my mental state. I was generally a happy person and it was now a daily battle to find my joy.

We were still in the beginning of our journey. One day, when Gene had left for a meeting and I was home alone, the doorbell rang. I opened the door and saw a deliveryman holding what appeared to be a covered bouquet. He smiled widely and said with a cheerful voice, "Are you Carol Kent?" I nodded and he continued. "Well, ma'am, it's your lucky day!"

My initial reaction was just in my head: *Mister, why don't you go make someone else's day lucky—I'm not in the mood!* However, I discovered that when you're feeling depressed, it's just easier to respond in a predictable way. As I reached for the delivery, he spoke again. "Someone must want you to feel very special because these flowers are for you."

I mumbled a "thank you" and walked to the kitchen, where I placed the arrangement on my counter. Removing the florist paper, I found a dozen of the most exquisite yellow roses I had ever seen and I wondered who had graced my day with this special gift. Opening the card, I discovered it was from two of my sisters. The note read:

Dear Carol,
  You once gave us some decorating advice that was very helpful. You said, "Yellow flowers will brighten any room." We thought you could use a little yellow in your life right now.
  Love,
  Bonnie and Joy[11]

I wept like a baby. I had never been so needy, and I had never felt so loved. Gazing at the flowers, I realized that my sisters, along with many

---

11. Some content taken from *When I Lay My Isaac Down*, by Carol Kent. Copyright © 2004, 2013. Used by permission of NavPress. All rights reserved. Represented by Tyndale House Publishers, Inc.

other people, were trying to let us know we were not alone. During this long vigil—of waiting for what would happen at Jason's trial and of dealing with fear over our income and his legal expenses—people were thinking about us, praying for us, and waiting with us. From that point on, yellow became my color of hope. The story of that delivery of yellow roses spread, and it ignited an entire community of people who began blessing us with gifts of Christian love, compassion, and encouragement for the long journey ahead. On many days the postman delivered cards in yellow envelopes. Packages filled with heartfelt gifts came in yellow wrapping paper. People sent yellow coffee mugs and yellow candles.

The people surrounding us were living out Colossians 3:12: "Therefore, as God's chosen people, holy and dearly loved, clothe yourselves with compassion, kindness, humility, gentleness and patience."

———

When we go through the arrest of a loved one, the greatest temptation is to hide. Sometimes we don't answer the telephone or the doorbell. Often, we don't respond to e-mails or text messages. It seems safer to pull away from people and remain alone. But God created us to live and breathe and work in community, and when we open ourselves up to receiving the sincere compassion of others, we find the courage to move forward.

Embrace those people in your life who respond in love like Jesus taught: "Here is a simple, rule-of-thumb guide for behavior: Ask yourself what you want people to do for you, then grab the initiative and do it for *them*" (Matthew 7:12 MSG).

### HIS WORDS OVER YOU

"I will redeem your life from the pit of depression and crown you with love and compassion. Talk to me. I love to give good gifts to those who ask. I am already blessing you with the presence and support of my people."

*Based on Psalm 103:4 and Matthew 7:11*

# 16. Bearing Each Other's Burdens

*No one offers the name of a philosopher when I ask the question, "Who helped you most?" Most often they answer by describing a quiet, unassuming person. Someone who was there whenever needed, who listened more than talked, who didn't keep glancing down at a watch, who hugged and touched, and cried.*

PHILIP YANCEY

Gene and I were used to showing compassion. But suddenly and unexpectedly we were the needy ones—emotionally, spiritually, and financially. This role reversal shocked us. We discovered it takes a lot of humility to tell people you have needs . . . and to be willing to receive assistance from them. Gene and I are both firstborns, independent people who had always prided ourselves on not needing a lot of help from others. But our real-life situation changed all that!

A few months after Jason's arrest, I received an e-mail from a friend who lived in Arizona. Kathe said that God was prompting her to network our friends through a monthly electronic newsletter, in hopes of providing support for us in the months prior to the trial. Within two weeks an almost identical e-mail arrived from Texas-based Becky. These women had never met each other, but since they each knew us, they joined forces. Kathe and Becky worked hard to provide regular updates—on the status of the trial and on our personal needs—to people who were praying for us and wanted to know how they could offer assistance.

Kathe called the group our "Stretcher Bearers," after a book entitled *Becoming a Stretcher Bearer.*[12] Several years earlier, she had heard the author, pastor Michael Slater, speak about his book, challenging people not to just pray for those in need but to be involved in active encouragement—to become stretcher bearers for them.

There is a powerful story of stretcher bearing in Luke 5:17–26. We learn that a paralyzed man needed help. His friends saw his need and interrupted their personal agendas to get involved. The Bible says, "Some men arrived carrying a paraplegic on a stretcher. They were looking for a way to get into the house and set him before Jesus. When they couldn't find a way in because of the crowd, they went up on the roof, removed

---

12. Michael Slater, *Becoming a Stretcher Bearer* (Ventura, CA: Regal Books, 1985). Formerly published under the title, *Stretcher Bearers*. Stretcher Bearer Ministries, P.O. Box 1035, La Habra, CA, 90633-1035.

some tiles, and let him down in the middle of everyone, right in front of Jesus. Impressed by their bold belief, he said, 'Friend, I forgive your sins. . . . Get up. Take your bedroll and go home.' Without a moment's hesitation, he did it—got up, took his blanket, and left for home, giving glory to God all the way. The people rubbed their eyes, incredulous—and then also gave glory to God. Awestruck, they said, 'We've never seen anything like that!'" (Luke 5:18–20, 24–26 MSG).

What a story! These "friends in need" got creative and good things happened. Our Stretcher Bearers were similar—they were friends who recognized our needs and took action, launching a campaign that helped us tremendously during the challenging months ahead.[13]

———

During World War I, teams of stretcher bearers were given first aid training to care for soldiers injured on the battlefields. They delivered medical aid as close to the front lines as possible, and later carried away the wounded on stretchers.[14] As families of the incarcerated, we know we are not in a flesh-and-blood war—but we definitely feel like we are on the front lines. Our wounds are not visible to the naked eye, but the pain and hurt below the surface need attention and God mercifully sends stretcher bearers to pray and to sustain us with hands-on help. As the Bible says, "Carry each other's burdens, and in this way you will fulfill the law of Christ" (Galatians 6:2).

### HIS WORDS OVER YOU

"You cannot carry all the burdens of your family members by yourself. You need friends to stand in the gap during this crucial time. Just as I did for Moses, I will enlist others to bear the load so you will not have to be weighed down. Be encouraged."

*Based on Numbers 11:14, 17*

———

13. Some content taken from *When I Lay My Isaac Down*, by Carol Kent. Copyright © 2004, 2013. Used by permission of NavPress. All rights reserved. Represented by Tyndale House Publishers, Inc.

14. Imperial College London. "Uncovering the unsung medical heroes of the Great War" by Andrew Czyzewski, February 4, 2013, http://www3.imperial.ac.uk/newsand eventspggrp/imperialcollege/newssummary/news_4-2-2013-9-52-58.

# 17. A Sister to the Rescue

*Did you ever take a real trip down inside the broken heart of a friend? To feel the sob of the soul—the raw, red crucible of emotional agony? To have this become almost as much yours as that of your soul-crushed neighbor? Then, to sit down with him—and silently weep? This is the beginning of compassion.*

JESS MOODY

I'm from a large family. Growing up, I knew the delight and the chaos of having four sisters and a brother. After our son's arrest, each of my family members wrote precious notes and called regularly to console me. It was the worst of times, but in an inexplicable way, it was also the best of times. I learned that God often uses the people closest to us to demonstrate the unconditional love and compassion of Jesus.

As month followed month, I had some days that were better than others, but some that were very dark. Almost a year had gone by and our son was still in the county jail. There had already been two postponements of his trial and time dragged on with no resolution in sight. The legal process moved at a snail's pace.

On the first anniversary of the murder, I found myself slipping into major discouragement. For my son, there was almost no hope for a positive outcome. I spent the day looking through family scrapbooks filled with pictures of happier days. There are times when we give ourselves permission to drown in our own grief—and this was my day. I finally escaped into a deep sleep.

At a later date, my sister Bonnie sent me the following note. She had typed it on her computer at almost the moment when I'd reached my lowest point:

> It was October 25, 2000, my husband's fiftieth birthday. I usually make birthdays a celebration; however, on this day, I woke up feeling deep sadness. One year earlier we received a call telling us that my nephew, Jason, had shot and killed a man, believing he was protecting his stepdaughters from potential abuse. Yet, here I was, one year later, in severe pain. I could barely breathe. The grief was beyond understanding.
>
> At noon I called Carol, hoping to gain some relief, but when I heard her voice, I burst into tears. No words would come. . . . That night I took my husband out for a birthday dinner celebration and

once again I broke down and wept. I told him it was as if J. P. (Jason Paul) was my own son.

When I read my sister's note, I realized she'd been sinking under the load of my sorrow. It was almost as if she carried the weight of my emotional pain. I was encouraged to know I had a sister who fully understood the depth of my sorrow and the overwhelming upheaval in my life. I was comforted by her call and thanked God for putting Bonnie in my family.

———

In Exodus 17, Joshua led Israel's army to a major victory over the enemy Amalekites. The Bible says, "Moses, Aaron, and Hur went to the top of the hill. It turned out that whenever Moses raised his hands, Israel was winning, but whenever he lowered his hands, Amalek was winning. But Moses' hands got tired. So they got a stone and set it under him. He sat on it and Aaron and Hur held up his hands, one on each side. So his hands remained steady until the sun went down. Joshua defeated Amalek and its army in battle" (Exodus 17:10–13 MSG).

In this story Moses is weary. He no longer has the strength to hold his own hands up. But when his hands go down, Amalek begins winning the battle; when his hands are up, Israel wins. Moses needs the combined support of his brother, Aaron, and a fellow Israelite, Hur, to hold up his hands for a victory to take place.

That story reminds me that God often uses *our* family and friends to come alongside when we can no longer carry the weight of our impossible situations. Sometimes just being there for us or calling to see how we're doing—basically, feeling our hurt—is just what we need to make it through the day.

We sometimes think there is no one in our lives who really cares, but it may be that we're just tempted to pull away from others. During the first few months following my son's arrest, it often seemed easier to pull down the window shades, to *not* answer the phone or e-mails or text messages, to try to make everyone around me think I was "fine." But I'm discovering that when I allow people to help carry my grief as I talk with them, spend time together, and open up about the tough days, my problem seems lighter. I realize I'm not alone.

That's what this book is all about—waiting *together,* instead of stubbornly trying to hide our pain and resisting the support of those people closest to us. We really do need each other!

## HIS WORDS OVER YOU

"Be quick to embrace love. Allow people to be kind and compassionate to you. As you open your heart, you'll discover that I'm able to do immeasurably more than you could ever imagine."

*Based on Ephesians 4:32 and 3:20*

# 18. Hold Me

*Holders are people who stand beside us even when things are unpleasant; they have a capacity to stay unshaken for the long haul.*

KAREN BURTON MAINS

Gene and I soon discovered there were two kinds of comforters. Both were sincerely trying to help us, but their approach to encouragement differed greatly.

The first type of comforter came to our house, wanted to hear all the details of our son's arrest, and started quoting Bible verses. Especially this one: "And we know that all things work together for good to them that love God, to them who are the called according to his purpose" (Romans 8:28 KJV). Even though I had been a Christian for years, I became irritated when someone who was not going through my extremely difficult circumstances tried to comfort me with what felt like a pat response.

The second type of comforter is what we called a "holder." These people already had tears in their eyes when they walked into our home. Often they would put their arms around us, simply holding us and weeping with us. Very few words were exchanged, as they had no expectation of a long explanation about the horrible thing that had happened.

The holders recognized that there were practical things they could do to help us. Some brought meals, and those who understood our shock knew that a light meal of soup and salad would be much more appreciated than a heavy dinner. Others said, "I know you have calls to make and personal matters to handle. I'm just going to tidy up the kitchen and vacuum the carpet so you can concentrate on more pressing matters." They looked around, saw what needed to be done, and took care of it.

Still other people did "long distance holding." An unexpected letter was sent to one of the women who sent out our monthly e-mail updates. It came from our former next-door neighbor, Tony:

> The Kents are among the nicest people I have ever met, so it stands to reason that Jason's wife is very special also. I would tell you I'm not a very religious or devout person. But I do believe in a higher power and on occasion do pray to give thanks. I am sending a check to Jason's wife today. I don't know if I can be a Stretcher Bearer, but I will carry the Band-Aids.

We loved that note from Tony. He wasn't helping our family because he was pretending to be a Christian—he honestly admitted that he wasn't religious, but still wanted to do what he could.

Our holders donated frequent flyer miles, because Jason was incarcerated in Florida and we were living in Michigan. Others sent books to Jason on a regular basis. A few sent encouraging gifts and notes to our step-granddaughters, knowing the children were going through a drastic change too. Our holders reminded us that they were going to stick with our family for the long haul.

———

Perhaps like me, you have not always appreciated people who seem to have all the answers—those who try to give advice without first experiencing the pain you are feeling. I had moments when I felt like slugging the know-it-alls. I had to learn to take a breath and realize that many were genuinely trying to help, responding the only way they knew how. That enabled me to forgive them more quickly.

The Bible says, "Those of us who are strong and able in the faith need to step in and lend a hand to those who falter, and not just do what is most convenient for us. Strength is for service, not status. Each one of us needs to look after the good of the people around us, asking ourselves, 'How can I help?'" (Romans 15:1–2 MSG). I think the secret of being an effective holder is in those verses. The people who help the most are the ones asking questions rather than giving answers—and the most important question is, "How can I help?"

We can actually assist the people who want to help us by making a list of the needs in our family—for both the incarcerated person and those at home. It can feel awkward to do this, but when people ask how they can serve you, they'll be grateful. They can know that they are providing assistance or sending gifts that are truly needed, rather than guessing at what might be helpful.

### HIS WORDS OVER YOU

"I will give you the strength to endure over the long time you are caring for your family both inside and outside the prison walls. I am not giving you a grim, 'grit your teeth' kind of strength, but a strength that endures the unendurable and spills over into joy. I want you to take part in everything I have provided for you through my people."

*Based on Colossians 1:11–12 and 2 Corinthians 1:3–5*

# 19. How Are You?

*I would rather walk with a friend in the*
*dark than walk alone in the light.*

HELEN KELLER

On the day we received the news of Jason's arrest, we made a few calls to close relatives to tell them what happened. Actually, Gene did the calling while I cried in the background. Sadness was washing over me in waves, and tears were flowing. It had been a hard morning.

Then a call came in for us. It was Jan, my best friend from high school. We had known each other since we were fourteen. Jan had an alcoholic, absentee father who had been in and out of prison during her growing-up years. She and her two sisters knew the gut-wrenching experience of having their dad, newly released from prison, showing up at their front door, looking for a handout.

As our friendship grew, we often talked about what we would do when we entered adulthood. After Jan graduated from high school, she majored in education, becoming a teacher and eventually a principal. We both led busy lives, so we weren't in regular contact, but we always had a sixth sense for knowing when the other needed prayer. At this time, we had been out of touch for several months.

When I answered the phone, Jan immediately asked, "How are you?" The question took me completely by surprise. Jan's call was unexpected— and her question was spot-on for the explosive news we had received overnight.

"Not very well," I muttered. Trying to catch my breath amid the emotion of hearing Jan's voice, I blurted out, "How did you know to call me *today*? Jason has been arrested for first-degree murder."

Jan wasn't prepared to hear those words, but she knew God had prompted her to call me. We were two redheads who had encouraged each other for decades, women who had prayed for each other's most secret needs and hurts for a long time. Jan had watched my son grow up from infancy; she loved him dearly and understood the severity of my anguish. Because of her troubled father, she also knew how prison tears families apart. I don't remember many specifics of that day's conversation, but I knew I was not alone.

A couple of weeks passed. We made the deposit on Jason's legal fees, with an agreement to pay off the rest of the bill in ten large, monthly payments. Humanly speaking, we had no idea how we could cover such a big bill every month. In my self-employment, as a speaker and writer, there are some good income months every year—and some that are much more meager.

One day in the mail I saw a letter from Jan. As I opened the envelope, a check fell out. It was written for the exact amount of one of our monthly attorney payments. The note said, "Carol, God prompted me to write this check. You may not need it right now, but I want you to put it in the bank and know it's there for any time you fall short of what you need as you await Jason's trial. Love, Jan." Over the next ten months there was always just enough to pay the monthly fee. At the end of that time, we were able to send Jan's gift back with thanks for giving us an ongoing peace of mind while the enormous bill hung over our heads.

———

Sometimes we forget that there are people who would *love* to assist us—if they knew their gift would be received. Often, pride gets in the way, as many of us don't want to be looked upon as needy. Here is a Bible verse that helped me choose humility: "Pride leads to disgrace, but with humility comes wisdom" (Proverbs 11:2 NLT).

Do you have a friend who doesn't even know what's happened yet? Perhaps you think it's too embarrassing to tell that person that your loved one has committed a crime and you are awaiting a trial. Take the risk and call. When your friend asks, "How are you?" answer honestly. I have discovered that, when they learned my secret, very few people looked down on me as a parent. Most people felt my pain and offered assistance.

If you feel you have no friends left, remember that God wants to be your friend. "Friendship with God is reserved for those who reverence him. With them alone he shares the secrets of his promises" (Psalm 25:14 TLB).

## HIS WORDS OVER YOU

"I hear you when you call for help and I can save you from your troubles. I am your refuge and strength, a tested help in time of trouble. Be alert. Your true friends will always be loyal. Allow them to bless you."

*Based on Psalm 34:17, Psalm 46:1, and Proverbs 17:17*

# 20. When Nobody Cares

*Compassion is understanding the troubles of others,*
*coupled with an urgent desire to help.*

Megiddo Message

The woman who approached me had tears in her eyes. "Our family didn't have the kind of support you and your husband had when your son was arrested," she said. "When our son went to jail because of illegal possession of drugs, I felt like the people closest to us were judging us for being bad parents, making us feel like it was our fault that he made such bad choices. We felt very alone, and we still rarely talk about what happened now that the trial is over and our son is in prison."

She went on. "I honestly felt jealous when I read about how your family and friends helped to encourage you in tangible ways—both financially and with meaningful gifts. For some unexplainable reason I even felt mad at you. I didn't even know you personally, but there was jealousy bubbling up inside me. It felt unfair that your family had so much support, when we were just as needy but had nothing."

More than a handful of people have voiced similar comments. My first reaction is great sadness that there aren't more compassionate people—the kind who see needs, listen to the heartbeat of those who hurt, and ask how they can be of assistance. But then God reminded me of something important: even when *we* are in the middle of great pain, if we look around we will be able to find at least one other person who needs help more than we do.

I've discovered it doesn't require money to bless someone. Taking care of children while a mom visits her incarcerated husband is a gift that costs us nothing but time. It doesn't cost a cent to pray over the phone with someone who has a child in the prison of drug addiction. The gift of waiting with someone during jury deliberations does not have a price—but it does have a high value.

In the months following our son's arrest, I rode a roller coaster of emotions. Some days I could make it, and other days I withdrew from the public and tried to hide. I even remember closing the blinds and turning out lights sometimes, so it looked like nobody was home.

One day a small padded envelope arrived from my friend Diana. She had experienced an abusive marriage, a difficult divorce, devastating financial challenges—all kinds of faith-shaking hardships. She had endured the harsh judgment of church people who thought she could have saved her marriage if she had only been "a better wife." Diana knew pain. She knew the ache of the soul. She had earned the right to speak to me about my own paralyzing hurt.

When I opened the package, out fell a tiny pewter figurine—only an inch high and a half-inch wide. Gazing closely, I saw it depicted a hand completely cradling a child. It was heavy for its small size, and it fit perfectly in the palm of my own hand. Diana's note said:

> During my worst days, when I didn't know how I would feed my children or pay the bills or hold my head up, I clutched this figurine in my hand and was comforted, knowing that God himself was my safe place. He was all I had left, and that was enough. I am passing this gift on to you. Cling to the truth of the Bible as you find comfort on the hardest days as you wait for Jason's trial. You are loved.

My greatest lesson was the mysterious way God allows us to comfort others. The gift of the figurine from Diana was of much greater value to me than money. It was offered by someone who knows what it feels like to be needy, but she gave what she had.

Diana comforted me with something that had comforted her—the reminder that no matter what happens, we are safe when we are sheltered in God's hand. The Bible says, "Hide me in the shadow of your wings" (Psalm 17:8). That day, through the image of the figurine, I understood that I could hide in God's embrace.

Who around you is hurting right now? Make a list of ways you can serve and encourage that person without writing a check or spending money that you don't have. Pick one thing on that list and follow through with action. Note what happens to your spirits. I know from experience that when you do what you can for others—even when you think no one cares about *your* needs—a splash of joy refreshes your heart.

## HIS WORDS OVER YOU

"My child, when you feel that no one cares about your impossible situation, come to me. I will be your refuge and your safe place. In my presence you will find comfort. Just as a hen covers her chicks with her feathers, I will be your protector. If you dwell in me, I will be your fortress when trouble comes. Then, as you are comforted, encourage others."

*Based on Psalm 91:1–4 and 2 Corinthians 1:4*

# 21. Creative Friends

*What did you do today that only a*
*Christian would have done?*

CORRIE TEN BOOM

Almost two and a half years dragged by as we awaited Jason's trial. After seven postponements, it was finally scheduled for April 2002. My friends Karen and Bette Jo contacted me to ask if they could plan a girls' getaway sometime before the trial. At one point all of us lived in the same city, but due to business and ministry moves, we had settled in three different cities several hours apart. Karen's family owned a cottage in northern Indiana, and that was designated as our meeting place.

When I arrived, Karen and Bette Jo were already there. They suggested that I unpack while they worked on dinner, and I soon realized they were treating me as their very special guest. That evening we had a glorious time of remembering shared experiences—highlights of a bygone season of our lives. We recalled things that made us laugh out loud and other memories that brought joy-filled reminders of a happier time in my life.

I felt encouraged. Since Jason had been arrested, I had not left my husband's side to spend time with girlfriends. As I laughed with my friends and relished this mini vacation, I had to suppress occasional feelings of guilt—the false guilt that says we're wrong to enjoy our own lives when a loved one is incarcerated.

The next morning we stayed in our bathrobes until noon and drank coffee on the deck overlooking the lake. It was unhurried. Quiet. Peaceful. Uninterrupted. I felt like I had entered a haven from the chaotic world of planning for my son's first-degree murder trial. All of us who live in this world of courtrooms and prisons should look for moments of respite, times when we can set aside our "real life" for a while.

That afternoon it was overcast and we were inside. Karen said, "We just want to encourage you," and she and Bette Jo opened some old-fashioned hymnbooks, the kind you might have seen in a church pew many years ago. They had selected songs to prepare my heart for the most challenging week of my life.

My friends started by singing a song I had heard from my earliest years in church: "Great Is Thy Faithfulness." They sang all of the verses, then turned a page and sang, "A Mighty Fortress Is Our God," followed by "Amazing Grace." For an hour these dear friends, a choir of two, sang to me—an audience of one. Karen and Bette Jo are not trained musicians, but out of love for me, they performed a concert of some of the great songs of the faith I had grown up on, reminding me of God's faithfulness.

Afterward, they pulled out their Bibles and read Scripture verses to prepare my heart for the week of my son's trial. One verse that stayed with me was Isaiah 41:10: "So do not fear, for I am with you; do not be dismayed, for I am your God. I will strengthen you and help you; I will uphold you with my righteous right hand." Another passage that comforted me during that worst week of my life was Psalm 23: "The LORD is my shepherd, I lack nothing. . . . Even though I walk through the darkest valley, I will fear no evil, for you are with me; your rod and your staff they comfort me" (verses 1, 4).[15]

———

I used to think "showing compassion" meant feeling sorry for people in difficult circumstances. I was wrong. When my son was arrested I learned the real meaning of compassion. Compassion is when we respond to someone's need both emotionally and practically. That's what Karen and Bette Jo did for me, and it gives us an example of what we can do for others. My friends saw my pain and did something tangible to help me know I was loved.

As I shared the story of what my friends did for me, other people began doing similar acts of kindness for their friends who were struggling. Creative compassion spread like wildfire. Have you experienced a unique act of compassion since your loved one was arrested? If so, can you "pay it back" to someone else in need? Even if you haven't enjoyed such a blessing, you'll benefit from showing compassion to someone nearby.

For example, think of those families you meet on the jail or prison visitation days. What is one thing you could do to ease their loads and show that you care, even as you wait in the security line?

You and I have the privilege of revealing to those in our unique circle of "the loved ones of the incarcerated" that "the LORD is good, a refuge in times of trouble. He cares for those who trust in him" (Nahum 1:7).

15. Some content taken from *When I Lay My Isaac Down*, by Carol Kent. Copyright © 2004, 2013. Used by permission of NavPress. All rights reserved. Represented by Tyndale House Publishers, Inc.

"I love to comfort my people—that's you! I tenderly care for those who are beaten-up and broken-down. My love never runs out. It's new every morning. Stick with me. You can rely on my faithfulness."

*Based on Isaiah 49:13 and Lamentations 3:22*

# 22. The Best Gift

*Hope begins in the dark, the stubborn hope that if you just*
*show up and try to do the right thing, the dawn will come.*
*You wait and watch and work: you don't give up.*

ANNE LAMOTT

A few months before Jason's trial was to begin, I had a speaking engagement in Southern California. It was a women's conference that ended on a Saturday afternoon. Some friends who received the monthly e-mail updates on our family asked if they could take us out for dinner after the event. We made plans to join them.

Judy was a fellow speaker, and we had known each other for years. She was hilariously funny and would often use humor to warm up a crowd before making important, life-changing points. When I heard that she'd married a man named Orvey Euclid Hampton Jr., I just knew she had to have a sense of humor! But Judy told me the funniest part of the story was that the person who typed up their marriage certificate spelled her husband's name O-V-A-R-Y. Whenever I spent time with Judy, I felt encouraged.

On the evening of our dinner, conversation was comfortable, uplifting, and encouraging. Judy and Orvey had followed the story of Jason's arrest, and they had been in touch often to let us know we were not forgotten. At one point, Jason told us they had written to him at the jail, sending books that were of great interest to him.

As our evening neared its end, we lingered over our last cups of coffee. We had thoroughly enjoyed our time with friends who were part of the team who prayed for us regularly. Then Judy pulled out a package. She said, "Orvey and I have a gift for you."

Opening the bag, she pulled out a copy of the Bible. She leaned toward us to present the gift and explained, "I have gone through every chapter in this book and I have highlighted every verse that has the word *hope* in it." Tears began to stream down my cheeks. I knew what a busy person Judy was, and I couldn't imagine how much time it had taken to prepare such an encouraging gift. She went on, "We thought you just might need to read some of these verses before the week of the trial."

It was an evening Gene and I will never forget. Anxiety was hanging over our heads as we approached our trip to Florida for the trial. Knowing our son had committed the crime and faced the probability of a harsh sentence was overwhelming. When I opened the Bible Judy gave me, I found myself immediately drawn to these yellow-highlighted verses:

- "But God will never forget the needy; the hope of the afflicted will never perish" (Psalm 9:18).
- "Be strong and take heart, all you who hope in the LORD" (Psalm 31:24).
- "We wait in hope for the LORD; he is our help and our shield" (Psalm 33:20).

———

Every one of the verses our friends had highlighted reminded us to wait with *hope*. There was nothing in Scripture that said we would win the trial, but we were encouraged by the reminder that God would be our help and protection. We were feeling very needy—and one of the highlighted verses said that God would not forget us.

Perhaps you, like my husband and I, have grown tired of waiting for your family member's trial. The days turn into weeks, and the weeks turn into months, and the months sometimes turn into years. In our case, it was a two-and-a-half-year wait for resolution. At times it felt unbearable. And then we discovered that waiting was much easier when we allowed people who cared to wait with us. To pray with us. To eat with us. Just to hang out with us.

Who in your life is willing to wait with you? Whether it's waiting for a trial, waiting for a sentence to be completed, or waiting with you throughout a sentence of life without parole, let these dear friends know that they are helping you to wait with hope.

### HIS WORDS OVER YOU

"It's a good thing to quietly hope for help from me. You'll make it through the hard times. When your life situation seems heavy, pray. Don't run from trouble. Wait for hope to appear. Allow my people to wait with you."

*Based on Lamentations 3:25–31*

# 23. Hope's Beginning

*Hope keeps you alive. Faith gives your life*
*meaning, blessings, and a good end.*

Rex Rouis

After my son was arrested, there were days when I questioned God. From the time I was a little girl, I had learned that God is all-powerful and all-knowing. *So if He's that powerful and knows everything and loves people,* I thought, *why didn't He prevent this crime that has totally ruined the hopes and dreams of two entire families—the family of the deceased and my family? Surely He was capable of giving Jason a flat tire before he got to the parking lot where the murder took place. Why did God allow this horrible thing to happen?*

As I struggled to hold on to my own hope and faith, my mind went back to my childhood. I remember, at the age of five, listening to a radio program called *Unshackled.* It was an outreach of the Pacific Garden Mission in Chicago, Illinois, which reenacted the stories of people who'd had dramatic changes in their lives. As I listened to the narrative unfold that afternoon, I was captivated.

When the program ended, I turned to my mother. "Mama," I said, "I am such a sinner. Do you think that Jesus would come into my heart?" My mother realized that even at my young age, I knew I needed to invite Jesus into my life and find my hope in Him. She took her Bible and read to me, "For all have sinned, and come short of the glory of God" (Romans 3:23 KJV).

I knew that was true. There was no doubt in my mind that I was a sinner.

Then Mama turned to another Bible verse, reading, "For the wages of sin is death; but the gift of God is eternal life through Jesus Christ our Lord" (Romans 6:23 KJV). She explained that Jesus—the perfect, sinless Son of God—came to this earth as a baby in Bethlehem, grew to maturity, and at age thirty began to minister to others and teach them about God. "Religious leaders mocked Him and said He was not the Savior of the world," Mama told me, "and when He was thirty-three years old, they hung Him on a cross to die." She explained that because Jesus was without sin, He could take on *my* sin—and the sin of the whole world—and pay the price for all our wrongdoing.

That day my child-heart understood the truth, and with Mama by my side, I prayed a simple prayer. I bowed my head and told Jesus I was sorry for my sins. I invited Him into my life. It was the most important choice I ever made, the beginning of a lifetime of genuine faith and unstoppable hope.

The choice I made that day became a marker in my life. It pointed my future in the direction of hope. It reminded me that my life had a purpose and that it would have a good end—because I would eventually live in heaven with Jesus. I had (and still have) a lot to learn about hope and faith. But the decision I made as a five-year-old girl became a touchstone I went back to, again and again, when I felt my faith flagging after Jason's arrest.

———

Throughout the incarceration of my son, I have learned that hope is not an emotion or a feeling. It isn't just wishful thinking that has no power to make something happen. *Real* hope, the kind the Bible talks about, is solid. It is concrete evidence based on Hebrews 6:18–19 (MSG): "We who have run for our very lives to God have every reason to grab the promised hope with both hands and never let go. It's an unbreakable spiritual lifeline, reaching past all appearances right to the very presence of God."

Think back on the important choices you've made in your life. Has there ever been a time when you made a definite decision to say yes to Jesus? Have you ever invited Him into your life? If not, you can do that today by praying:

Lord, I need you in my life. I'm tired of trying to pick myself up by my own bootstraps. I'm tired of trying to fix my family members who have made bad decisions. Right now, I say yes to you. I confess my sins and I invite you to come into my life. I want to be a follower of Jesus. Thank you for giving me the secure hope of heaven as my final destination.

If you just prayed that prayer, you have a sure hope. That does not mean your problems are over—but it means you have begun a personal walk with Jesus. He will guide you as you make tough decisions regarding your incarcerated loved one.

### HIS WORDS OVER YOU

"Personal faith in me is the beginning of a solid hope. Your hope is like faith that cannot be moved by tough circumstances. You can rest, knowing that when you ask me for wisdom, I will give it to you."

*Based on Job 11:18, Hebrews 11:1, and James 1:5*

# 24. Is the End in Sight?

*Hope is the thing with feathers*
*that perches in the soul*
*and sings the tune without the words*
*and never stops—at all.*

EMILY DICKENSON

Jason's trial was delayed several times before he actually appeared in court to face the first-degree murder charge. Twenty-one months after his arrest, in late July 2001, we prepared for a scheduled trial.

Tension hung like a thick cloud, enveloping me in an eerie fog. For almost two years, to visit our son at the jail, we had made the expensive trip from Michigan to Florida every four to six weeks. Now, the possibility of resolution was finally within reach.

Family members knew we needed support, and they made plans to be at our side during the week of the trial. I struggled with the sacrifices they were making, doing the mental math on what it would cost them to drive or fly to Orlando, pay for a hotel, and eat in restaurants for multiple days. To sit through our son's trial for first-degree murder, they were giving up time and money they might otherwise have spent on a vacation. Out-of-state friends, meanwhile, offered to care for our step-granddaughters, removing them from the midst of great anxiety and unwanted publicity. It was hard to accept such sacrificial love—but I realized we couldn't make it without these people.

One creative couple rented a houseboat, supplying a few of our family members with no-cost lodging. It also provided a place where inexpensive meals could be made. They decided to call the boat *Hope Floats,* after a movie starring Harry Connick Jr. and Sandra Bullock.

Jason and his wife had seen the film when they were dating. On their way out of the theater, Jason picked up his fiancée and carried her as the main character in the movie had done. With the *Hope Floats* marquee in the background, this fairy-tale moment was photographed by a bystander. A friend who had flown in from California to be with us for the trial had the picture enlarged and laminated. It served as a welcome banner on the houseboat, reminding all of us to hold on to hope.

Jury selection began on Monday morning and several of our family members were in the courtroom. Throughout that day several jurors were chosen, and things seemed to be moving ahead as planned. But around noon on the second day, we could see that the attorneys working on Jason's case were engaged in a heavy discussion. The prosecutor had referred to a specific page number in the evidence documents, which our attorneys discovered they didn't have. We ultimately learned that the prosecutor's office had not sent 250 pages of important paperwork to our legal team. This was a major problem. The judge asked our attorney to confer with Jason to ask if they should go ahead with the trial, or if he wanted a postponement. With so much paperwork undisclosed, the decision was made to delay the trial yet again. The emotional toll on all of us was huge.

There had been so much prayer and so much preparation—and so much money spent by so many family members and friends to be with us—now all of that was going up in smoke! It felt like a cruel joke. Jason was placed in handcuffs, a waist chain, and leg-irons, and led out of the courtroom for transport back to the jail.

———

In the lead-up to your loved one's trial, have you ever had your hopes smashed into a million pieces? There was a part of me that wondered if God had a supernatural reason for this delay, some plan to bring good out of it. But then I found myself getting angry, yelling in my mind, *Hello, God? What is the whole point of this major postponement? Do you love us? Do you care?* At that moment my hope was not floating—it was sinking fast, and I was miserable!

How have you reacted during the waiting times—of not knowing what to expect, or facing delay after delay, or having family and friends come to your aid only to suffer another major disappointment? I found myself wondering, *How many times will the system cry "Wolf!" before we have no one with us in the courtroom?* I felt sad and hopeless.

Much later, I opened my Bible and read, "Let all that I am wait quietly before God, for my hope is in him. He alone is my rock and my salvation, my fortress where I will not be shaken" (Psalm 62:5–6 NLT). I wish I would have known and lived up to that verse in July 2001—and though I know the verse now, I could still do better putting it into practice. It is an ongoing goal in my life.

### HIS WORDS OVER YOU

"Dear one, I know you are tired and worn out, waiting to be rescued. Put your hope in my Word. Always remember that victory and honor come from me. If you quit resisting, I will be your refuge and your rock."

*Based on Psalm 119:81 and Psalm 62:7*

# 25. Flashbacks of Better Days

*I can usually manage a crabby hope that there is meaning*
*in mess and pain, that more will be revealed, and that*
*truth and beauty will somehow win out in the end.*

ANNE LAMOTT

When Jason was born, we were given lots of baby gifts. Along with the usual things, we received a remarkable assortment of pink and blue quilts (this was before you could discover the gender of your baby in the womb), handmade afghans, and heirloom-quality blankets—christening blankets trimmed in exquisite white lace and others with soft satin borders. These items were knitted and crocheted by the hands of praying grandmothers and family friends. Our son's nursery was stocked with the most elegant baby blankets I had ever seen.

Time passed and it soon became obvious that J. P. (Jason Paul) had become attached to the only truly ugly blanket in the pile. His favorite was a polyester "Blue Light Special" from K-Mart. It didn't take long for the white comforter to take on a grayish hue and develop disgusting balls of knotted material on its surface. The binding started to shred and dangled precariously at places along the perimeter.

The blanket was a public embarrassment to me. Several times I hid Jason's treasured rag, replacing it with one of the exquisite blankets from the nursery closet. But they were all rejected by my son. He had developed a fierce loyalty to his blanket.

Several months went by and I decided Jason was now old enough to be permanently severed from the tattered blanket. I thought about how often it had been dragged across floors, rationalizing that it was no doubt covered with harmful bacteria. It was time to retire this thing—so one day, while he was busy at play in another room, I replaced it with a blanket of much finer quality. I quietly and carefully placed the polyester castoff in the kitchen wastebasket.

Within an hour, I realized that he had found it. I looked up from my work and saw Jason on a kitchen chair, clutching the "blankie" to his face as tears streamed down his cheeks. He had recently started praying with his own words (instead of just repeating the memorized prayers we had taught him earlier), and he bowed his head over the precious blanket that he had moments earlier rescued from the wastebasket. I heard his sweet voice say, "Dear Jesus, you're just like a blanket and I won't ever stop loving you."

Throughout our son's long wait in the Orange County Jail, followed by many years of imprisonment, one of my greatest temptations has been to linger over memories of better days. Even recalling this story of Jason's blanket sends chills down my spine. My thoughts and questions go in multiple directions:

- What happened to my son that after his precious childhood innocence he was able to shoot and kill a man in his young adulthood?
- What signs along the way could have been warnings to us?
- Did it mean nothing that I prayed over my child every night when I tucked him in?
- Why did other people's children, who were much more difficult to raise, turn out fine while my child committed a heinous crime?
- Did my son's faith, a major part of his background, not "take"? Why else would we face this nightmare?

I am discovering that when I dwell on all the mistakes Gene and I might have made as parents, or when I concentrate on the "what might have been" scenarios of our lives, I destroy my ability to cope. And I have a choice. Will I keep wallowing in the past or will I choose to cling to the hope that God is not finished with my loved one—even if, in his current situation, everything looks doomed to failure?

How often have you wondered what you could have done to prevent the crime that took place? Does fatigue play a role in your looking back, rather than forward? Are there family members or friends who destroy your hope because they won't quit talking about the past?

One great reminder in the Bible helps me out of this self-deprecating mood. "One thing I do: Forgetting what is behind and straining toward what is ahead, I press on toward the goal to win the prize for which God has called me heavenward in Christ Jesus" (Philippians 3:13–14).

### HIS WORDS OVER YOU

"Do not allow yourself to be consumed by reminders of better days. There are people who want to pull you down and destroy your hope. But if you know me, your real home is in heaven. Look ahead. Be purposeful in putting your complete confidence in me as you continue to put one foot in front of the other."

*Based on Ecclesiastes 7:10 and Philippians 3:18–20*

# 26. Praying at the Courthouse

*What's the answer to hopelessness? It's to hope in God,*
*the God of all hope, the God who hears the cry of the*
*desperate and who answers according to His mercy.*

KAY ARTHUR

It was April 2002. Jason had been in jail for two and a half years, and it appeared that after seven postponements, his trial would finally take place. We knew many people were praying for us, and we wondered what influence that would have on the outcome of the legal process.

The trial was to begin on a Monday morning, so Gene and I flew to Florida on Sunday afternoon. We rented a vehicle and met our daughter-in-law at the downtown courthouse. It was a massive complex that took up an entire city block; the main building was more than twenty stories high. We felt intimidated.

The three of us planned to walk around the complex, praying for all aspects of the trial before jury selection began the next morning. We made this decision based on the Bible story of Joshua, who did a "prayer walk" around the walls of a place called Jericho. After his seventh trip around, the walls came tumbling down. (We were not expecting the walls of the courthouse to fall down, but we did know there is power in prayer—and we wanted to be sure we had our bases covered!)

Our walk around the huge building took a long time. We took turns praying out loud for the jury selection process and for the family of the deceased. We also prayed for the judge and the prosecutor, for Jason's attorneys, and for Jason himself.

A wave of guilt came over me as I prayed for the jury. More than once I had been asked to serve on a jury, and now I remembered trying to *avoid* the duty, because I was "just too busy." I did eventually serve, but I wondered how many people have figured out how to avoid doing this job. And I wondered what kind of jury pool is left when so many people have no desire to serve and seek ways to be excused.

With my own son approaching trial, I realized it is a duty and a privilege to serve on a jury—and I felt gratitude for the people who, in spite of the inconvenience, sacrifice their time for the sake of our justice system. I prayed that the jury that would serve during Jason's trial would be honest and fair. And I kept coming back to Jason, as I begged God to protect him and cover him with strength and wisdom, especially if a plea bargain should be offered.

On our final turn around the front of the building, we paused at the main entrance. Security devices were in plain sight and I could see the metal detector that all of the key people in the trial would walk through the next morning. In that moment our audible prayers were getting bolder, louder, and more forceful. My faith was big and my hopes were high. We reached out and touched the doors of the entrance as we continued to pray.

And then the security guards came running toward us! I can imagine them thinking, *Who are these strange people, talking out loud and putting their hands on the courthouse entrance?* We quickly explained that we had come to pray for a family member whose trial would begin in the building the next day. The guards rolled their eyes and looked at each other as if to say, *These people are crazy, but they seem to be harmless. Let them be.*

As they walked away, we prayed—with all the hope and faith we could muster—for the weighty decisions that would be made in that building during the coming week.

———

You may be awaiting the trial of your loved one. Or maybe the verdict is already in—and now you're dealing with visitation issues. Either way, you're probably wondering how long you can keep up with the multiple demands that are placed on the family of a prisoner.

One of the best ways I've found to make it through each day is to take time to pray. I have started praying with my eyes wide open. Sometimes I'm in my car. At other times, I'm in the kitchen or outside. Wherever I am, I hold on to hope by asking God to protect my son and give him opportunities to make meaningful contact with a fellow inmate, a corrections officer, or a volunteer on the compound.

My hope is always renewed when I take the time to pray. Why don't you try too? Start by praying this verse: "O my God, may your eyes be open and your ears attentive to all the prayers made to you in this place" (2 Chronicles 6:40 NLT).

### HIS WORDS OVER YOU

"I help those without hope. Keep your eyes open and your ears attentive as you pray. Listen for my instructions. You will find answers in my Word."

*Based on Isaiah 40:31 and Proverbs 23:12*

# 27. The Week of the Trial

*I'm realizing that I can feel God's presence easily and joyfully
in moments of delight. I find him in the light but lose him in
the dark. When I'm anxious . . . I can't touch him or sense his
reality. That's when he comes in the guise of other people.*

LUCI SHAW

Looking back, I can say there was no time in my life when I experienced
more intense anxiety and emotional pain than the week of Jason's trial.
We had advance warning that there would be lots of publicity. We
knew *Court TV* cameras would capture every moment of the trial, and
there was nothing we could do to keep them out of the courtroom. The
trial lasted five days, and it was carried live on the *Court TV* website.
Eventually, an edited version was aired on *Dateline NBC*. Television
reporters and print journalists repeatedly tried to interview family members as they entered and exited the courtroom.

On Monday morning the jury selection process began. Our attorney
told me, Gene, and our daughter-in-law that we would not be allowed
inside the courtroom until later in the week because of Jason's "not
guilty by reason of temporary insanity" plea. Since all three of us had
been witnesses to Jason's declining mental state before the murder took
place, we could not be present when the psychiatrists were questioned
by our attorney and the prosecutor.

I began to experience the meaning of the word *wait.* We were more
than ready for resolution, looking forward to answered prayers without
even knowing what that would look like. But we were feeling the weight
of being outside the courtroom doors for the first three days of the trial.
Even with hope in our hearts, waiting was excruciating.

During that time I wrote in my journal:

The anxiety in the air is so thick I could cut it with a knife. This
day is so odd . . . I can't concentrate. I try to pray, but then realize
I am already praying for my son, for this trial, and for all parties
involved with every breath I take. We need resolution, but I am so
afraid of resolution.

By the end of the first day, half of the jury members were selected.
By noon on Tuesday, all twelve jurors were in place. On the third day
we were allowed to sit in the waiting area outside the courtroom. While
watching the psychiatrists go in and out of the courtroom to present

their testimony, I sat on a high-back Chippendale sofa and absorbed the formal look and feel of the lobby.

As I waited in that formidable place, I read the letters in a three-ring binder sent to us by a praying friend. Titled *Prayer Changes Things*, it was filled with notes from many people who had been on a forty-day prayer vigil for us. The first note was from Kathy:

> These Scripture, quotes, and prayers have been compiled during our prayer vigil for your family. Our hearts have been turned toward a *holy God* who has penetrated our own hearts as we have been on our faces for each of you and the fragrance of our worship is permeating heaven. . . . You are loved. We are embracing what God has arranged.

The notebook was arranged with letters on one side of the page and pictures of the people who were praying for us on the other side. Gene and our daughter-in-law gathered around me as I read. We knew all three of us would take the witness stand the next day—God was sending us hope through the reminder that we were being prayed for. I remember reading one of the verses in the notebook out loud: "I call on you, my God, for you will answer me; turn your ear to me and hear my prayer" (Psalm 17:6).

—

When someone you love is on trial for a crime, a courtroom is a very frightening place. Everything about the formality in the courthouse is unfamiliar and intimidating. At the courthouse, my husband and I experienced a total loss of control over our circumstances. Sometimes it felt like we were watching a movie, when we suddenly realized the movie was about our family. Perhaps you've felt that way too.

We discovered the best way to hold on to hope—to make it through the exhaustion of the trial—was to read God's words of hope about overcoming fear. One of my favorites is a verse that my friends Karen and Bette Jo shared on our girls' getaway, Isaiah 41:10: "So do not fear, for I am with you; do not be dismayed, for I am your God. I will strengthen you and help you; I will uphold you with my righteous right hand."

We were so grateful for the encouraging words from our friends— the hope-filled Scriptures they shared in the notebook, and the prayers they were so faithful to offer on our behalf. Having supportive people during this process is a great comfort. If anyone has offered to be with you in any way, be sure to allow them that opportunity.

"Why are you downcast and disturbed? Put your hope in me and praise me. Remember, I am the Lord your God and I will take hold of your hand. Don't be afraid; I will help you."

*Based on Psalm 42:11 and Isaiah 41:13*

# 28. The Verdict

*And once the storm is over, you won't remember how you made
it through, how you managed to survive. You won't even be
sure, in fact, whether the storm is really over. But one thing is
certain. When you come out of the storm, you won't be the same
person who walked in. That's what this storm's all about.*

HARUKI MURAKAMI

Before we left the courthouse on Wednesday we were told that Gene
and I, along with Jason's wife, would be called upon to testify the next
day. I suddenly had heart palpitations and erratic breathing. Random
thoughts whirled in my mind: *What should I wear on the stand? I don't
want to look too professional, but I need to look credible. What if I say the
wrong things? What if I hurt my son's chance for a sentence that would
involve an eventual end-of-sentence date? I can't eat before I go. . . .* I had
a hard time sleeping that night.

On Thursday morning other people were called to the witness stand,
and then there was a lunch break. That afternoon Gene was called to testify, followed by our daughter-in-law, and finally, me. I walked into the
courtroom and looked over at the jury. *Are they fair people?* I wondered.
I looked at the judge and asked myself, *Is he a father? Does he know my
son's true heart?* I looked at the prosecutor. She was educated, articulate,
and gifted at her job, which she'd been doing for twenty years. I looked
at Jason and he was looking at me. I mouthed, "I love you, Son." His
lips moved and I saw him silently voice his love for me too.

I remember second-guessing everything I said in response to the
questions that afternoon, wondering if I had in any way hurt my son's
opportunity for a favorable outcome. But even if he was found not
guilty by reason of temporary insanity, he would still face many years
in a mental institution before he would ever be able to walk in freedom
again. As the proceedings ended that day, we knew closing arguments
would be presented the next morning. My heart was heavy.

We arrived at the courthouse early the next day and Gene and I,
along with family members who attended the trial, gathered for a short
prayer with the pastor of the church where Jason and his wife had met
each other in a Bible study. Closing arguments were made and by noon
the jury was taken out to begin their deliberation. It was a long afternoon. We made seven prayer walks around the courthouse that day,
praying for a miracle of mercy.

At 5:30 p.m. we were called in. The jury had reached a verdict. *Court TV* cameramen scrambled to get set up and Jason was brought back into the courtroom. The judge asked if the jury's decision was unanimous. It was, and the verdict was read: "We, the members of the jury, find Jason Paul Kent guilty of murder in the first degree." An audible reaction broke out as people in the courtroom heard the announcement.

Since this was Jason's first and only crime, the prosecutor knew it would be hard to get a jury to agree to a death sentence, and that had been taken off the table earlier. Florida is a state with mandatory minimum sentences, so there was no need to wait for a sentencing decision. The judge asked our son to stand, then said, "I sentence you, Jason Paul Kent, to live out the rest of your life in a Florida state penitentiary, without the possibility of parole." The gavel came down.

Jason was immediately put back in handcuffs attached to a waist chain, and then he was led toward the exit. He looked in our direction, and through my sobs I mouthed the words, "I love you, Son." *Court TV* cameras tried to zoom in on the grieving mama. It was the worst invasion of privacy I had ever experienced.

I have heard it's possible to die of a broken heart. Though I didn't die that day, I felt very, very close to the edge. My strong hope for a better outcome was in shambles. I had believed that with all the prayers we and others had prayed there would be a more favorable decision. That night I suffered the agony of dashed hopes and dreams for my son. I identified with the Bible verse that says, "I am worn out calling for help; my throat is parched. My eyes fail, looking for my God" (Psalm 69:3).

———

Has there been a time during this journey when you lost all hope? Perhaps you tried to pray and felt like your words were going nowhere. Or you might have expected your loved one's attorney to do a better job or a jury or judge to be more merciful, only to be sadly disappointed. I understand those feelings.

There are times when we are too exhausted to be angry. We are just worn out. The entire ordeal—from the initial arrest, through jail visits, getting an attorney, paying legal fees, waiting for the trial, sitting through the trial, and hearing the final verdict—is more than your heart can bear. You want to hold on to hope, but you have had enough.

Give yourself permission to grieve. Everything is *not* all right and it hurts to the core. Sob out loud and let God himself hold you. If the verdict is harsh, try to remember Hebrews 10:23: "Let us hold unswervingly to the hope we profess, for he who promised is faithful."

"My child, don't give up. Even though on the outside it looks like things are falling apart for your family, on the inside, I am making something new. Not a day goes by without my unfolding grace. Choose hope. There's much more here than meets the eye. The things you see now are temporary. The things you can't see now will last forever."

*Based on 2 Corinthians 4:16–18*

# 29. I Want to Know Why

*Life is filled with unanswered questions, but it is the courage to
seek those answers that continues to give meaning to life. You
can spend your life wallowing in despair, wondering why you
were the one who was led towards the road strewn with pain, or
you can be grateful that you are strong enough to survive it.*

J. D. Stroube

When Gene and I got the news of our son's arrest, we were filled with
tough questions. *Why did he commit this murder? What happened to his
sense of right and wrong? Did he run away from his Christian upbringing?
Were we terrible parents?*

We were left without complete answers to those questions for a long
time. Because our visits to the jail were monitored and all of our phone
calls were recorded, anything that we or our son said could be used
against him during the trial. You may have run into the same problem.
You are desperate to know *why* your loved one committed a crime—
but you do not have enough privacy to ask that question without fear
of what might happen if someone overhears the response. When that
process goes on for months, you feel like you're in limbo . . . and in our
case it went on for over two years! That was a long time for us to wonder
what propelled our son to unravel to the point of taking a life.

We had a few answers, but not to the biggest question. We knew
that our son feared for his stepdaughters' safety if they were left alone
with their biological father, due to the multiple allegations of abuse.
But we didn't know why he thought murder was the only solution to
the problem.

We had been involved parents. We knew we had raised our child
to know right from wrong. Throughout Jason's growing-up years, we
watched him make mostly good choices. He was a peacemaker, not a
violent person. He had compassion for people who were abused and
mistreated. Our son wasn't perfect, but he was heading in the right
direction. We were optimistic about his future. What could possibly
have led him to believe he had no choice but to take matters into his
own hands?

Soon after Jason's arrest he talked about what prompted him to
make such a devastating choice. However, it was in 2009—ten years
after the murder—that Jason wrote us a letter with a more detailed
answer to that question.

As I write now, it is almost impossible to recall exactly what led up to my actions. I do remember the intensity of my emotional angst as my ability to protect my beloved stepdaughters appeared to be slipping away. . . . I imagined my daughters coming to me in the future, sobbing out: "Daddy, couldn't you have done anything to protect us?" In my determination not to abandon my little girls, I was losing my grip on reality and my ability to reason.

I would brood on our family's situation while I was at work, and when I came home I would play with the girls and be filled with a desire to protect them. I'd wake up at night and feel I was a failure as a father in my duty to provide safety and security for my family. I lost sleep and became exhausted and fixated on my fear. As my trust in God eroded I became more and more restless and angry and frustrated, and by the time my hope died completely, I took the life of the father of my stepdaughters.

———

Over time, Jason filled in the missing pieces to the puzzle of his actions. His ability to think rationally suffered as he compartmentalized his feelings instead of dealing openly with his intense fears. In that one letter, we didn't learn everything about his reason for the murder, but the answer to that question was unfolding little by little.

There is often a long period between the arrest and the trial or plea bargain. During those months, feelings and emotions that were initially heated and intense are sometimes softened. Looking back, your loved one may not even remember all the details of what led to the illegal act. We on the outside want answers—but sometimes our incarcerated family member doesn't know how to respond to our questions.

During my wait, I was comforted by Psalm 145:15–16: "The eyes of all look to you, and you give them their food at the proper time. You open your hand and satisfy the desires of every living thing." I believe there will be a time when our desire for answers will be satisfied. In the meantime, we wait.

### HIS WORDS OVER YOU

"Wait patiently for me to act. Turn to me and I will hear your cry. Hope for the answers you do not have yet, and wait patiently."

*Based on Psalm 40:1 and Romans 8:25*

# 30. Is My Loved One Remorseful?

*Remorse is the punishment of crime; repentance, its expiation. The former appertains to a tormented conscience; the latter to a soul changed for the better.*

JOSEPH JOUBERT

*Is he sorry for what he did?* The television interviewer was unrelenting. I was on a program to tell the story of my journey with my son. I had thought the focus would be on what it's like for parents to experience the shock of their child's arrest and the difficulty of going through the trial. In the preinterview process, the questions were much simpler: *Who was the first person you called after you received news of the arrest? How did you break the news to your extended family? What did the need for legal representation do to your finances? How long did it take for you to feel comfortable going back to work? What kind of security checks do you go through when visiting your son in prison? What has changed about your life and your goals as a result of your son's incarceration?*

By the time of this interview, I had been publicly discussing my son's crime and I was not surprised by most of the questions from journalists. But when this well-known host asked, "Is he sorry for what he did?" the emotion and force of the question gave me pause.

For a moment, my mind whirled. Jason *was* sorry for what he did. He was filled with remorse over all the loss and grief his actions had brought about. When we visited him, I saw him weep over his wrong choices and I heard genuine angst in his voice. A mama knows when her son is genuinely repentant and sorry for what he did. During that interview, I came up with some pat answer—but looking back, I still think about the process of remorse.

In the beginning, soon after the crime, Jason was filled with the emotions that had made him spiral downward—extreme fear for the safety of his stepdaughters, and a feeling of helplessness, of not being able to protect the girls. It was much later, when the full impact of his crime hit him squarely in the heart, that he experienced the level of remorse I wished he could have felt earlier. Even though Jason had expressed remorse while still at the jail awaiting his trial, it was a decade after his crime that he wrote out his thoughts in detail:

> As I slowly reconnected with reality, the immensity of it all—
> including the harm I had inadvertently done to those I sought to

protect—began to sink in. I was empty, exhausted, depressed, and felt like a failure. I thought about the huge shame for you, Mom and Dad, as I destroyed our family name, and I envisioned what you and my wife would experience as you were dragged through the trial. I had no idea how much pain I would put all of you through. And I certainly had not considered the huge loss and sorrow of my victim's family. I can only imagine the pain I have caused the father of the man I killed. I stole from him his relationship with his son.

Only in retrospect can I recognize how arrogant, self-righteous, and self-reliant I became in the weeks leading up to the murder as my fears consumed me. My lack of trust in God to intervene on behalf of my family left me feeling like I was the only one who could rescue them. I still believed that God existed and He'd sent Jesus to secure our eternity through His sacrifice, but I didn't believe He would come through in the present for my family. My lack of faith in God led me to take action that did the opposite. My actions brought death, devastation, and the destruction of everything my life previously represented. I am so sorry!

---

When a person we love is first arrested, the fact that he or she committed the crime is so sad and disgusting to us that we want them to say immediately, *I was wrong. I am so sorry. I made the worst decision of my life. I want to help the person I hurt. I was so wrong to bring shame to my family.*

But the truth is that they have probably not yet fully processed the devastation their actions have brought not only to their victim, but also to the family of the victim, and to their own family. It takes time to process the full impact of their actions.

In time, your family member may express the remorse you long to hear. We were blessed to hear deep remorse from our son. But what if that doesn't happen? Sometimes remorse is blocked by mental illness, narcissism (extreme self-absorption), or depression (giving up on life, lacking the energy to respond to anyone else). At other times, due to a loved one's drug use or repeated poor choices, you are left with never-ending questions about whether they even care about the long-term impact of their crime.

In times like this, it's helpful to acknowledge your grief. Realize that you cannot control the mental or spiritual state of your loved one. Psalm 35:14 says, "I went about mourning as though for my friend or brother. I bowed my head in grief." Sometimes we weep for our incarcerated loved one; at other times we weep for the victim and their family. When you have done all you can do, wait for God to move in the heart of your family member.

## HIS WORDS OVER YOU

"I love your deep desire to hear contrition and remorse. Distress that drives us to God turns us around. We never regret that kind of pain. Encourage one another. As you express your love to others, my love and peace will be with you."

*Based on 2 Corinthians 7:10 and 2 Corinthians 13:11*

# 31. Is Prison Dangerous?

*Fear of danger is ten thousand times more*
*terrifying than danger itself.*

Daniel Defoe

At the time my son was arrested I had never been inside a jail or prison. My only understanding of the workings of local jails and state corrections departments was from books, television, and movies. I thought of every penal institution as a place where horrible things happened— gang rapes that went unreported, corrupt corrections officers who didn't always protect those behind bars, and maybe even prompted fights between inmates for entertainment.

All of these thoughts swirled in my mind as I worried over the safety of my son. Then he was beaten at the jail, as you read earlier. That incident confirmed my worst fears. *All jails and prisons are filled with corrupt people and my son is not going to survive,* I thought. *And even if he does, he'll probably be in a wheelchair for the rest of his life!*

After being taken to the Central Florida Reception Center for evaluation following his conviction and sentencing, Jason was moved to the Avon Park Correctional Institution near Sebring, Florida. Soon after this move, I developed a new concern.

When you are new on the prison compound, you have not yet developed a group of inmate friends who can help to protect you in an altercation. Some confrontations are planned, directed attacks by gangs that can form within the prison population. But more frequently, the confrontation arises from a lone-wolf troublemaker. These are the inmates who, by their own actions, have alienated themselves from friends and families, doing what got them into trouble in the first place—lying, stealing, and abusing people. And Jason describes an entirely different category of inmate, the ones who are simply evil. They have no place in their lives for God or for anything resembling responsible living. They have embraced the wickedness around them, and plot depraved things to do to other inmates.

When Jason had been in his first prison for less than two weeks, we were talking on the phone. I asked if he felt safe. As he answered, I could hear a crack in his voice. "There's this big two hundred and fifty pound guy who's been stalking me," Jason said. "He hides in unexpected places and periodically he jumps out at me. Then he yells, 'I'm gonna get ya, Kent. I'm gonna get ya!'" I felt sick to my stomach. My boy was "the new kid on the block," and I knew Jason was being threatened with rape. This corrupt inmate was just waiting for a time when he could get away with his crime. The sound I heard in my son's voice was fear.

After the call I picked up my Bible and looked for verses that said, "Fear not." Before long I found Isaiah 41:13: "For I am the LORD your God who takes hold of your right hand and says to you, Do not fear; I will help you." How I needed that reminder!

———

Over time Gene and I have discovered that there are well-run jails and prisons with competent and compassionate staff members. There is an equal number of poorly run facilities. In those without good leadership, inmates face much more danger.

If you are concerned about the safety of your incarcerated loved one, try to get to know the warden, the chaplain, and the program director at the prison. Your inmate might not be able to meet the warden personally, but he or she will have opportunities to connect with the other leaders. Encourage the one you love to attend programs in the chapel or the educational building. This helps them to form friendships among inmates who already care about bettering themselves—and these relationships will become a layer of protection in the yard or cellblock.

Jason quickly discovered it's important to not look like a victim. "I learned to walk around the compound like a military man, confidently, with my head up," he said. "Most prison rapists are looking for easy prey, and they are looking for someone who appears fearful and weak." Jason's stalker eventually moved on to easier targets.

Jason actually had some help from one of the local newspapers when it printed that he was a Navy SEAL. The truth was that Jason had only taken pre-SEAL training; he was actually in Special Operations. But word spread like wildfire: *You better watch out for Jason Kent. He's a Navy SEAL!* That reputation did not hurt his ability to stay safe.

Prison *is* a very dangerous place, but God is capable of protecting our loved ones. Most of all, pray for the safety of the prisoner you love, who is now in a place where threats and violence are common.

## HIS WORDS OVER YOU

"Do not fear threats, do not be frightened. I will meet you more than halfway and calm your anxious heart. I set up a circle of protection around you while you pray."

*Based on 1 Peter 3:14 and Psalm 34:4, 7*

# 32. How Do We Prepare for Prison?

*I don't spend a lot of time asking "Why?" Instead I focus*
*on what I should do now or how I should react.*

JEFF DIXON

The woman was upset. She had read one of my books and she wrote me a desperate letter.

Dear Carol,
. . . I, too, am the mother of a son who committed a dreadful crime. Only in my case, my son was not reacting impulsively and obsessively in a way that he believed was saving children from a predator. My son *is* the predator. He married a previously married woman who had two children by her first husband and he was caught in an unthinkable act—sexually abusing one of his step-children. He is currently in jail, awaiting his trial, and he will no doubt receive a very long sentence.

My heart is torn. I am angry with him and sick at heart that he repeatedly abused an innocent child. There is a knot in the pit of my stomach when I realize I gave birth to someone who could do such a horrible thing—something that will negatively impact the life of that child for the rest of his life. My son does not fit the image of what I think a child molester looks like. He's from a good Christian family, has a university degree, and before his arrest, he had a job that provided very well for him and for his family.

I am forcing myself to visit my son at the jail and I'm praying for the grace to forgive him for what he's done. As a mother, I'm also concerned about the safety of my own son as he will inevitably face a long sentence. Would you ask Jason how I can best prepare my son for the life he faces behind bars?

As I finished the letter, I realized she was asking the same question I'd wanted to have answered before Jason received his sentence. I've learned a lot about life behind the razor wire over the past few years, but on a recent visit I asked my son what warnings he would give to someone who was about to be sentenced. He instantly responded with his top three recommendations:

1. *Don't participate in gambling.*
   Jason explained that due to boredom in prison, inmates very

easily fall into the habit of playing card games—and in many of the games, a wager takes place. My response was, "How can they bet when they have no money?" He assured me that there were all kinds of favors done on the compound, and that men make wagers with food items out of the commissary—things purchased with money that is placed in their accounts. If a prisoner has won major bets, he can be a target for stealing—which often leads to fights.

2. *Don't get involved in drugs.*

There is always great speculation regarding how drugs get inside a prison compound—whether they're smuggled in by visitors or by corrupt corrections officers. Either way, there are plenty of drugs (or their synthetic equivalents) in most prisons. Jason warns that once an inmate is addicted, he will do just about anything to feed his habit . . . and the results are always devastating.

3. *Stay away from homosexuality.*

My son explained that many prison fights and deaths are due to "lovers' quarrels." If it appears an existing inmate relationship is threatened by a third person, jealousy often brings on threats that eventually end in destructive actions. This was the cause of the recent murder of an inmate in the correctional institution where my son is located.

———

You may be like the woman who wrote to me. You love your child, spouse, brother, or sister who has been arrested, but the behavior that got them into this predicament is so disgusting that you're tempted to turn your back on them. It's hard to visit your loved one in jail or prison when you can barely stomach their recent behavior.

The fact that you are reading this book tells me that you do still care—that you want to do something to help turn around your family member's life. Sometimes, of course, advice from you is not appreciated or wanted. It may take several visits before you find an opening to bring up the warnings Jason offered. Be wise. Remember to pray first, and then be willing to truly listen to your loved one's side of the story. These are often the first steps to softening a heart, and eventually opening it to guidance. And this counsel from the Bible is good both for inmates and their family members: "Wisdom is found in those who take advice" (Proverbs 13:10).

"My child, you desperately want to help prepare your family member for the rough life inside a prison. All you can do is wait on my timing to speak truth, but always wait with hope. I will help you. Then rest in me. Trust me with the results."

*Based on Psalm 33:20 and Psalm 62:1*

# 33. Should I Go to Visitation?

*For true success ask yourself these four questions:*
*Why? Why not? Why not me? Why not now?*

JAMES ALLEN

As I was signing her book at a speaking engagement, the woman leaned over and whispered, "Thanks for sharing your story. I have a brother who's been incarcerated for the past six years and I've never visited him in prison. Your talk gave me pause, and I'm wondering if I can get over my fears enough to go to visitation."

"What are you afraid of?" I asked.

I instantly knew that I had asked her a hard question. "Well," she said, seemingly unsure if she had an appropriate answer, "I think there's a list you have to get on—some kind of an approval is needed, but I'm not really sure what's involved with the paperwork." After more hesitation, she added, "And I'm kind of afraid of going to a place where there are so many criminals."

She thought for a moment and then continued. "Also, in the beginning, I didn't want to speak to my brother because I was angry over what he did—I thought visiting him would make him feel like I approved of his behavior. The years kept going by and I tried to pretend he's not even a part of my family. At reunions we don't speak of him and I never show pictures of him to my children." After one last pause, she said, "But I'm not sure my response is the right way to handle this whole situation."

I think this woman speaks for thousands of family members of inmates, people who don't go to visitation for a variety of reasons: inconvenience, anger, fear, financial challenges, even disgust over the family problems that have come about as a result of what has happened. These family members may feel occasional guilt, but it can be easier to avoid the incarcerated person than to make decisions that culminate in regular visitation.

Why? Because visitation is hard. It's inconvenient. You have to research how to get on the visitation list. It costs money to drive to the prison and to feed a family from the food window or vending machines. You have to give up a day in your weekend to sit in a prison instead of going to the beach or a park with the rest of your family. Your visit is limited to the time and place and rules set by the facility, and you have to converse with your incarcerated family member during the entire visitation time. Sometimes you run out of things to talk about, but if you leave early, it may look like you don't care or you're eager to get away. That can be awkward. It's not normal for us to sit at a table for hours in a restricted environment without "doing" something, even if we're with someone we love. Let's admit it: prison visitation stinks!

So why go? Probably the best answer to that question is found in the Bible, when Jesus describes how God will separate "the sheep from the goats" at the end of time. "The King will say to those on his right, 'Come, you who are blessed by my Father, inherit the Kingdom prepared for you from the creation of the world. . . . I was in prison, and you visited me.' . . . And the King will say, 'I tell you the truth, when you did it to one of the least of these my brothers and sisters, you were doing it to me!'" (Matthew 25:34, 36, 40 NLT).

But there are plenty of other good reasons. Prisoners who have ongoing relationships with their family and friends have a much better chance of staying out of prison in the future. You'll slowly begin to understand the true heart of your incarcerated loved on. You can become an advocate for him or her. You'll meet other inmates' family members, people who are going through what your family is experiencing, and you can encourage each other. And that's one of the best reasons I've found for visiting: I have become a different, more compassionate person, weeping with others who hurt and brainstorming with my son and others about how to initiate positive change in a harsh environment.

If you've never gone to a jail or prison visitation, begin by contacting your local or state Department of Corrections. You can find their websites with a simple Google search. Then click on the link that gives you information on visitation.

When you're going to a jail (that is, prior to a trial), you will face fewer restrictions. Once your loved one has been assigned to a prison, you'll need to submit additional personal information so a security check can be run. In most cases, you'll soon be informed that you've been approved for the permanent visitation list. If you're bringing a child with you, you may need to have their birth certificate on hand. If one of the child's parents is not with you, some states require a notarized approval from the custodial parent, giving you permission to take the child into the prison. Guidelines vary from state to state, so be as prepared as possible. It's not a hard process, it just takes initiative to get started.

Before you arrive, make a mental list of things to talk about—shared memories, updates on the family, current happenings in your church or community. Talk about a book you've read or about an interesting movie or TV show you've seen. Our son loves to hear about new movies, because he only gets to see old television reruns in the prison day room—and that's only after all of the inmates have agreed on what station to watch. Usually, there are games available on a table in the visitation room—sometimes it's easier to have a long discussion while playing a game together. That makes the time go quickly, and also brings a sense of normalcy to you and to your loved one.

Know that your visits are your loved one's window to the outside world. It's worth the effort it takes to go. Visitation is time well spent.

## HIS WORDS OVER YOU

"I hear the groans of the prisoners. When you visit those who are incarcerated, it is as if you are showing kindness to me."

*Based Psalm 102:20 and Matthew 25:40*

# 34. Can There Be Purposeful Life in Prison?

*Purpose in life is not just something we do. It involves*
*who we are and our way of being in this world. . . .*
*Our heart is broken by what breaks God's heart,*
*and we devote our energies to those purposes.*

JAN JOHNSON

In the weeks following our son's arrest, we kept hearing from distant friends and acquaintances who had just received the news. Though we appreciated their calls of concern, it was hard to revisit our family trauma again and again. Most people understood our pain and were gracious—but others struggled to come up with appropriate things to say. One woman I had known for many years said, "It's too bad that Jason didn't just shoot himself after shooting the victim. That way you would go through a time of mourning, and then you could get on with the rest of your lives. But the way this has happened, the pain is never really over."

It was hard for me to pull myself together and form any kind of response. Was this woman saying that because my son had committed a murder, he should also take his own life? Did she mean that if a man is sentenced to life in prison, there is no more need for him to exist? Was she saying that Jason could never find purpose and meaning in his life if he was in a prison until he died? Certainly, this woman did not understand the concept of redemption—the idea that something good can come out of something bad.

Many parents of incarcerated children have written to us, asking questions about the life their children will lead behind bars. What they ask is important:

- My son has been in prison since he was sixteen years old. Can he get a high school equivalency diploma while he is incarcerated?
- Can inmates have jobs that they are paid to do?
- Can my incarcerated husband teach classes behind the razor wire? He's a gifted mechanic and would love to use his expertise to equip other inmates to be able to make a living on the outside.
- My daughter was married only three years before she was arrested for a white-collar crime. Can she have conjugal visits with her husband?

- Can I put extra money in my loved one's inmate account so she can share with other inmates who have nothing?
- Can I send clothing and food items to my son for Christmas?
- Can inmates get college or seminary degrees while they are locked up?

This list could go on and on. And each different question boils down to one central question: Can there be purposeful living when you are incarcerated?

———

The answer is a resounding *yes*—there can most definitely be purposeful living in prison. But exactly how purposeful depends on the inmate and his or her desire to do something meaningful to help others.

Our son began to realize that many inmates were not good at financial management—that weakness resulted in the wrong choices that led some of them to prison. Through the chaplain, Jason got permission to facilitate Dave Ramsey's Financial Peace University course. In the prison where our son is located, more than seven hundred men have now gone through training that helps them balance a checkbook, write out a budget, and be disciplined with the use of their income.

Answers to some of the questions posed earlier depend on the rules of the facility where your loved one is incarcerated. Some prisons do allow inmates to receive a small stipend for their prison job, but most do not. In Florida, there are no conjugal visits for married couples, but that is not true in every state. Some prisons have educational programs that allow inmates to earn their high school equivalency diplomas and their undergraduate degrees, but others do not. Most of the time, if you have the resources to put extra money into your loved one's prison account, they can encourage other inmates with gifts of food or postage stamps. And no . . . none of us can send in clothing or bring a holiday dinner to our loved one during visitation.

The key is to ask questions of the warden, the program director, or the chaplain, to find out what education and training and other opportunities are available in the institution where you have an inmate. Sometimes, outside family members can get answers even faster than the inmates can, especially if your loved one is in a large facility that is short on staff.

Time in prison doesn't have to be wasted time—in fact, it can be a tremendous opportunity for an inmate. We are happiest and most productive when we are busy doing work with purpose and meaning. Christians believe that we are meant to do good work with our lives, as we imitate God, who does good work himself. "For we are God's hand-iwork, created in Christ Jesus to do good works, which God prepared in advance for us to do" (Ephesians 2:10).

## HIS WORDS OVER YOU

"I gave life to the ones you love and I have created them to use their gifts. Encourage them to develop their talents and not to hide them. My gifts and my call are irrevocable. Gifts are for the purpose of blessing other people."

*Based on Matthew 25:14–30 and Romans 11:29*

# 35. When No Answers Are in Sight

*Sometimes questions are more important than answers.*

NANCY WILLARD

After I had written *When I Lay My Isaac Down,* a book on our son's arrest and conviction for murder, I received many letters from parents and spouses who had hard questions. Since these people didn't know me personally, they weren't afraid to be honest. Some of them asked:

- Why did my son molest a child? I am too humiliated to tell anyone what my son's crime is—because it's despicable.
- My husband has a life sentence and I have three children at home. I have spent the past six years going to visitation almost every weekend. I'm tired and there is no hope he will ever walk in freedom. I'm a Christian and I want to do the right thing, but I would also like a normal home life for my children and for myself. Does God expect me to stay in this marriage?
- My daughter is a three-time drug offender. She has two young children I'm raising while she's in prison. We've mortgaged our home and used our retirement funds for drug treatment programs, but she continues to go back to using drugs time after time. She wants us to bring her children to visitation at the prison, but she doesn't deserve to see them. What should I do?
- My husband was caught viewing child pornography. His computer was confiscated and he has been arrested. How can I cope? I am so angry. He is sick mentally. I still love him, but I don't know if I can stand by him in the courtroom.
- My wife worked for a major corporation and began using the company credit card for large personal purchases. She was caught after two years and is now in prison. She is not the woman I thought I married. Please give me advice about whether I should stay with her or begin the process of divorcing her?
- Since the incarceration of my husband, my life has turned upside down. I have no social life, except going to the prison. I work all day and every night I get calls from the prison that begin with a digitized message, asking me if I'll accept the charges in order to talk to my husband. The calls are fifteen minutes long and he wants to call several times because he's lonely. I am weary. I have to take care of the kids, make the money for our household

expenses, put money in his inmate account, and spend my weekends visiting him—and I am exhausted. I feel like I need someone to take care of me, but I have no one. Is that thought selfish, or do I deserve it?

- My son was convicted of armed robbery. He stole from a wealthy family and feels absolutely no remorse for stealing from a family that has a lot of money. I have prayed for my son, but I am also so frustrated with him that I can hardly stand to visit him. Are these feelings wrong?
- My finances are in shambles due to my husband's incarceration. I cannot afford groceries for my family, gasoline to get to the prison, and money for his account. Where can I get help?

---

When someone we love is behind bars, we have more questions than answers. As I've sifted through letters that come in, I've realized there are specific types of questions that are the most pressing:

- Is it wrong for me to leave my marriage over what has happened?
- How can I take care of myself when I'm overwhelmed with helping everyone else?
- Should I take children to visitation when their incarcerated parent repeatedly makes the same wrong choices?
- When there is no remorse for the crime, how should I respond to the person I love?
- Where can I get financial and/or legal aid?
- Why did my loved one do something so horrible?

That last question is the toughest of all—but I have found a certain Bible story helpful. One time, the disciples asked Jesus why a man had been born blind. They wanted to know if the blindness was caused by the sin of the blind man himself or his parents. But Jesus told them, "You're asking the wrong question. You're looking for someone to blame. There is no such cause-effect here. Look instead for what God can do" (John 9:3–4 MSG).

Usually, we don't receive immediate answers to the practical questions. But we know that we can ask God for wisdom, and He will give us the ability to make good choices. Sometimes He answers through a support group, a church, or an organization that can refer you to written and videotaped resources. At other times He responds through the Bible or a wise Christian friend, impressing your mind with the ability to make hard decisions.

These questions are hard. It's okay if you don't always have answers. But keep looking to God—and in time, the answers will come.

## HIS WORDS OVER YOU

"When you need answers, ask me your direct questions. Seek my truth, and look intently for wisdom. Ask boldly, believingly, without a second thought. I love to help you."

*Based on Matthew 7:7 and James 1:5–7*

# 36. Mad at God

*Part of me was afraid that if I raised my fist to the sky and*
*demanded an answer now, I would hear a thundering*
*and calloused, "Because I said so," from God in heaven.*
*And I may not ever want to speak to Him again.*

SARAH THEBARGE

Jason's verdict and sentencing came down on his wife's birthday. Why did God allow *that* to happen?

After the hearing, Gene drove our daughter-in-law and me back to her home. There were no words, just low, intermittent sobs from all three of us. We entered the house, clung to each other and wept. At that moment, I didn't recognize it—but our crying was the sound of fear. Fear about Jason's safety. Fear about what the future would hold for his family. Fear about how we could ever go on living after such a traumatic experience. I never knew fear had a sound until I heard it through my own sobs.

I wrote in my journal:

The trial is over. We lost. On the birthday of Jason's wife, we lost. On every birthday for the remainder of her life she will be reminded of this great sorrow on what should be the happiest day of her year. This is beyond cruel. "Lord, I want to pound my fist at you and yell at the top of my lungs until you acknowledge my anger and understand how disappointed I am in you. But, honestly, I don't even know how to find you. Are you even listening to me?"

My spirit is groaning with a grief I've never known before. I am nauseous from a depth of mourning that is high and deep and wide. I don't know if I can continue to live. "God, do you even care about what's happening to us?"

I had never been so bold in a prayer. Who was I to be that angry with God? How could I have talked to Him in such a harsh tone? But at that moment, I didn't care. The honesty of yelling out my pain—even if only on paper—felt strangely comforting.

An hour later there was a knock at the door. It was my seventy-seven-year-old mother and my sister Bonnie. They told me they knew that if they had called first, Gene and I would have told them we needed to be alone. But we fell into their arms as Mama said, "We know you need to be with us tonight, so we are here—and we are staying!"

As we melted into the warm embrace of family members, I remembered what my friend Lael had written in the *Prayer Changes Things* notebook: "He will cover you with his feathers. He will shelter you with his wings. His faithful promises are your armor and protection" (Psalm 91:4 NLT). I slowly realized that even when I was too angry, hurt, and disappointed to communicate with God in a civil way, He would still use His people to offer me protection and unconditional love.

On the day after the verdict, a large package arrived from Phoenix, Arizona. Addressed to Gene, our daughter-in-law, and me, it had been shipped via overnight delivery. When we opened the package, we found boxes of Kleenex in every imaginable color and size. Under the tissues, we discovered scented candles in matching colors. The package was huge, but the note was brief:

Dear Ones,
    We are praying that you will feel God wrapping His arms around you in this time of unspeakable grief. Please know how much you are loved.
    Rich and Kathe Wunnenberg

We suddenly felt like we were burrowing into the soft feathers of a mother hen who was covering us with her protective wings. These special friends knew we didn't need twenty-five Bible verses and a sermon—only a safe place to cry and a private moment to vent our pain.[16]

———

At what point in your loved one's legal process did you feel the most anger? If the process is ongoing, you may be feeling anger now—and if you haven't yet, you probably will. Anger can arise toward people and situations. Sometimes we are angry at the family member whose criminal actions caused our pain, or at the legal system for being unfair, or at the politicians who set harsh, mandatory minimum sentences so they can look tough on crime and get reelected. Sometimes we are simply mad at God because He does not seem to be rescuing us.

When I was angry, one of the things that helped me most was to write out what I was feeling. Why not try journaling your own experience? It was easier for me to "scream" in written form than it was out loud, and that helped me to be honest with myself and with God.

I began to understand Psalm 51:6 (NKJV): "Behold, You desire

16. Some content taken from *When I Lay My Isaac Down*, by Carol Kent. Copyright © 2004, 2013. Used by permission of NavPress. All rights reserved. Represented by Tyndale House Publishers, Inc.

truth in the inward parts." Before the arrest of my son, I never thought to tell God exactly how I felt about Him when I was unhappy with things He allowed to happen. Slowly, I realized that He desires honesty from me—even when I am expressing disappointment in Him.

## HIS WORDS OVER YOU

"Cast all your cares on me because I care about what happens to you and to your loved ones. Remember that there is a time to weep and a time to mourn. Hide in the shelter of my presence. I will keep you safe."

*Based on 1 Peter 5:7, Ecclesiastes 3:4, and Psalm 31:20*

# 37. A Toe-Tag Sentence

*No one ever told me that grief felt so like fear.*

C. S. Lewis

We were starting to learn an entirely new vocabulary as we spent more time with inmates and their families. Jason had been given a "toe-tag sentence": in prison vernacular, that means an inmate will never leave prison until he is dead—on a slab with a tag on his toe. I had a hard time digesting the unending nature of that phrase.

The unspeakable pain was also affecting my husband, Gene. Following the verdict, he wrote:

> God, I am broken. I am undone and I am lost in my grief. Have mercy on my son. Be close to him. Bless him and prepare him for the days ahead. New struggles. New opportunities. Father, give me wisdom with Carol. Help me to know how to love her.

Both Gene and I were consumed with fear over what the next stage of this process would contain for our young, blond, blue-eyed son. As a mother, I was gripped by the fear that my son would be hurt during some kind of initiation, much like the beating he received at the Orlando jail soon after his arrest. Jason would soon be in a high-security prison, where there is even the threat of being raped by other inmates.

Then my mind went back to the day we had received the verdict. About three hours after we arrived at the home of our daughter-in-law, the phone rang. We were surprised to receive the digitized message we had often heard in the past, asking if we would accept phone charges from an inmate. Soon, Jason was talking:

> After the sentencing, I was transported to the jail and they took me back to the faith-based area of the building. The inmates there had already heard about my conviction and sentencing and these maximum-security prisoners were weeping as I entered the cellblock. One of them spoke up and said, "Jason, if a man like you got a sentence like this, there is no hope for us. There is absolutely no hope."

Jason had been in the county jail awaiting his trial for two and a half years. During that time, he had become the cell coordinator in the faith-based area and many maximum-security inmates had accepted Christ. Jason told us, "God gave me the ability to stand up and preach. I said, 'Men, if we know Jesus, we will all one day walk in freedom.'"

I felt the passion in his voice. I knew the brokenness he had experienced and the sorrow and remorse he had expressed for taking the life of another human being. There was a strong boldness in his voice, something that could only come from a man who was walking with Jesus, seeking to do His work no matter where he was or how hopeless the future looked. I sensed that God's Holy Spirit, who lives inside everyone who invites Christ into their lives, was comforting Jason, giving him a purpose beyond what anyone might expect.

My fear and grief produced bursts of tears, but Gene and I began to realize that God *was* at work answering our prayers for our son—just in a far different way than we anticipated. Since there was no end-of-sentence date, Jason was already viewing his toe-tag sentence as an opportunity to speak hope and faith into the lives of other prisoners, no matter where the Department of Corrections moved him.

God gently calmed my fears as I read Isaiah 43:19: "See, I am doing a new thing! Now it springs up; do you not perceive it? I am making a way in the wilderness and streams in the wasteland."

———

What is the most fearful thing you've experienced during the incarceration of your loved one? After my anxiety about Jason's safety at the jail, I now had more intense fear as he was about to be placed in a maximum-security prison. We simply have no control over how our loved one—the inmate we care about—will be treated.

Our fear and grief are intensified when another family member struggles. It was hard to see my usually optimistic husband experiencing waves of deep sorrow. Even so, after all that had transpired, we were both beginning to see that our son was in a much better place spiritually.

One of the most well-known chapters in the Bible, Psalm 23, includes this verse: "Even when I walk through the darkest valley, I will not be afraid, for you are close beside me" (verse 4 NLT). Try reading that short chapter yourself, and look for ways God is beginning to work in the life of your incarcerated loved one.

### HIS WORDS OVER YOU

"I see your grief and I know the fears you are experiencing. You may think I have turned my back on your family, but my thoughts are not your thoughts, neither are your ways my ways. I am at work in ways that currently don't make sense to you."

*Based on Isaiah 55:8–9*

# 38. The Lure of Cynicism

*A cynic is not merely one who reads bitter lessons from the past;*
*he is one who is prematurely disappointed in the future.*
SYDNEY J. HARRIS

The couple e-mailed to ask if they could meet with Gene and me following a speaking engagement in northern Minnesota. "We don't have the same story," they wrote, "but there are similarities and we would appreciate the opportunity of talking to you." Gene made arrangements for us to share a meal after the event ended.

At the restaurant I was struck by how attractive and personable these people were. We chatted about their jobs and about the speaking engagement that had brought Gene and me to their part of the country. It seemed hard for them to begin the conversation on the real reason they had requested this meeting.

Suddenly Jim blurted out, "We have three children. Our middle child is a son who is a high school math teacher, and he's single. He became attracted to a young woman in one of his classes and she was very enamored with him. We were shocked to find out that they had begun an affair—and even though it was a consensual relationship, she was slightly underage. When her father got the news, he went ballistic, called the police, and had our son arrested."

Jim's wife, Cindy, started weeping and continued the story. "When the news hit the local paper, our son was dragged through the mud and portrayed as a sexual predator," she said. "People in our church reacted with disgust, anger, and a lot of finger-pointing at our son and at the two of us. Our family was portrayed as perverted and disgusting. The local prosecutor was trying to make a reputation for herself, and she threw the book at our son during his trial—when he was found guilty, the judge gave him the maximum sentence allowable in our state. The young woman admitted that the relationship was something she wanted, but because she was underage, it did not lessen the charge."

Gene and I felt this couple's intense pain. Their son had worked hard to get his education and to pursue his career, but because of an attraction to a student, made a wrong choice. He was portrayed in the news media as a molester of children, though his parents pointed out he had fallen in love with a young woman who was just two months shy of legal age. Jim and Cindy were overcome with grief over what appeared to be the unfairness of the justice system.

As the evening progressed, the couple also told us they had been very involved in their church: Jim was on the board and Cindy was a codirector of women's ministries. When the news of their son's case came out in the paper, though, their pastor asked both of them to resign. Over a period of months, they told us, when they went to church, people didn't know what to say. Jim and Cindy felt alienated, even by good friends.

"In addition to feeling shunned by the church, we found ourselves mistrusting the legal system," Jim told us. "After watching our kindhearted son maligned in multiple headline articles and in television news reports where his mug shot was aired repeatedly, we were sick at heart. We were disillusioned with both the church and with our local community.

"Since our son was sentenced and placed in prison," he continued, "we have learned that for the rest of his natural life he will be labeled as a sex offender. That means he will have restrictions on where he can go in public. He will never be allowed to teach school again. He will be thrown into the despicable mix of child molesters and predators—and there is nothing we can do about it. It is beyond unfair!"

Cindy looked up and said, "We never thought this would happen to us, but we have become cynical and reclusive."

———

The experts don't classify cynicism itself as an emotion, but it can trigger many emotions that will suck the life out of you: hostility, anger, frustration, impatience, bitterness, resentment, hatred, rage, and fear. When we become overly distrustful of human nature in general and the motives of other people in particular—especially those in authority—cynicism creeps into our lives.

As year follows year, Gene and I face the same temptation as Jim and Cindy do—to become hardened in our hearts, doubting that any good can come from our son's conviction and sentence. Cynicism is an unproductive reaction to disappointment. It springs from the helplessness we feel when we're disappointed by other people or by our circumstances. At that point we make ourselves detached observers rather than active participants.

Cynicism clouds our thinking and pushes us toward irrational accusations and wrong decisions. That's why it's important not to make major decisions when we're feeling disillusioned. And it's much better for us not to hang out with cynical people.

Jim and Cindy's approach to their situation is what had helped us to heal: we reached out to others who had experienced the incarceration of a family member. When you have a loved one behind bars, when you feel there has been misunderstanding or even injustice, it helps to discuss those feelings with people who have known a similar pain.

Review the truth in Hebrews 3:13: "But encourage one another daily, as long as it is called 'Today,' so that none of you may be hardened by sin's deceitfulness." If you struggle with cynicism, ask God to break your "hard shell."

## HIS WORDS OVER YOU

"Above everything else, guard your heart, for everything you do flows from it. I will give you a new heart and put a new spirit in you; I will remove your heart of stone and give you a soft heart."

*Based on Proverbs 4:23 and Ezekiel 36:26*

# 39. Shedding Shame

*If we can share our story with someone who responds with empathy and understanding, shame can't survive.*

BRENÉ BROWN

The woman approached my table cautiously. I was signing books after speaking at a conference, and she was next in line. She had trouble making eye contact, and spoke in a whisper. "My husband's been incarcerated for the past eighteen years, and nobody knows," she said. "He's getting out in one month."

Realizing she did not want our conversation to be heard by others, I responded quietly. "Is he coming home to live with you?"

With a bit of hesitation, she nodded. Then, suddenly, she stood to her fullest height, put her shoulders back, looked at me directly, and spoke confidently. "Thank you for sharing the story of your experience with your son's incarceration," she said. "Today you've given me the courage to start telling my own story. I'm going to quit hiding in false shame and false guilt, and I'm going tell people what's happened to our family. I want to give them hope the way you've given me hope."

I had a momentary flashback to the beginning of our own story, and I reviewed the experiences and thoughts that produced my own false shame:

- humiliation when the news of our son's arrest hit our local papers
- apprehension regarding how our neighbors would feel about living close to the parents of a murderer
- embarrassment in front of local people at the grocery store, the bank, or the hair salon
- guilt over what we must have done wrong in our parenting
- awkwardness when running into old friends who might or might not have known what had happened
- fear over the possibility of losing our livelihood in a career that involved speaking and writing

Shame is a tricky emotion. In reality, it's "a painful feeling of humiliation or distress caused by the consciousness of wrong or foolish behavior."[17] In light of this definition, everything I listed above is actually a *false* shame—a burden I have taken on myself due to the actions of my

---

17. Google. "Shame." https://www.google.com/#q=What+is+shame.

son. Nonetheless, it is a powerful feeling that all of us who have loved ones in prison understand extremely well.

Shame makes us feel like we are defective as people. It makes us think that if anyone knew what we were like, we'd be rejected. We often live in fear of being exposed—that woman who spoke to me at the book table had lived through almost two decades of her husband's incarceration, telling me, "nobody knows." Shame keeps us focused on how bad we are (or on how bad our incarcerated loved one is), and pushing us toward isolation. It can thrust us into destructive behaviors including alcohol and drug abuse, eating disorders, and damaging relationships. It can make us feel worthless and unlovable, putting us in a prison of our own making. It handcuffs us to the past and steals our joy.

———

So where is the hope? Start by recognizing that shame is a lie. None of us is ever worthless or beyond repair. Shame can come from our own wrong choices, but false shame comes from taking on guilt for the wrongdoing, mistakes, and sin of our incarcerated family member. Though you love that person, you are *not* that person. Reject the thinking that makes you feel responsible for their criminal actions.

Then share your story with someone else. Begin by talking to one other person you trust, perhaps someone else who has a family member in prison. When we honestly discuss what we've experienced and receive empathy in return, the painful feeling of false shame begins to dissolve. We know we are not alone.

Now, some shame is real—so ask yourself if there is any wrong in your life that needs to be dealt with. If the answer is no, reject false shame. If the answer is yes, take action. The forgiveness you seek can come only from God. One of my favorite verses is 1 John 1:9 (NLT): "But if we confess our sins to him, he is faithful and just to forgive us our sins and to cleanse us from all wickedness."

Shame ends right there!

### HIS WORDS OVER YOU

"Instead of shame and dishonor, embrace a double portion of honor. Know that I am merciful and gracious, slow to anger, and abounding in steadfast love. I do not deal with you according to your wrongdoing. My love toward you is as high as the heavens are above the earth and as far as the east is from the west."

*Based on Isaiah 61:7 and Psalm 103:8–12*

# 40. The Green-Eyed Monster

*Jealousy . . . is a mental cancer.*
B. C. FORBES

Gene and I were slowly getting into the rhythm of our "new normal." On Labor Day weekend, I was scheduled to speak at a church in London, Ontario, and we had flown from Tampa to Detroit and rented a car to lower our travel expenses. We drove on I-94 east to Port Huron, crossed over the Blue Water Bridge, and entered Canada. An hour later we were in London.

During our twenty-six years of living in the area, Gene and I had often crossed this border. Our son was raised in Port Huron, and we knew many people in both countries. The weekend was filled as we caught up with longtime friends in between speaking at four church services on Saturday night and Sunday morning.

On the return trip, we planned to visit Gene's best friend, Dan, and his wife, Joan, back in Port Huron. Their son, a young attorney, was visiting that weekend, so we eagerly anticipated the added delight of seeing Carl, his wife, Julie, and their six-year-old twin boys. But something came up that we did not anticipate. Here is how Gene recorded his experience:

> He was not my son, but he could have been. Blue eyes. Straight teeth. Flashing smile. Quick to discuss everything—politics, Christianity, history, college, raising kids. His winsome personality and positive attitude about life were disarming and contagious. He was helpful with his children and looked lovingly at his wife. His fingers were often entwined in hers in an affectionate, lingering manner.
>
> Carl was trim, athletic, confident, and stylish. He was articulate and energized as he talked of participating in a fifteen-mile run. I was captivated by his maturity, discernment, and wisdom. Later I watched Carl play catch with his boys in the front yard.
>
> Without warning an unexpected emotion leaped into my heart. I instantly recognized it as jealousy. Wasn't *Jason* the energized and articulate young man I saw before me now? Wasn't he going to use *his* education, leadership, and potential in a great career the way Carl was doing? Wasn't *he* going to be a great dad who interacted with his children in meaningful ways?

Carl is the picture of what I envisioned my boy would look like at the same age. In reality, I see my son behind barbed wire in a blue uniform with white stripes on the sides of his trousers. Instead of meeting his family for days at the beach, followed by engaging conversations in our home, I see him in an institution where there are big grey cement block buildings arranged on a grid with guarded sidewalks between them. Momentarily, the green-eyed monster took a bite out of a much-anticipated visit. It took some effort to shove that emotion aside so I could enjoy our remaining time with these valued and caring friends.[18]

When our son was arrested, it never occurred to me that my husband and I would deal with jealousy. But we did. You, too, may have experienced a time when the green-eyed monster seemed to come out of nowhere—when you suddenly realized another family had the life you wanted.

I thought back to a time when I read in the Bible, "Anger is cruel, and wrath is like a flood, but jealousy is even more dangerous" (Proverbs 27:4 NLT). Is it true that jealousy is more hazardous to our mental and spiritual lives than anger? I had always thought of jealousy as a passing wish for something (or someone) that belonged to another person. It never crossed my mind that jealousy is like a cancer in the brain—often slow moving, but constantly growing in size until it crowds out the ability to be happy for other people.

My husband eventually told Dan about the jealousy he felt. Gene explained that he'd had some unexpected emotions over the success of Dan's son when compared with our own son's life sentence. They were able to talk openly and transparently with each other—and this honest exchange brought about an even closer relationship between Gene and his best friend.

If you feel jealousy toward someone, consider the potential benefit of talking through your feelings with that person, when the time is right. (By the way, if you are struggling with jealousy, you are normal!)

---

18. Adapted from Carol Kent, *Between a Rock and a Grace Place* (Grand Rapids: Zondervan, 2010), 66–67.

"As you look at the happy lives of others, it's tempting to be jealous of people who are enjoying favorable circumstances. Sharing honest words about your feelings with others can be painful. Seek my wisdom as you move forward. Nothing you desire can compare with it."

*Based on Proverbs 8:11 and Job 6:25*

# 41. The Benefits of Doubt

*One of the worst feelings in the world is having to
doubt something you thought was unquestionable.*

UNKNOWN TEEN BLOGGER

The woman lingered in the back of the auditorium. After almost every-one left the room, she moved to where I was seated near the book table and said, "Do you have time to talk?" I nodded and we found a couple of chairs in a quiet area.

We sat down and she told me, "My daughter is in prison for the possession of illegal drugs. She was a little girl who loved life and gave her heart to Jesus at an early age. As a teenager, she was actively involved in sports and church youth activities, and she was intent on pursuing her dream of becoming a registered nurse."

I could see the pain in Sarah's eyes as she continued. "She graduated from high school with honors and then she began her university studies. My husband and I moved her into the dormitory and prayed with her before we left. Over the next couple of months she called home less and less. By the time Christmas came, she informed us that she would only be home for two days because she was planning to spend most of her holiday vacation with friends. This was a surprise to us, but we were happy that she was forming good relationships with her classmates."

"Did something happen after that to cause concern?" I asked.

"Yes," she answered. "In the middle of February we received a call telling us our daughter had been arrested for the possession of illegal drugs." By this time, Sarah was wiping tears and found it difficult to go on. "We discovered that she had dropped out of college and moved in with friends—and she had never told us about these plans. My husband and I borrowed money to pay for an attorney, but our daughter was eventually convicted of her crime and sentenced to three years in prison. She will probably have to serve a minimum of sixteen months of her sentence before being placed on parole."

I could tell there was more to Sarah's struggle. "Carol," she went on, "I have been sitting here all weekend at this conference hearing you say that God is faithful in the middle of unthinkable circumstances—but right now I am doubting that there even is a God. If He is real, why would He allow such bad things to happen?"

I couldn't answer all of Sarah's questions to her satisfaction. But I instantly sympathized with her, realizing how easy it is to move toward doubt when you have a child or spouse behind bars. I heard Sarah saying:

- I doubt that God would allow our family to suffer financially and personally if He is all powerful.
- I doubt that I was a good enough parent.
- I doubt that my child ever really believed in God, since she made these terrible choices.
- I doubt that any good thing can come out of what's happened.
- I doubt that God exists.

———

When we begin to feel uncertain about long-held beliefs—when we start to question the reality or truth of things about which we've always been confident—doubt has stepped into our lives. Unchecked, it begins to make slow but steady cracks in our once strongly held faith. None of us experiences a perfect trust in God, but when doubt creeps in, uncertainty can take root.

I love that the Bible says, "Be merciful to those who doubt" (Jude 22). Doubt can actually help us if we are quick to ask questions—about our uncertainties themselves and about our faith. Doubt can mean we are still open to wisdom and truth, even if our life circumstances have made us question if God or anyone else cares about us.

In the Bible, in Mark 9:14–29, we read about a man who brought his son to Jesus. The boy was possessed by an impure spirit that robbed him of his speech and threw him to the ground. He experienced other difficulties that complicated his life and made his condition obvious to other people. Jesus asked the man how long his son had been in this condition, and the man said the boy had suffered from childhood. Then the father asked Jesus to take pity on him. Jesus said, "Everything is possible for one who believes" (verse 23).

The man responded, "I do believe; help me overcome my unbelief!" (verse 24). Following so many physical challenges with his son, this father struggled with doubt, wondering if there could ever be healing for his child. But that day Jesus commanded the impure spirit to leave the boy, and he was healed. There is no record of this man being scolded for his lack of faith—and that tells me we can be honest with God about our doubts.

I learned after Jason's arrest that it's okay to voice my fearful questions to people who can offer me wise counsel. I even learned that it's okay to pound my fists into the floor and state my doubts about God directly to Him. I told Sarah that on one of my most difficult days, I shouted at the top of my lungs, "God, are you for real?" He can handle it.

Theologian Paul Tillich wrote, "Doubt is not the opposite of faith; it is one element of faith." It is nothing to be ashamed of, but something that can and should push us to God. When we keep an open mind and seek His truth, we will find it—and *that* is a great benefit!

## HIS WORDS OVER YOU

"Talk to me about your doubts, even if you feel you have little faith. You will find me when you seek me with all your heart. Have the courage to ask me for what you need and I will give it to you; seek me and you will find me; knock, and I will open the door for you."

*Based on Jeremiah 29:13 and Luke 11:9*

# 42. Confronting Discouragement

*Discouragement neutralizes optimism, assassinates hope, and erases courage. Perhaps no other human emotion is so commonly experienced and yet so infrequently exposed.*

DENNIS RAINEY

As a preacher's kid I was used to covering up my feelings of disappointment and discouragement. In retrospect, I think I wanted to make sure that my mental attitude did not reflect badly on my parents. As the years went by, I mastered the art of people-pleasing. I became a perfectionist and a workaholic. So to cover up my discouragement when Jason was arrested, I began to work even harder and immerse myself in doing things more perfectly. Whether I intended it or not, all that exhausting work meant I could fall asleep more quickly at night, and not lie in bed for hours ruminating on Jason's incarceration.

Discouragement involves a loss of confidence or enthusiasm. Author William Arthur Ward says it is "dissatisfaction with the past, distaste for the present, and distrust of the future. It is ingratitude for the blessings of yesterday, indifference to the opportunities of today, and insecurity regarding strength for tomorrow."[19] However, when you and I experience discouragement, we aren't thinking in those terms. We simply feel downhearted, hopeless about any positive change, and highly aware of our personal misery. Discouragement usually builds over a long period of loss, heartache, and the inability to change circumstances for ourselves or our incarcerated loved ones.

Gene and I have both gone through periods of discouragement. One of the things that wears him down is the grinding routine, week after week and month after month, of the visitation process. Gene writes:

> I enter my prison visitation ID number on the well-worn keypad and press my hand into the machine for the imprint to be verified by an officer. I return through the abrasively loud staggered lockout doors, but before leaving the building, I must account for everything I walked in with—a belt, a watch, a ring, sunglasses, one car key, and a jacket. I pass through the metal detector, exit through the front entrance and walk toward my car. I'm discouraged—and

---

19. Bible.org. "A Definition of Discouragement," February 2, 2009. https://bible.org/illustration/definition-discouragement.

then it hits me. What must it be like for Jason to go back to his cell after visitation?

I unlock my car, open the windows, and let the hot, humid, Florida air blow through the vehicle. Then the thought slams into me like a fist. My son has been sentenced to life without the possibility of parole. Is this all we have to look forward to for the rest of our lives—visitation at the prison? In my mind I rehearse the endless questions. *Who will be his advocate when Carol and I are gone? Who will care enough to visit him? Who will send books and materials to the prison for the classes he facilitates?*

More than a few times when I've felt this discouraged, I stop for junk food—something to dull the pain. On one of those trips I forage for crunchy cookies and find Famous Amos Chocolate Chip Cookies on a two-for-one special. I make my purchase and go home.

After walking in the back door, I pour cold milk in a large mug and place fifteen cookies on a plate. One by one I dunk the cookies and eat them all while rehearsing my grief. I go back for more cookies and polish off the entire bag in one sitting. In some ways, my behavior isn't much different from the pleasure of alcohol, or drugs, or whatever addictive behavior numbs pain for other people. I am discouraged.

———

You are living out the consequences of your loved one's actions. When you find yourself without hope that these hard things will change anytime soon—or perhaps ever—discouragement begins to produce sadness, insecurity, indifference, numbness, and even distrust. The obvious cause of your discouragement is that a person who is important to you is a prisoner.

However, as we look more closely, we find that exhaustion often triggers discouragement. We are mentally and spiritually fatigued by going through the legal process. And even after that process is over, we face "doing time" with our loved ones.

Discouragement also comes from frustration—over visitation issues, caring for children left behind, wrestling with finances, going through appeals. Nothing about the process is easy. And discouragement also arises from fear—mostly the fear that things are not going to change, except for the worse.

So what is the cure for discouragement? For one thing, we need rest. We're so busy juggling everything it is hard to make that choice—but will anything improve if you keep going like you are now? Sometimes we need to reorganize our lives and take a break from the never-ending routine. For example, skip an occasional visitation day when other family members or friends can go. Finally, resist fear. Listen to this wisdom from the Bible: "Be strong and courageous. . . . Do not be afraid or discouraged, for the LORD God, my God, is with you" (1 Chronicles 28:20).

## HIS WORDS OVER YOU

"I will go before you and I will be with you. I will never leave you or desert you. I will keep you in perfect peace when you keep your mind focused on me."

*Based on Deuteronomy 31:8 and Isaiah 26:3*

# 43. Choose Life

*We are all faced with a series of great opportunities*
*brilliantly disguised as impossible situations.*

CHARLES SWINDOLL

As the news of Jason's arrest spread to friends and acquaintances in faraway places, cards started arriving at the house. Gene and I read many kind notes of condolence from people who had known us in other places we had lived or who had met us through speaking engagements. I placed each card in a big basket, knowing a day would come when we would want to read through these caring notes again.

One day, sifting through the cards, I was stunned to notice that a majority of them were sympathy cards—the kind you receive when someone dies. I know there isn't a Hallmark line for the parents of children who've been arrested for murder. Our friends were simply trying to find the most appropriate sentiment for our unusual circumstances. But a wave of emotion washed over me. I picked up the cards and threw them in the air. "My son is not dead!" I shouted. "He is alive!"

Then it hit me once again: someone else's son *was* dead—at the hands of my child. There was a father, a stepmother, and a sister who had planned a funeral for their loved one while we awaited Jason's trial for first-degree murder. Grief for the family of the deceased overwhelmed me. I imagined what it must have been like for them to receive the call telling them their loved one had been shot and killed. I began to weep for this family and their excruciating loss, for their shattered hopes and dreams, for their future reunions with an important part of their family missing and never to return.

Gene and I had to address a big question: would *we* die too—emotionally, physically, and spiritually—or would we choose life? Eventually we came to understand that we could do absolutely nothing to change the facts of what had happened. But we could choose, every day, how we would live our lives in the midst of uncertainty, emotional agony, financial challenges, deep disappointment . . . and razor wire.

One day Gene put his arms around me and started to pray. He knew I was discouraged and filled with fear about the future—both for our son and for us as a couple. "God, we are hurting so badly at this moment," Gene prayed, "that we would much rather exit the hardship we're in the middle of and go straight to heaven to be with you. But we know that's not possible. So right now, we choose life instead of a slow, sickening emotional death. We're counting on you to help us, because we are too tired and weak to make it alone." I found myself gathering strength from my husband's faith. That was the beginning of my rediscovery of hope. We knew we would live—but we also recognized we would be living a different kind of life. Our future would be more like author Ken Gire describes: "When suffering shatters the carefully kept vase that is our lives, God stoops to pick up the pieces. But he doesn't put them back together as a restoration project patterned after our former selves. Instead, he sifts through the rubble and selects some of the chards as raw material for another project—a mosaic that tells the story of redemption."[20]

---

Incarceration permanently alters life. From the point of the arrest and onward, family dynamics change. Our dreams are thwarted. Our finances, reputations, work situations, and church and community interactions are all affected by the wrong choices of our loved one. Sometimes the humiliation and the hurt are so bad that even suicide feels like a plausible way of escape.

One day I picked up my Bible and found a verse I had memorized as a child, the words of Jesus in John 10:10 (KJV): "I am come that they might have life, and that they might have it more abundantly." I knew the choice was mine. Hope or despair? Death or life? Choosing life would mean a new kind of existence—harder, but in some ways better than before. More honest. Richer because of the pain.

When you are living amid harsh circumstances, it can be hard to find hope. But it's worth trying. Can you think of any good things you've experienced during this difficult time? It doesn't matter how small they might be: Did someone bring you a cup of coffee while you were waiting? Did a police officer answer your questions in a kind way? Did you meet anyone in the security line who shared your grief for a moment, even if no words were spoken? Write down any and every little thing that represents *life*. It took me a while to grasp the idea—but life is a courageous choice!

### HIS WORDS OVER YOU

"Dear one, I place before you life and death. Choose life. Listen to me and embrace me. I will renew your life and sustain you. I will redeem your life from the pit and crown you with love and compassion."

*Based on Deuteronomy 30:19–20, Ruth 4:15, and Psalm 103:4*

---

20. Ken Gire, *The North Face of God* (Wheaton, IL: Tyndale House Publishers, Inc., 2005), 120.

# 44. Choose Trust

*Never be afraid to trust an unknown future to a known God.*
CORRIE TEN BOOM

"We just don't know who we can trust."
The man sounded fearful and uncertain. He and his wife had asked to meet with Gene and me after we spoke in the Sunday services of their church. As this couple gave details of their story, they both wept. Their son, who I'll call Brad, had been a highly achieving teenager and an award-winning athlete in high school. He received scholarship offers from several respected universities, and he quickly decided on his first choice.

During the fall of his freshman year, Brad's fraternity hosted a party after the college won a football game. Brad drank too much and woke up with a hangover the next morning. An hour later there was a knock on his door, and a police officer told Brad that he was under arrest for raping a girl the night before. Officers read him his rights, put him in handcuffs, and transported him to the local jail.

"He remembers partying, drinking, and celebrating the win in football," Brad's father said, "but has no memory of forcing a woman to have sex with him. He admits he was so drunk that he recalls almost nothing of what transpired at the party. Tests confirmed that he was intimate with the young woman making the accusation—but we don't know if the act was consensual or not. Needless to say, we are heartbroken. If our son is convicted of rape, he will be locked up for a long time."

Then Brad's mom spoke up: "We have no one we can trust. The details of the case have been all over our local papers and we see people staring at us in the supermarket, at the bank, and even in church. Their eye contact might be compassionate, but right now their glances feel intimidating and piercing. We know we're hypersensitive, but it feels so invasive. We're grieving for all of our son's losses; we feel deeply for the awkwardness and embarrassment of our two younger children who are still in high school; we need support, but we don't know how we can trust anybody. What advice can you give us?"

Even as she asked the question, I recalled dealing with the same issue early in our experience. When you and I cope with the arrest and trial of our loved one, we long to have someone who will wait with us, listen to us, keep our confidences, and be our advocates throughout this strange and foreign place called the legal system. *Trust* is defined as an "assured reliance on the character, ability, strength, or truth of someone."[21] Our question is this: who is the person we can believe in like that?

---

When Gene and I responded to this couple, the first thing we said was that there will be people who will fail them—by breaking confidences or gossiping about their son—but there is One who is trustworthy. As people of faith, Gene and I fully embrace these words from Psalm 9:10: "Those who know your name trust in you, for you, LORD, have never forsaken those who seek you."

However, choosing to trust *people* is a different thing entirely. When your loved one has been arrested for a serious crime, don't look for a large group of people to support you. Start with one person—that one who really seems to care about you and treats others with consideration. Be alert. When you're with others, watch whether they talk negatively about people or are wise in their communication. Look for a reliable person who keeps his or her word, is honest, and seeks the well-being of others.

Are there people in your life that you can trust, people who are honest and reliable? If you believe in God, pray that He will help you make wise choices about who to trust with the details of your situation, as well as your secret hopes and fears. When I pray, I expect an answer—and I have discovered that God loves to meet my needs.

Remember, choosing to trust one person will not keep you from being hurt by other people. It will not stop some people's criticism. It will not eliminate gossip about your loved one. But it *will* give you a friend who stands by you when your heart is breaking—and that is a great gift!

### HIS WORDS OVER YOU

"Trust in me. I will be your strength and shield. Don't be afraid. What can people do to you? I will be your refuge and fortress and you can rely on my character."

*Based on Psalm 28:7 and Psalm 56:4*

---

21. *Merriam-Webster's Collegiate Dictionary*, 10th ed. (Springfield, MA: Merriam-Webster, 1996), s.v. "trust."

# 45. Choose Vulnerability

*Owning our story can be hard but not nearly as difficult as spending our lives running from it. Embracing our vulnerabilities is risky but not nearly as dangerous as giving up on love and belonging and joy.*

BRENÉ BROWN

It was Christmas Day, and Gene and I were at the prison with Jason. In the middle of the afternoon, I left the main visitation room to use the restroom. While in a stall, I heard a woman come in the main door. She was sobbing, cursing, and hyperventilating. "I hate this place!" she yelled. "I hate these people!"

Though I couldn't see her face, I understood her pain.

The old "professional me" would have stepped out of the stall, quoted my five best Bible verses on suffering, and prayed for this woman. But the new, broken, hurting, "mama-of-a-lifer me" instantly identified with her. Gently opening the door of the stall, I stepped out and put my arms around her.

I did not quote any Bible verses. I did not say a prayer. I just cried with a stranger. For a moment, two women who'd never met shared an unspoken moment of frustration and pain. Without describing our personal stories, we recognized the similarity in our journeys—and understood each other's heartache. That moment of vulnerability enabled us to communicate very personally at a later date.

Over the past few years, many people have told me secrets about their incarcerated family members—things they don't share with people in their own circles. Sometimes they tell me these personal things during my speaking engagements, when we have a chance to connect during a break in the program. At other times they e-mail their comments to me, or send me private messages on Facebook. They say things like this:

- I've never told anyone that my brother is incarcerated.
- People in my church don't have any idea that my grown daughter is in prison.
- No one in the office I work in knows that my husband is in prison. I'm not sure my job would be secure if my story was common knowledge.
- I wish I could be as open about my incarcerated family member as you are, but I'm too afraid if I opened up, I would face rejection by people in my community.

One thing is certain: vulnerability is risky. But it is also rewarding. It takes courage to open up to others, especially when we're being honest about the incarceration of one of our family members. Normally, we put up emotional shields to protect ourselves from the possibility of being hurt. But when we take the risk and speak openly with another person, we experience a new kind of freedom. Our openness prompts others to be real about their own messy and broken lives, and we find out that imperfection in our families is not unusual. A bond of mutual trust is formed with others.

What are the risks? Some might criticize us or handle our story carelessly, opening us to verbal attacks by others. A few people might choose to move on, rather than continue in friendship with us. But I believe the risk is worth it. I've discovered that vulnerability breaks down walls of hurt and destroys suspicions. It eliminates whispering behind our backs, encouraging people to be direct in their conversations with us. The alternative to vulnerability is to conceal our secrets, hide our hurts, lock up our feelings, run from caring people, and live in the dark shadows of loneliness.

When we recognize our need for others and the benefits of vulnerability, we start to develop emotionally healthy relationships. And it all begins by being honest with God. Psalm 38:9 is a favorite Bible verse of mine: "All my longings lie open before you, Lord; my sighing is not hidden from you." When I believe that God knows everything about me, I realize that I'm not alone . . . and that gives me courage to trust others with my real self.

### HIS WORDS OVER YOU

"Nothing in all of creation is hidden from me. Everything is exposed before my eyes. Open your lips and speak truth from your heart."

*Based on Hebrews 4:13 and Psalm 15:2*

# 46. Choose Gratitude

*Gratitude . . . turns what we have into enough, and more. It turns denial into acceptance, chaos into order, confusion into clarity. It . . . makes sense of our past, brings peace for today, and creates a vision for tomorrow.*

MELODY BEATTIE

One weekend, while visiting Jason at the prison, I casually asked, "How do you hold on to hope in the middle of a life-without-parole sentence?"

He looked up and said, "Mom, I have a gratitude list. Every time the cloud of depression starts to settle on top of me, I get a piece of paper and write down everything I have to be thankful for."

Jason went on. "I'm thankful I have two parents who will be my advocates for as long as they live. The average number of years a 'lifer' like me even gets visits is five—and then no one comes to visit them anymore. No one puts money in their account for the basics of personal hygiene items, postage stamps, and occasional snacks. I have family members and friends who place enough in my account that I can share with those who have nothing. That's a lot to be thankful for." He paused and then continued. "I'm also grateful that on a compound that houses up to seventeen hundred men I can be a missionary in a very dark place."

Later, as I thought about what Jason said, I realized how much my son had accomplished inside a maximum-security prison. He has facilitated classes, brainstormed with us about how to help inmates and their families, contributed to books I've written on our unexpected foray into the world of incarceration . . . and encouraged Gene and me when we felt hopeless.

When I was a child, my mother encouraged me to memorize 1 Thessalonians 5:16–18. I had no idea how handy those verses would be later in my life. In the Bible version called *The Message,* they read, "Be cheerful no matter what . . . thank God no matter what happens. This is the way God wants you who belong to Christ Jesus to live."

My mother is full of compassion and encouragement and she's always concerned for Jason's well-being. Some time ago I told her how disappointed and angry I was over some harsh changes at his prison. Following my tirade, the first thing she said was, "Carol, have you thanked God yet? There's power in intentionally giving Him praise. Taking that action will keep your heart and mind in the right place.

If you choose thanksgiving over anger and fear, you will find hidden treasure in this situation."

She was right. Praying out loud, I praised God for what I knew to be true about His character. As I focused on Him, not on the circumstances that upset me, I started to *feel* grateful. I realized I was grateful for my son's growing maturity, and for his remorse over the pain he had brought to the family of the deceased and to his own family. I found myself grateful for his deepening humility and his spiritual growth.

That was my unexpected treasure!

———

I still occasionally struggle with being grateful. There are days when it feels good, even justifiable, to be *un*grateful. Do you feel this way? Are you angry at the system, at your loved one, at the seeming unfairness of it all? Do you ever feel justified in being ungrateful?

After more than a decade on this journey, I can tell you that when our hearts and minds give up on gratefulness, it can be devastating. My son is in prison for the rest of his life and there is nothing I can do to change his never-ending sentence. Sometimes, on the surface, it feels good to be ungrateful—until I realize what takes place in my mind and heart when I make that choice. When we are ungrateful, we are less able to cope with stress. We have trouble accomplishing our goals.

Scientists tell us that gratitude is associated with better health. A researcher at Duke University Medical Center once stated, "If [thankfulness] were a drug, it would be the world's best-selling product with a health maintenance indication for every major organ system."[22]

Gratitude is a thankful appreciation for what we've been given. We can look back and recognize blessings in our history. We can look outside our own misery and see the good in people around us, recognizing those who have supported us, waited with us, encouraged us, and wept with us.

It helped me to begin my own "gratitude list," and I encourage you to do the same. Date the top of the page, whether paper or electronic, because that will give you a point of reference when you look back. Itemize *everything* you have to be thankful for, being sure to include all the unexpected benefits that have come from the incarceration of your family member. I once talked to a woman who said, "Going to

———

22. Mercola.com. "Developing an Attitude of Gratitude Can Help You Live a Longer, Happier Life," November 27, 2014. http://articles.mercola.com/sites/articles /archive/2014/11/27/thanksgiving-gratitude.aspx#_edn2.

prison saved my son's life." Now that's a lot to be thankful for! Share your list with at least one other person as you begin to realize the power of gratitude.

## HIS WORDS OVER YOU

"Your grateful praise is music to my ears. Learn to give thanks in all circumstances. Don't be troubled. In every situation bring your requests to me, and my peace will guard your hearts."

*Based on Psalm 147:7, 1 Thessalonians 5:18, and Philippians 4:6–7*

# 47. Choose Forgiveness

*When we forgive, we set a prisoner free and*
*discover that the prisoner we set free is us.*
LEWIS B. SMEDES

After Jason's arrest we become very close to his wife and stepdaughters. All of us were still in a state of shock, and we needed each other desperately. At that time Gene and I were living in Michigan and our little extended family was in Florida. During the two-and-a-half-year wait for the trial, we called back and forth often, providing emotional support for each other. Every Saturday night at the jail, Jason enjoyed visits from his girls.

Following his conviction, Jason was moved to his first prison. Now the girls were allowed Saturday and Sunday visits from 9:00 a.m. until 3:00 p.m., which was a huge investment of time every week. And these visits involved a much longer drive for his family. Still, for another three and a half years, Jason's wife faithfully brought the girls to visit.

Then in 2004, four major hurricanes hit the state of Florida. Three of those colossal storms went directly through the town where Jason's family lived, causing massive damage to our daughter-in-law's home. There were roof leaks and wallboard damage. Moisture, combined with the Florida heat, quickly caused mold to set in, aggravating our daughter-in-law's allergies.

Jason's wife is a licensed artist, and her exquisite, hand-painted murals on the walls were being warped. In the midst of so much difficulty and disappointment, I saw something in her spirit die. I now believe she was experiencing a sense of hopelessness, a feeling that nothing would ever change for the better.

In the summer of 2005, Gene and I moved to Florida to be close to Jason and his family and offer more hands-on help. But soon after our move, Jason's wife came to us and said, "I need to give the girls a more normal life. They need soccer on Saturdays and church on Sundays. It isn't normal for little girls to spend every weekend in a maximum-security prison." Then she spoke words that were hard for us to hear: "I'm planning to leave the state, and if I separate from Jason, I will no longer be in touch with the two of you."

I felt a wail coming out of the depths of my being. I understood how hard and how endless this journey was. Gene and I were coming to grips with the difficulty our daughter-in-law was having. She had to live her own "new kind of normal" with no hope that she would ever have Jason return home to be a typical husband and father. The endless sentence combined with the hurricane damage to the house had taken their toll. She packed up the girls and all of their earthly possessions, and moved out of state.

We understood our daughter-in-law's desire to move on, to settle in a place far away from so much sorrow. But as this major transition took place, I found myself playing the blame game. There were plenty of people to blame: my son, for pulling the trigger; the prosecutor, for being so harsh; Gene and myself, for not being better parents; our daughter-in-law, for leaving. And, of course, there was God, who allowed all of this to happen.

It didn't take long to realize that I had unforgiveness in my heart. And I soon discovered that forgiveness is a process, a *daily* choice, not just a one time decision.

———

Archibald Hart says, "Forgiveness is giving up my right to hurt you for hurting me."[23] Forgiveness grants relief to the person who "owes" us for what they've done to us . . . or allowed to happen to us. When you have an incarcerated loved one, it's easy to blame him or her for ruining your life—for not thinking about the impact their crime would have on family members. It's also easy to point fingers at other people, or even the justice system. Perhaps you're struggling with forgiveness issues right now.

In Matthew 18:21–22 (MSG), Peter asked Jesus, "Master, how many times do I forgive a brother or sister who hurts me? Seven?" Jesus answered him, "Seven! Hardly. Try seventy times seven." Jesus knew that forgiveness, for most of us, is a process, a decision that needs to be repeated often. It is rarely a one time choice that lasts a lifetime.

Forgiveness doesn't negate the wrong done to you; it sets you free from bitterness and anger. Forgiveness frees you to move forward—out of the hurts of the past and toward a productive life. It is always worth the effort.

23. Archibald Hart, quoted in James Dobson, *Dr. Dobson's Handbook of Family Advice* (Eugene, OR: Harvest House Publishers, 1998), 87.

"Forgive others as quickly and completely as I have forgiven you. Don't repay evil for evil and don't respond with insults when people insult you. Instead, pay them back with a blessing. Above everything else, wear love. It's your basic, all-purpose garment."

*Based on Colossians 3:13–14 and 1 Peter 3:9*

# 48. Choose the Gift

*I've heard hundreds of tear-filled stories. . . . I always whisper*
*the same thing to them: "Look for the gift in your pain." If*
*you look for that gift, believe me, you will find it. If you don't*
*look, it's all too easy to become enslaved by your misery.*

SEAN STEPHENSON

We have received numerous letters from prisoners over the years. "Charlie," a thirty-six-year-old inmate who had been incarcerated with Jason, wrote that he had read my book *When I Lay My Isaac Down* and wanted us to know how it affected him.

> When I started to read your book, I only made it through a few pages and I began to cry, something I almost never do. I was able to feel the unconditional love of a mother and father for their son. I wasn't crying for my loss, for I have never received such love. I cried because I knew what a priceless gift I had been denied. I was openly hated by my parents from my earliest memories in life. Thank you for showing me that real love exists.

As we began a correspondence with Charlie, we realized that our "new normal" is very different from what we had planned for our own future. But it is nevertheless fulfilling, exciting, uplifting, and purposeful. We've met many inmates like Charlie who had no positive examples in their homes—no adults who nurtured or mentored them and no spiritual training that would have given them a basis of faith. It's little wonder that they didn't develop a clear view of right and wrong. Nobody cared.

I discovered a growing love in my heart for these prisoners, the ones who did not have mothers or fathers who poured out life-giving truth in their growing-up years. In time, I realized that this love was a gift from God. And I've chosen to use this gift to help and encourage prisoners as much as I can.

Sometimes Gene and I send books to inmates. At other times, donors provide funds that we can designate for food packages through the official Department of Corrections vendor. We have found that a small thing means a lot to inmates: receiving a new greeting card and envelope they can send to someone they care about. Sometimes our gift is simply to talk with the struggling parent of an inmate.

About a year after Jason's arrest, a friend sent me this Bible verse: "I will give you hidden treasures, riches stored in secret places, so that you may know that I am the LORD, the God of Israel, who summons you by name" (Isaiah 45:3). It had never occurred to me that a "gift" could arise out of the messy, ugly, and uncertain circumstances of our lives. How could any good thing come out of so much sorrow?

But Gene and I started to think of the opportunities we had encountered, which were actually gifts we might never have received apart from having an incarcerated son: compassion for people who are going through similar experiences, opportunities to help families that are struggling financially and emotionally, invitations to speak in jails or prisons and offer hope to prisoners. And it was amazing to meet inmates who have been transformed by true faith in Jesus Christ. The list could go on and on.

———

What dreams from your past have had to be adjusted due to these new circumstances in your life? When you feel discouraged and miserable, how do you normally respond?

- Do you withdraw from people and hide your feelings?
- Do you get together with a friend and have a pity party?
- Do you escape into a favorite addiction—work, perfectionism, food, alcohol, prescription drugs, pornography?
- Do you talk to God about how miserable you are?
- Do you brainstorm creative ways to use the new opportunity you've been given?

It helped me tremendously to think about the hidden gifts in my unwanted circumstances. A Bible passage that I appreciate is Proverbs 24:3–4: "By wisdom a house is built, and through understanding it is established; through knowledge its rooms are filled with rare and beautiful treasures." I began to pray that God would give me wisdom to fill my life with new treasures—treasures that have come only because of my son's incarceration.

The gifts we receive aren't always visible to others. Our acts of compassion may not be noticed, but I send up instant, silent prayers for people I meet who are struggling with any hard issues, not just the incarceration of a loved one. On the surface, the person I pray for seems to be the recipient of the gift—but the truth is, *I'm* the one who benefits most. Instead of being consumed by the harsh circumstances in our own family, my focus turns to others. *That* is a treasure I never expected!

Take a moment to list the gifts you've been offered in your new and different life as the family member of a prisoner. It's okay to start small—but be sure to act on whatever gift you've been given. When you choose to embrace your opportunity as a gift, you begin to find joy again.

## HIS WORDS OVER YOU

"Dear one, when life is different from what you want, look for my creative ways of giving you the desires of your heart. Delighting in me is the first step. I love to give you good gifts."

*Based Psalm 37:4 and Matthew 7:11*

# 49. Choose Perseverance

*Perseverance is not a long race; it is many*
*short races one after the other.*

WALTER ELLIOTT

The woman gave me a desperate look. She was standing next to me in the seemingly endless line of people waiting to get through prison security. "How long have you been doing this?" she asked.

I sensed her frustration at the inefficiency of the intake process, the hours of wasted time, week after week and month after month. Only two corrections officers were assigned to record every item of jewelry we were wearing. They had to count the amount of cash we were carrying for the vending machines—it could not exceed fifty dollars, and no denomination higher than a twenty-dollar bill would be accepted.

Before I could answer her question, the woman continued: "Last weekend, after waiting an hour and a half to get to the front of the line, I had to return to my vehicle because I had a small ring attached to my car key."

When she paused, I answered her original question. "We went to the jail to visit our son for two and a half years, and since he was sentenced, we've been standing in these lines for another thirteen years at four different prisons," I said. "How long has it been for you?"

She flushed with embarrassment and said, "Nine months. I guess I shouldn't complain." I assured this woman that whether it had been fifteen years or nine months, the waiting is never easy. She nodded in agreement.

I thought about the waiting the families of prisoners do—sometimes over short periods of time, sometimes for many years:

- waiting for the news to hit the local paper
- waiting to obtain the money for legal expenses, or waiting for a court appointed attorney
- waiting for a plea bargain, or for a trial to take place
- waiting for the case's final resolution
- waiting for the right time to express your sorrow and condolences to the family of the victim
- waiting to be placed on the approved prison visitation list
- waiting in visitation processing lines
- waiting for financial recovery after so many expenses
- waiting for true remorse in the life of our loved one

- waiting on answers from God about why He allowed our family to endure this misery

I never really understood the meaning of perseverance until I lived "in the meantime"—waiting for the explanation for, the resolution to, and the results of my son's crime. *Perseverance* is defined as "steadfastness in doing something despite difficulty or delay in achieving success." It can also mean, "continuance in a state of grace leading finally to a state of glory."[24] I know that sounds complicated. I'm learning that this too is a process.

---

During the past fifteen years, as I've grappled with learning the art of perseverance, I have realized some things:

1. Life is short—no matter how long the days feel.
2. Delayed answers can make an eventual result more meaningful.
3. God reveals the "glory" part of the experience much more slowly than I would like.

You have already figured out that my faith is important to me. The Bible says, "The testing of your faith produces perseverance" (James 1:3). I hate the process of testing, but I'm already experiencing positive results of perseverance. It has allowed me to meet some incredible people who are going through the same thing my family is experiencing. It has taught me that I often miss important opportunities because I'm usually in a hurry—being forced to slow down has given me a chance to learn the needs of inmates and their families. Because of perseverance, my husband and I have been able to help some of those people through Speak Up for Hope, the nonprofit organization we started.

Have you learned to persevere because of your experience so far? Is there positive change in your life because of perseverance? If you are a person of faith, thank God for the things that don't go right. Remember that the testing of your faith develops perseverance.

## HIS WORDS OVER YOU

"Run your race with perseverance. I know your deeds and your hard work; I see your steadfastness in the middle of your challenges. Wait with hope for me. I will be your help and your shield."

*Based on Hebrews 12:1, Revelation 2:2, and Psalm 33:20*

---

24. Wordnik, s.v. "perseverance," accessed May 10, 2013, http://www.wordnik.com/words/perseverance.

# 50. The Package on the Porch

*Each day holds a surprise. But only if we expect it can we see,*
*hear, or feel it when it comes to us. Let's not be afraid to receive*
*each day's surprise, whether it comes to us as sorrow or as joy. It*
*will open a new place in our hearts, a place where we can welcome*
*new friends and celebrate more fully our shared humanity.*

HENRI NOUWEN

Over my son's incarceration, I have learned that my toughest time of the year is the Christmas season. It may have to do with the colorful decorations in the stores, or the lighted trees in people's yards, or the upbeat songs on the radio . . . or the envy I feel when the houses on my street have extra cars parked out front. Other people are enjoying family reunions while Gene and I go to the prison and spend the day behind razor wire.

We've been doing this long enough that I realize my malaise begins early in December and lasts for a full month. I can put on a plastic smile and appear fine, but I'm not. Perhaps you have that artificial smile too.

Several years ago, about two weeks before Christmas, I was startled by the doorbell at 9:15 p.m. It was way too late for a delivery and an unusual time for unexpected company. I hurried to the front door, turned on the porch light, and peeked out. When Gene joined me, we opened the door only to discover that no one was there. There weren't even any cars in sight. But as I glanced to the left, a brightly wrapped package caught my eye. The streetlight bounced off the metallic paper and I noticed a card on top. It simply said: *Mom.*

My immediate response was that the gift was a mistake, or perhaps a cruel joke. My only child was in prison and could not have delivered this package. However, it was on *my* porch and I *am* a mom. My curiosity got the best of me.

Opening the card, I discovered a note in my son's handwriting. Tears tumbled down my cheeks as I read the message:

Dear Mom,

It's been a long time since I was able to be home with you and Dad for Christmas. I miss you so much! You have poured love and encouragement into my life, and you've supplied me with many educational and ministry tools to help my fellow inmates here at the prison. I wanted to do something special for you this year. I hope you enjoy the gift. It would bring me lots of joy if it's something you like. I hope every time you wear it you think of how much you mean to me.

Love,

J. P.

Opening the lid of the large box, I found mounds of tissue paper covering the surprise. As the paper cascaded to the floor, there it was—the most stunning silk jacket I had ever seen, its russet color an ideal match for my red hair. Slipping it on, I headed for a mirror. It was the perfect size, as if a tailor had measured me for a custom fit. Best of all, the surprise was from my son!

I later learned that my friend Pam had exchanged letters with Jason, arranging for this gift to be delivered on his behalf. I felt as if God was saying, *I know your heart hurts. Your Christmases will not be the way you dreamed they would be, but be encouraged. I am comforting your son as I am comforting you.*[25]

––––

If you asked me about the most surprising moment of my life, it would be that time, in the middle of the night, when my husband and I received the news of our son's arrest. That was a heartbreaking surprise!

None of us want or expect bad surprises. Negative surprises can initiate tears, anxiety, hyperventilation, physical weakness, even the anticipation of danger. However, we're very fond of good surprises—the kind that make us suddenly aware of a generous act or a sacrifice made on our behalf. We love birthday surprises, balloons for special occasions, and unanticipated visits from people we love. Gene and I have learned that the families of prisoners often get unexpected surprises—of all sorts.

How do you respond to the bad surprises? Read through the following list and decide which way of coping you usually choose:

- I withdraw from people closest to me and give everyone the silent treatment.
- I get angry and yell a lot.
- I criticize the person or people who've caused my unwanted surprise.
- I talk to God and ask for wisdom.

––––

25. Adapted from Carol Kent, *Between a Rock and a Grace Place* (Grand Rapids: Zondervan, 2010), 13–14.

You may have read about my Christmas surprise and thought: *It must be nice to know people who are rich and connected enough to provide you with such a special gift! I've got nobody in my life that would ever do anything like that!* I didn't mention that I received the unexpected gift more than *seven years* after my son's arrest. It was the first time anyone had done something so unusual for me, and it *was* a good surprise. But I've had plenty of bad ones too.

I'm learning on this journey that we'll have surprises of all kinds—but because of the sorrow and grief we've experienced, the bad ones often overshadow the good. A Bible passage that has been meaningful to me is 1 Peter 4:12–13: "Dear friends, do not be surprised at the fiery ordeal that has come on you to test you, as though something strange were happening to you. But rejoice inasmuch as you participate in the sufferings of Christ, so that you may be overjoyed when his glory is revealed."

We can start by praying about the surprises we encounter, whether bad or good. Perhaps some of our prayers can start like this:

- God, the wind has been knocked out of me with news of the long sentence my husband received. . . .
- Lord, thank you for the unexpected bonus in my paycheck. With all the legal bills we've had, that was a great surprise. . . .
- Father, my thirteen-year-old had a positive attitude about going to the prison to visit her brother. Knowing how much she hates the dress code and how angry she is with her brother's bad choices, I'm grateful for this new beginning in their relationship. . . .

If you believe in prayer, run directly to God whenever you're hit with the surprises of life.

### HIS WORDS OVER YOU

"I long to bless you with good things. I want you to experience my lavish gift-giving by getting to know my Son personally. There has never been the slightest doubt in my mind that your story will come to a flourishing finish on the day Christ Jesus appears."

*Based on Ephesians 1:6 and Philippians 1:6*

# 51. Discovering Contentment

*We tend to forget that happiness doesn't come as a
result of getting something we don't have, but rather in
recognizing and appreciating what we do have.*

FREDERICK KOENIG

Since our family's dreams were shattered by Jason's crime and sentencing, I have struggled with discontent. It has often been hard to plan for anything remotely connected to having fun or enjoying life.

Once, I talked to the wife of an inmate, who told me, "I recently purchased the first new car I've ever owned, and it brings me absolutely no joy. I thought it might give me a sense of accomplishment, but to my surprise, it means nothing. With my husband behind bars facing a long sentence, I'm experiencing an uneasiness that permeates every day of my life, and it totally destroys any chance of future happiness."

What this wife expressed is something that most of us are familiar with—a lack of contentment with what we have, what our circumstances are, what our future holds, and what our day-to-day life feels like. The dictionary defines *contented* as "feeling or showing satisfaction with one's possessions, status, or situation."[26] Most of us with a family member behind bars can easily admit that it's hard to find contentment in the midst of an interrupted life.

One of the key ingredients of contentment is acceptance—accepting the hand dealt to us, our place in the world, the people closest to us, and the resources we have. I'm convinced that if there were a way to measure my own satisfaction and acceptance of my circumstances, there would be days when neither would register on a meter. My *dis*satisfaction, however, would be off the charts.

I asked my son to explain how he finds contentment.

Everything I own must fit into a small, one-foot-high, one-and-a-half foot deep, and two-and-a-half-feet long steel lockbox. All of the earthly possessions I care about are placed in this box, including family pictures, my Bible, books I'm reading, personal letters, and legal papers. . . . I'm learning to live comfortably with very little and I'm discovering it's good not to have too many things I can't let go of, because on any given day I could lose everything.

---

26. *Merriam-Webster's Collegiate Dictionary*, 11th edition (Springfield, MA: Merriam-Webster, 2003), s.v. "contented."

I'm also learning to enjoy the pleasures of this moment—a conversation, a letter, a phone call, a visit, a prayer, a hug—for the pleasures they are. . . . Experiencing contentment in my current circumstances is a daily choice, and some days are much harder than others. But I find that my times of pain lead me to my most intimate times of prayer. . . . I try to live in the moment and enjoy what this day has to offer and to have a thankful heart. If you are observant, there are many things to be grateful for in every event and even in every challenge. By practicing gratefulness for the way I am blessed and provided for, I am learning to be content.

---

I have received great advice and encouragement on the subject of contentment from my son—but also from a Bible character named Paul, who was also incarcerated. He said, "I have learned how to be content with whatever I have" (Philippians 4:11 NLT).

One Christmas day, Gene and I went through security and waited to see Jason in the visitation room. When he arrived, we shared greetings and hugs, then got into line at the canteen window to order our "Christmas dinner"—packaged tuna and crackers, frozen cheeseburgers, a slice of frozen pizza, Diet Coke, a couple of bottled waters, and a bag of popcorn. After standing in another line, this one to use the microwave oven, we eventually got our dinner warmed up. We bowed our heads at our table and thanked God for each other and for our meal. We enjoyed every bite of our food—but most of all, we celebrated the privilege of being together.

On the way home, Gene and I discussed the great day we'd had. With no big dinner to prepare, we enjoyed leisurely time with our son—and we were surprised by how relaxed and even contented we were.

We never wanted to spend our Christmas days in a prison—but this is our "new normal," and we found that Philippians 4:11 is true: we can learn to be content with whatever we have. On your next visit with your incarcerated loved one, talk about where you are on your journey to contentment. Have you learned to be content in this situation, or is it still a struggle? In what ways are you beginning to experience a different kind of contentment than in past days?

### HIS WORDS OVER YOU

"One day you will discover that knowing me brings the deepest contentment. When you focus on godliness, you will find it is all the wealth you need. Forget what is behind and press toward what is ahead."

*Based on 1 Timothy 6:6 and Philippians 3:13*

# 52. Just Say Yes

*Best Yes answers are much more likely to happen when we are
in the habit of seeking wisdom. We have to put our hearts and
our minds in places where wisdom gathers, not scatters.*

Lysa TerKeurst

I grew up in a home where there wasn't a lot of extra money. My parents
always paid their bills on time, but we didn't have an affluent lifestyle.
Before any purchase was made—even for what I would now call basic
necessities—choices were prayed about and strongly evaluated. But in
spite of our humble finances, my parents always said yes to helping people in need. As I grew up, their example of generosity made a profound
impression on me.

Two years after Jason's sentencing, Gene and I were becoming deeply
aware of the needs of many inmates and their families. God seemed to
speak to us through these Bible verses: "Speak up for the people who
have no voice, for the rights of all the down-and-outers. Speak out for
justice! Stand up for the poor and destitute!" (Proverbs 31:8–9 MSG).
We didn't have a lot of money to help prisoners and their families, but
we did have opportunities to talk about their needs in my conferences
and in interviews on radio and television. That's when we established
the nonprofit organization Speak Up for Hope.

I have long believed that God has blessed generous people who would
love to give to good causes—if they knew their funds were going to be
used for the intended purpose. Gene and I had previously sent books
to several inmates and occasionally we sent gift boxes to the wives and
moms of inmates, but we longed to empower Jason to help us determine
how best to bless inmates whose family no longer visited them or put
money into their accounts. That's when two generous families contacted
us, saying that God wanted them to give to prisoners. They considered
Speak Up for Hope a cause that mattered, and Jason their "man on the
inside" for distributing their gifts.

The Florida Department of Corrections had launched a program that
would allow families and friends of inmates to order up to a hundred
dollars' worth of food (including candy bars and hot chocolate mix) and
basic necessities (such as deodorant, socks, and T-shirts) to be delivered
directly to individual prisoners twice per year. Due to the kindness of
our donor families, Jason had the delight of surprising many men with
an unexpected package. One of the recipients was Rick, who wrote,

Thank you for the gift. Part of my testimony of how Jesus has transformed my life has to do with dog food. When I was growing up, we didn't have any food in our house a lot of the time, so I became acquainted with the taste of different brands of dog food. At various times I would go to neighbors' houses and partake of their dog's food. Some dogs would not like my choice, so I did not go back—I learned my lesson.

But one day at another house I was happily sharing some Purina with a toy poodle. The owner really loved this dog, because this food was good. All of a sudden the back door opened and an older lady stepped out with a startled look on her face. She said, "Young'un, what are you doing?"

Trying to swallow without choking, I managed to squeak out a soft response: "Eating." She asked me why, and I continued. "Because I'm hungry and your dog doesn't seem to mind."

Mrs. Hamilton asked me to come in, then gave me a glass of water and a toothbrush and led me to a sink to brush my teeth. After I finished scraping the dog food off my teeth, I was set down at a table filled with so much food it brought tears to my eyes. Mrs. Hamilton helped me to develop a desire to be kind, generous, and caring. Just like you. Thank you so very much for your surprising and unexpected gift of love that came in the form of a food package.

———

If you're like me, it feels easier to live in my own private world, to get involved in "prison matters" only when it is absolutely necessary. However, God keeps reminding me that as the family member of a "lifer," He has given me a front and center view of the needs behind bars. This ringside seat is one of the many unexpected surprises I've received because of my son's incarceration.

It's always easier to let somebody else do something—but that can no longer be my decision. As I seek wisdom from God, He reminds me that it is my privilege and responsibility to *do* something—by speaking out about needs, by managing the gifts of people who want to help, and by saying yes to blessing inmates with the love of God through something as basic as a food package. Jesus once told His followers that when we feed the hungry or visit the prisoners, it's as if we are feeding and visiting *Him*: "For I was hungry and you gave me something to eat" (Matthew 25:35).

God may one day direct *you* to do something. He may not ask you to create an organization—but there's so much need behind prison walls,

He can certainly show you some other way to make a difference. Be open to God's leading in your life. As you pray, trust Him to show how you can serve your loved one and other inmates too.

## HIS WORDS OVER YOU

"If you want to be a part of what I'm doing, make some sacrifices and follow my example. There are times it will be hard, but the result will be worth it. Those who put their hope in me will not be disappointed."

*Based on Matthew 16:24 and Isaiah 49:23*

# 53. A Day in the Life of an Inmate

*Every man can transform his world from one of monotony*
*and drabness to one of excitement and adventure.*
IRVING WALLACE

The television host had asked me to do a series of interviews that would spotlight the needs of inmates and their families and also discuss what different organizations and ministries were doing to help. "Let's definitely do a program on what a full day in prison is like for your son," she said. Before Jason was incarcerated, I would not have thought much about that topic.

Americans often define *freedom* as the opportunity to go where you want to go, choose what you want to do, and make decisions without being bound by the rules of someone more powerful. That sounds like the complete opposite of what my son experiences every day.

I thought I already had a pretty good idea of what happened behind the razor wire, but I asked Jason to write out the details of one day in his life. Here's how he responded:

5:00 a.m.: I wake up and listen to a news program on the radio—that is, if I can position my radio in a spot where I can receive a signal.

5:30 a.m.: My cell door opens and the lights come on.

6:00 a.m.: Inmates go to the chow hall for breakfast.

7:00 a.m.: All inmates go back to their cells and they're locked down for "count" and a shift change. (Inmates are counted by corrections officers several times a day. If the number doesn't come out right, they are counted again.)

8:00 a.m.: The cell doors open and some inmates go to their jobs on the compound while others exercise on the yard.

11:00 a.m.: The recreation yard closes and inmates go back to their dormitories.

11:30 a.m.: We are locked in our cells and another count takes place.

12:00 p.m.: Cells open and we go to the chow hall for lunch.

1:30 p.m.: The yard opens for recreation again. Some inmates take classes in the chapel or in the education building. Others go back to their jobs on the compound.

| | |
|---|---|
| 3:30 p.m.: | All inmates must return to their cells. |
| 4:00 p.m.: | We are locked in and another count takes place. |
| 4:30 p.m.: | Cells open and we go to the chow hall for dinner. |
| 5:30 p.m.: | The yard opens for recreation and sometimes chapel services are held. However, right now our new warden has shut down evening services due to security concerns. |
| 7:00 p.m.: | The yard closes. |
| 7:45 p.m.: | We are locked in our cells and another count takes place. |
| 8:15 p.m.: | The cell doors open and inmates can watch the television in the day room or stay in their cells. Often, fights break out when inmates disagree on which program to watch. |
| 10:00 p.m.: | We are locked in our cells and another count takes place. |
| 10:30 p.m.: | The cell doors open and we can watch television in the day room or stay in our rooms. |
| 11:00 p.m.: | We are locked in for the night. |

Reading this schedule, I was struck with one word—*monotony*! Most of us would have a hard time with the boredom and repetitiveness of this daily routine. My son's agenda is shockingly different from the variety represented in my day planner. He faces five mandated inmate counts every day—and no freedom of choice. The rules must be followed, and variation is not open for discussion. "It's prison, Mom," Jason reminds me. "It's just the way it is."

---

Just as I have, you've probably wondered how your loved one can find meaning in such a daily existence. But I've been surprised by the resourcefulness of inmates when it comes to using their skills to solve problems together—for educating, mentoring, and encouraging each other. Often, prisoners follow Jesus' Golden Rule in their problem-solving: "Here is a simple rule of thumb for behavior: Ask yourself what you want people to do for you; then grab the initiative and do it for *them*!" (Luke 6:31 MSG). I've watched prisoners share books so their inmate friends can take "mental vacations." Because Jason likes vigorous exercise, he helped to organize a marathon that took place within the perimeter of the prison fence.

But what can we on the outside do to help prisoners find meaning?

One of the best ways is to ask questions when you're visiting. Ask both prisoners and prison officials what is most needed on the compound. Sometimes athletic supplies, like volleyballs or Frisbees, are in short supply. Perhaps the chapel needs musical instruments for the worship bands. Maybe there are educational and recreational programs that you could suggest for the mental, physical, and spiritual well-being of the inmates. Try to team up with other inmate families or people in your community or church to donate equipment or set up programs the prison doesn't supply—anything that will improve the quality of life on the inside.

Call the chaplain or the assistant warden to learn the proper procedures for serving in this way. Inmates are surprised and grateful when we make their needs a priority—and you'll be surprised by the joy you'll experience in giving.

### HIS WORDS OVER YOU

"Whatever you do for someone who is overlooked or ignored, you do for me. Be generous with your lives. When you open up to people, you prompt them to open up to me."

*Based on Matthew 25:40 and Matthew 5:16*

# 54. Medical Emergency

*God may go to extreme measures to connect you to someone who is hurting. His divine connections are limitless and powerful. . . . Don't be surprised if His hope spreads in ways you never imagined.*

KATHE WUNNENBERG

When we became "family members of a prisoner," I found myself wondering what health care would be like for my son. I Googled many articles that described how the Department of Corrections took care of the physical needs of inmates. Many of those articles were not unlike this one, called "What's the Health Care System Like in Prison?" Author Christopher Beam says,

> It depends on the state. At best, it's about as good as a low-income health plan. At worst, it's almost nonexistent. In general, when a prisoner gets sick, he tells the on-duty guard. If it's not urgent . . . the guard will put his name on a list, and an appointment with the prison's in-house doctor may be set up for as soon as the next day. To handle emergencies, most prisons have a nurse on duty 24 hours a day. The majority of ailments are treated on-site, but inmates who are gravely ill can be taken to the nearest hospital. . . . At least that's the theory. In practice, many prison systems are so overcrowded that prisoners have to wait days to see a doctor, even in emergency situations. . . . In maximum-security prisons, an inmate may be taken to see the doctor in arm and leg chains, and left to wait in a cage.[27]

If you have worried over your loved one's health care in prison, you are not alone.

In January 2008, our phone rang. Gene answered, and soon whispered urgently to me, "Get on an extension! Jason's had emergency surgery."

Joining the conversation I asked, "What happened?"

"Ma'am, your son's appendix burst yesterday, and he had surgery at eleven o'clock last night," we were told. "He's fine, and he'll probably be back on the compound tomorrow."

Trying to sound calm, I said "Sir, my son had a ruptured appendix—

---

27. Slate. "Jailhouse Doc: What's the health care system like in prison?" by Christopher Beam, March 25, 2009. http://www.slate.com/articles/news_and_politics/explainer/2009/03/jailhouse_doc.html.

there are septic poisons throughout his body—and he is being discharged from the hospital *tomorrow*?" The caller told me the system doesn't keep inmates in the hospital very long these days. "Where is he?" I demanded. He mumbled something about that being confidential information, because Jason is a maximum-security inmate.

As we hung up, I was exploding with emotions. We knew our son had undergone major surgery, but we didn't know where he was. For the next five days, as we called to check on his status, we were told each time that Jason needed to stay another day. I knew he was alone and in a lot of pain, so I began to pray for someone to be like a mama to my boy.

After Jason was released and was finally well enough for a visit, he told us about his ordeal. He had two guards at his door at all times, but it was a nurse that he really remembered.

"One nurse stood out from the rest: Nurse Betty," Jason said. "A day after my surgery, I had severe back pain and had been taken out of my bed and placed in a chair for a change in position. A couple of hours later, Nurse Betty came in to get me back to bed. She reached around me in a 'hug' to help me stand, and although I let go after I was upright, she just kept holding me and told me to rest for a minute. For just that moment it was almost like having you giving me a big hug, Mom. I could feel tears in my eyes. I felt like God had sent an angel to my room at a time when I was hurting, needy, and lonely."[28]

———

I instantly knew God had answered my prayer. He had come through with the kindness of Nurse Betty, providing her to be "like a mama" to my boy in his hour of greatest need. When someone shows unexpected kindness to our incarcerated loved ones when they have physical needs, that surprise warms our hearts—and reminds us that God does indeed care about us.

When I was a child in church, I learned about a man named Job. He went through terrible hardships, but one Bible verse revealed that in the middle of his agony, somebody surprised him with kindness: "You gave me life and showed me kindness, and in your providence watched over my spirit" (Job 10:12).

Have you had a Nurse Betty experience? Not necessarily during a medical emergency, but anytime that someone surprised you with an

---

28. Adapted from Carol Kent, *Between a Rock and a Grace Place* (Grand Rapids: Zondervan, 2010), 49.

unexpected kindness, either inside or out of the prison setting? If so, take time this week to e-mail or write a note of thanks to that person.

## HIS WORDS OVER YOU

"You will discover me in your desperate places. I love you with an everlasting love and I draw you with unfailing kindness. I am full of compassion and gentleness. Be encouraged."

*Based on Jeremiah 31:3 and Isaiah 63:7*

# 55. The Job No One Wants

*God wants to surprise you; He wants you to be amazed at the*
*blessings He lays upon your life. When we begin to trust Him . . .*
*our outlooks and attitudes will change . . . as we begin to realize*
*our Heavenly Father enjoys surprising us with His goodness.*

DARRELL CRESWELL

All of us know there are two very different types of surprises. The bad kind includes the shock we experienced when we received the news of our loved one's arrest. The good kind of surprise is when we realize that unforeseen, positive opportunities are being birthed out of great chaos and heartache.

That was certainly the case for an inmate named Deric. I met him in the visitation area of the prison on a Sunday afternoon when I was visiting Jason. Deric was passing out games, coloring books, and crayons to inmates' family members. His smile could light up a room. I looked forward to seeing him during our regular visits with Jason.

Over time I learned that in the midst of his thirty-year sentence, Deric had become a Christian. Jason told us, "Deric and I work out and pray together. He lives out his faith and I am privileged to call him my friend."

One weekend he was noticeably absent. "Where's Deric today?" I asked my son.

"He was recently moved to a prison closer to where his family lives," Jason answered. "I'll miss him a lot, but I know he'll really appreciate seeing his family more often." I knew what a loss it would be for my son to lose his daily interaction with this friend who loved vigorous exercise as much as Jason did—someone who had become a close confidant and a spiritual encourager.

A few months later, a letter arrived from Deric:

Dear Mr. and Mrs. Kent,
 I hope and pray all is well with you and with Jason. You may know I was moved to a prison closer to the area where my mom lives. Being here will make it easier for my stepdad and mom to visit more often. . . . Zephyrhills is a medical prison facility and it's now my job to care for the dying, elderly, and disabled inmates who will more than likely finish their lives here. I bathe them, brush their teeth, change their diapers, and empty their catheter bags.

Nausea swept over me as I realized the sacrifice Deric made to move to a prison closer to his family. His letter continued.

Every day while I feed them and shave them I tell them about Jesus, or sometimes I just let them talk and get things off their minds. I've had the privilege of comforting several who were crying and freaking out. Recently, I read Scripture to an eighty-one-year-old inmate who had cancer. Five hours later he died. This is a sad, hard, dark place, but I know God wants me here and I want to be here.

I can tell God has changed me a lot in the two months since my transfer. I just want to be like Jesus. I want to do God's work and not be afraid to ruffle feathers or to take verbal abuse because of my obedience to God. . . . Tell Jason I miss him and hope to see him again—if not here on earth, then in heaven where we'll all meet up and hang out.

Your friend and brother in Christ,
Deric[29]

Many of us have discovered a harsh reality of prison: that an inmate can be moved to another facility without any advance knowledge—without even an opportunity to say good-bye to friends. For security reasons, these transfers usually take place in the middle of the night. And with few exceptions, inmates are not allowed to write letters to inmates in other prisons.

Even as I grieved the departure of Deric, an inmate that my son and I both enjoyed, I realized that God had surprised Deric with an unanticipated opportunity. He was now making a significant difference in the lives of dying inmates—comforting them, encouraging them, pointing them to an eternal hope. Deric was living out the truth of James 1:25: "Whoever looks intently into the perfect law that gives freedom, and continues in it—not forgetting what they have heard, but doing it— they will be blessed in what they do."

Take time to consider the surprises you've experienced during the incarceration of your family member. What positive opportunities or unforeseen blessings have you encountered? If you don't think you have, ask God for insight into His surprising ways. You might realize there have been good surprises after all!

---

29. Adapted from Carol Kent, *Unquenchable* (Grand Rapids: Zondervan, 2014), 155–56.

"When you are in a desperate place, I delight in surprising you with my purpose in your situation. You will be blessed if you wait for me. Allow my purpose to prevail."

*Based on Isaiah 30:18 and Proverbs 19:21*

# 56. Startled by an Inmate

*Most people want to be circled by safety, not by the unexpected. The unexpected can take you out. But the unexpected can also take you over and change your life. Put a heart in your body where a stone used to be.*

DENVER MOORE

I had long been told that it was impossible to be on the visitation list of an inmate and to volunteer as a guest speaker at that inmate's correctional institution. That was understandable. No doubt it was part of the security protocol.

However, an awards program was going to be held at the prison where my son is located and I was recommended and approved to be guest speaker. It was an unexpected opportunity, and I wondered: *What material do I have to share with inmates that could possibly apply to their lives?*

I decided the best thing to share was my own story—of how our family had been affected by our son's arrest, trial, conviction, and life sentence. Then a fearful thought quickly followed: *My son will be in the audience. What will it be like for him on the prison compound if my presentation embarrasses him?* Jason assured me of his full confidence in my comments, and that he could handle any repercussions from my talk.

On the day of the program, Gene and I went through the usual prison security procedures—going through the metal detector; listing what we were carrying—the one car key we're allowed to take in, jewelry, belts, watches, and a small amount of cash; undergoing the usual pat-down. Then we entered the visitation room where the meeting would take place. About one hundred chairs were set up in rows, and there was a lectern and a microphone at the front of the room.

Inmates were starting to arrive, and it was obvious that this was a program day. Instead of being limited only to our son, we were allowed to mingle with all the men in the room. We chatted about how they were doing and what was happening that day. A couple of the inmates had read my book *When I Lay My Isaac Down*, and let me know it had helped them.

The mood in the room was upbeat, encouraging, and definitely a change from a usual day at the prison for the men in attendance. One of the inmates provided technical help for me, plugging in my flash drive so everyone could see my PowerPoint slides.

As I was introduced and took my place behind the podium, I found myself overcome with emotion. Looking out at these men, I realized each one was somebody's son. No doubt their mothers and fathers had hopes and dreams for their children, just like I did for mine. The lump in my throat was getting bigger and I was fighting back tears.

I tried to use a bit of humor to warm up the crowd, and showed a few pictures of Jason in his growing-up years. The guys chuckled and I saw inmates seated near Jason poking him in the ribs in a friendly way.

Then I told about the call we received in the middle of the night, telling us of our son's arrest for murder. I described the horror we experienced as parents wrestling to believe the shocking news. Gene was seated nearby, and I asked him to come up and talk about a dad's tears.

You read earlier in this book about Gene's journaling, his record of his own tears. Gene began by describing his tears of joy when Jason was born. He told about the fun he'd had as Jason grew up—hiking with him in the provincial parks of Canada, reading the same books together, watching him become a high achiever in school and then receive an appointment to the U.S. Naval Academy. Gene spoke of more happy tears when Jason married a lovely woman who had two adorable daughters. But then Gene paused and spoke of another kind of tears when Jason was arrested. Fighting back his own sobs, Gene spoke of his sorrow and anguish over all that had happened. I could hear men quietly weeping.

I stood up and said, "I know, statistically speaking, only 6 percent of you had a father like Gene Kent. Most of you had an absentee dad and many of you had an abusive father." Suddenly, an inmate on the front row was overcome with emotion. He fell off his chair sobbing, looking toward Gene and shouting, "I need a Daddy like that!"

———

The inmate's loud, poignant exclamation surprised me. The longing in his voice was obvious, and I thought of a Bible verse I had read: "No, I will not abandon you as orphans," Jesus said. "I will come to you" (John 14:18 NLT).

Later, as I thought about that man who longed for a loving father, I realized that you and I have an opportunity—that as the family member of a prisoner, we can invest in the lives of more than just our own loved ones. Consider a tangible act of love and kindness you can do for an inmate who no longer has anyone in his or her life who cares.

God longs to surprise us with opportunities to enrich the lives of others and enhance our relationship with Him. When your life is hard, remember that God wants to renew your hope with opportunities to enrich the lives of others.

## HIS WORDS OVER YOU

"If you get to know me, you will understand how wide, how long, how high, and how deep my love is for you. I want you to experience the complete fullness of life and love that comes from me. Let me soften your heart with a love that never gives up, never loses faith, is always hopeful, and endures through every circumstance."

*Based on Ephesians 3:18–19 and 1 Corinthians 13:7*

# 57. Megan's Example

*Waiting on God requires the willingness to bear
uncertainty, to carry within oneself the unanswered
question, lifting the heart to God about it
whenever it intrudes upon one's thoughts.*

ELISABETH ELLIOT

Most of us have become experts at waiting, though we're usually better at describing the feeling than defining the word. *Waiting* actually means "the action of staying where one is or delaying action until a particular time or until something else happens."[30] The whole concept is filled with delay, discomfort, and a desire for resolution—the longing for an end to the reason we are in limbo.

When we have a loved one who is incarcerated, we experience all the types of waiting—waiting for the trial, waiting for the verdict, waiting for the sentence, waiting in the visitation lines, waiting for a better life. In this unwanted place, it may help to know that we are not the only ones who wait. Perhaps you know others who have experienced

- waiting for a clean bill of health
- waiting for a marriage proposal
- waiting for a better-paying job
- waiting to get pregnant
- waiting for a rebellious child to come home
- waiting for an apology
- waiting for a relationship to improve
- waiting for an answer to prayer
- waiting for a happier life

All of us can admit that, on our journey with an incarcerated loved one, there are good days and bad days. When I was having one of my lowest days, I cried out to God in prayer: "How long do we have to endure this sadness? Why don't you give us any reason for hope? Why do families of prisoners have to live in their own kind of prison? I am sick and tired of waiting on answers from you!"

That same day, this letter from twenty-nine-year-old Megan arrived in my mailbox:

---

30. Google. "Waiting." https://www.google.com/#q=What+does+waiting+mean%3F.

Dear Carol,

You don't know me, but I have been encouraged by reading your book *A New Kind of Normal*. I too am in my own prison. It isn't a "brick and mortar" building—it's my body. I was diagnosed with multiple sclerosis and have gone from living a physically active life to spending every day in a wheelchair. My immune system has attacked the protective sheath that covers my nerves. This damage disrupts communication between my brain and the rest of my body. I'm still "in here," but my nerves are deteriorating. I've had a couple of remissions, but this is currently an irreversible process. . . .

I want you to know that I pray for your family every day and I know what you are going through seems "irreversible." My prayer is that God will give you daily glimpses of hope as you wait on resolution, perhaps for the rest of your lives. I am enclosing a bookmark with one of my favorite Bible verses on it: "I waited patiently for the Lord; he turned to me and heard my cry" (Psalm 40:1).

---

When you and I get tired of waiting, we should follow the example of Megan—to be alert to people within our sphere of influence who need help more than we do. Yes, there is a funk that comes with the exasperation of waiting indefinitely. But the fastest way to get out of that funk is to take our eyes off our own impossible situation and help someone else.

That day, without saying it specifically, Megan reminded me that I still have a healthy body. I have the ability to write encouraging words in my books—even on days that I'm not living up to my own advice. Her example reminded me that I can (1) encourage someone else who is hurting; (2) pray for specific people who are going through challenging circumstances; and (3) get out of my self-imposed misery by focusing on others.

If you are sick and tired of waiting, follow Megan's example. Then think about this encouraging word from the Bible: "The Lord longs to be gracious to you, therefore he will rise up to show you compassion. For the Lord is a God of justice. Blessed are all who wait for him!" (Isaiah 30:18).

## HIS WORDS OVER YOU

"Be strong and let your heart take courage. Wait for me. If you turn to me, I will give you a blessed hope—the glorious appearing of your God and Savior, Jesus Christ."

*Based Psalm 27:14 and Titus 2:13*

# 58. Is Clemency Possible?

*Let perseverance be your engine and hope your fuel.*

H. JACKSON BROWN JR.

I was in the atrium of a hotel, walking to my room after a speaking engagement. "Wait!" I heard someone call out. "You forgot to tell us the end of the story!"

"Excuse me?" I said. "What do you mean?" The woman answered, "You didn't tell us about when your son got released from prison."

"That's because he's still in prison," I said, trying to be calm. "He has a sentence of life without the possibility of parole." This woman's persistent desire for a different response was unsettling.

I have come to understand that many people long for a happy outcome for those of us with incarcerated loved ones. Their intentions are good, but sometimes their communication is awkward. What they are really asking is this: "Is clemency possible?"

After Jason's trial and sentencing, we went through all the steps of appealing his case at both the state and the federal levels, but to no avail. It was a long and expensive process. All of us realized a life had been taken and that there is rightfully a heavy price to be paid. Though some would argue the only justice is for Jason to spend the remainder of his life in prison, we longed with hope that Jason would eventually walk in freedom.

One day an e-mail arrived from an influential governmental official in Florida. He had read my book *When I Lay My Isaac Down* and said in his note, "I feel strongly your son should make application for his case to be heard in front of the Florida Clemency Board in December." With a surge of hope, I thought, *Someone in a position of leadership in the state of Florida believes that Jason is not a threat to society—that he doesn't need to be locked up for the rest of his life.* At that moment I believed that God had not only heard my prayers but was in the process of providing the path to an eventual positive resolution.

I responded to this official, expressing some doubt that clemency could be an option. "Many people don't understand that clemency doesn't always mean instant release," he answered. "The clemency process can result in a commutation of a sentence, which means setting an end-of-sentence date. In your son's conviction of first-degree murder, you would definitely not be looking at instant release. The most you could hope for would be to receive an *eventual* end-of-sentence date."

With our hopes growing, Jason submitted an application for clemency and Gene and I began doing what we could to support the request. We contacted people who knew our son both before and after his conviction, asking if they would be willing to write in support of Jason. The response was overwhelming, and we sent their letters to the state capital while we waited.

After about four months, we received a call from the governor's office. A woman who identified herself as legal counsel to Governor Jeb Bush spoke politely, but firmly. "I have discussed your request with the governor," she said, "and Jason's case will not be fast-tracked—because he is not desperately ill and he has not been incarcerated for a prolonged period of time." My mind whirled as my heart sank.

"Your son's case will be in the system, and it will eventually rise to the top," she continued, "but of course that will be under another administration, because Governor Bush will be leaving office at the end of December." Then her voice softened. "Jason Kent has the best advocates any inmate could have. You have a wonderful family." And she hung up.

During this entire experience, I clung to a Bible verse: "LORD, I wait for you; you will answer, Lord my God" (Psalm 38:15). Perhaps He *had* answered, just very differently from what we had waited to hear. I felt sick. The disappointment was bitter and I wept uncontrollably.

---

You and I are in a tough position. In most cases we know our loved one is guilty, yet sentencing seems harsher for some inmates than for others who have committed similar crimes. Or we sometimes see the changed heart of our family members and, knowing they would not be a threat to society, we wish for a lesser sentence. Our waiting gets longer and longer, and often our hopes are dashed.

We persevere, though, when we wait with hope. I'm learning that sometimes my "hope" is for a specific thing like a shorter sentence. But desperation drives me deeper into a relationship with God—and He is my only real hope.

Think of the times in your life when it seemed that God did not answer your prayers. Take a moment to ask yourself: *Have I come to a place where I can see Him at work in other ways? Am I able to recognize His presence in my situation?* If you're not there yet, it's okay. But answering these questions honestly can help you begin to make sense of your current situation.

## HIS WORDS OVER YOU

"Put your trust in me. I will be your help and your shield while you wait. Lay your requests before me and wait expectantly."

*Based on Psalm 33:20 and Psalm 5:3*

# 59. Another Chance

*When in doubt, do nothing, but continue to wait on God. When action is needed, light will come.*

J. I. PACKER

One afternoon a call came from our attorney. "I have good news," he said. "Jason's clemency application finally came to the top of the pile and I've just received word that the Florida parole commission has recommended that his case be heard at the next clemency hearing."

I was shocked. After the previous administration had turned down the fast-tracking of Jason's case, this was a great surprise! To my knowledge, we had no advocate in the current administration.

Our attorney continued. "In order to get that hearing, Jason has to be granted a waiver by the clemency aides [attorneys and other professionals] who work for the four members of the clemency board: the governor, the chief financial officer, the attorney general, and the head of the department of agriculture. You will need to come to Tallahassee to present the case and request the waiver." My heart raced. We had been turned down so quickly by the previous administration.

On the scheduled day, we drove to the state capital. In the building where the hearing was to take place, we were handed a piece of paper explaining that we would have five minutes to present our case. Our anxiety mounted. *How could it be possible to present the facts of such a huge case in five minutes?* We were allowed to observe two cases before it was our turn.

My stomach twisted as Gene and I, along with our attorney, took our seats. We were at a desk, with all of the clemency aides sitting at a large desk situated at a higher level. They could look down on us from a higher vantage point. It was intimidating.

Our attorney made some opening comments and then said, "Carol, why don't you begin. Share what Jason was like in his growing-up years, along with your understanding of what happened, and why you believe he should be given an opportunity for his case to be heard at the next clemency hearing."

I could hear a tremor in my voice as I began to talk. The clemency aides leaned forward, listening carefully and asking appropriate questions. I began to sense the favor of God in that room, and I found courage to respond to the questions of this powerful group of officials. Then Gene was asked to speak, followed by more questions: *Are there inmates and family members of inmates who would write letters in support of your son's work in the prison as an educator, mentor, and positive example? Are there jail and prison volunteers who've gotten to know Jason who would write letters on his behalf?* We answered with a wholehearted "Yes!"

Panel members asked us to gather and submit these letters so that a decision could be made. One hour had passed since the hearing had begun. Our attorney told us that he had never seen that much time given to a case at a waiver hearing.

As we returned home, our hearts were singing. We believed we might be in the first stages of a positive result. But we still felt nagging doubts that anything good could happen.

———

In all of our waiting—before, during, and after the trial or plea bargaining of our loved ones—there are days when we feel like progress is being made. Doors open. Hopes rise. Connections with people in authority happen in unlikely ways and with better timing than we would expect. We think that, finally, things might be working out for the better.

But then we realize we're actually living in "the meantime"—that period between our loved one's arrest and what we hope will be a resolution that brings peace to the chaos in our lives. Proverbs 13:12 describes what this time feels like: "Hope deferred makes the heart sick, but a longing fulfilled is a tree of life." While we wait, we realize that everything about this process changes us—our mental outlook, our peace of mind, our spiritual health, and sometimes even our physical well-being.

A realistic view is vital. I'm learning that I won't always get the answers I want instantly. But that's why we pray, asking God for wisdom, direction, strength, and patience. He typically gives just enough light for the next step.

### HIS WORDS OVER YOU

"I will strengthen you with great endurance and patience. I am the light of the world. If you follow me, you will have the light. When anything is exposed to the light, it becomes visible. Wait with patience."

*Based on Colossians 1:11, John 8:12, and Ephesians 5:13*

# 60. The Decision

*There are some things which cannot be learned quickly, and time, which is all we have, must be paid heavily for their acquiring.*

Ernest Hemingway

During the eight weeks following Jason's hearing, we worked feverishly to contact key people and collect the letters requested by the panel. One inmate wrote, "I was nothing but a no-good addict before coming to prison, and Jason Kent led me to Jesus Christ." Clearly, Jason was making a major difference in the lives of many inmates.

Exhaustion was setting in as we assembled eight identical notebooks for the clemency aides. We also collected DVDs of television programs that had been aired on Jason's case. Carefully placing everything in a box, we prayed that God would use this information to reveal Jason's true character to those who would evaluate him—the people deciding whether or not he would receive a clemency hearing. Then we shipped the box to Tallahassee.

Three days later, our attorney called. We could tell from the sound of his voice that the news was not good. "I'm sorry to tell you," he said, "I've received a form letter from the attorney to the governor and it's stamped 'Denied.' Jason will not receive a clemency hearing. There was no additional explanation with the letter."

Sobbing, I fell into Gene's arms. We had poured every ounce of energy, passion, and commitment into contacting people to ask for their letters of support. It was obvious that there hadn't been time for eight people in four executive offices to read through the notebooks and meet to decide what to do. It would have taken at least a day for the shipment to reach the state capital and another day for the contents to be distributed to the various clemency aides—and the rejection call came on the third day.

We knew this was a rubber-stamp denial from the governor's office. Had it been a ridiculous farce that we'd even been asked to collect the letters? We felt like we had simply been appeased at the waiver hearing.

By law, Jason would have to wait five years to fill out another application for clemency. Then it would take another three to five years for his paperwork to rise to the top of the pile. It seemed like an unending wait. A hopeless process.

The following day was a scheduled visitation. We would tell Jason what had happened in person, since we are not allowed to call him at the prison. Along with a group of committed Christian inmates, Jason had been fasting and praying as we awaited this decision. We feared the news would be a bitter disappointment.

I was too upset to go to the prison the next morning. We decided that Gene would go in early, and I would arrive at noon. Tears cascaded down my cheeks as I walked through the heavy metal door where Jason was waiting. I sobbed into his shoulder. "I'm sorry, Son," I said. "So much work has been done and we've prayed so hard. My heart aches for you and your friends in the prison who have fasted and prayed so fervently."

But I saw the peace of Jesus on Jason's face. "Mom," he said quietly, "if we were given the waiver, we might have thought it was because we had the best attorney, or we might have thought it was because we had the favor of politicians." He paused. "The way this has happened," he continued, "we know the only way I'll ever walk in freedom again is when God says I've served enough time and I can help Him more on the outside than I can on the inside. And if that doesn't happen on this earth, we need to realize life is short, and we'll all walk in freedom in heaven very soon."[31]

———

That day my son consoled me, and I understood these verses in a more personal way: "And we boast in the hope of the glory of God. Not only so, but we also glory in our sufferings, because we know that suffering produces perseverance; perseverance, character; and character, hope" (Romans 5:2–4). Jason understood the power of perseverance—the kind of "waiting with hope" that is not defined by the immediate results I was praying for.

When we don't get the decisions we hope for, it's easy to feel disappointed or angry, or even forgotten. But though it's sometimes hard for me to admit, the difficult things I've experienced have brought me perseverance—the "waiting" has the benefit of developing my character and deepening my complete dependence on God.

What other benefits might waiting have, whether or not you are a person of faith? Have you experienced any of these benefits? Do you need to address any attitudes that are holding you back?

---

31. Adapted from Carol Kent, *Unquenchable* (Grand Rapids: Zondervan, 2014), 53–55.

## HIS WORDS OVER YOU

"My child, you are exhausted from crying for help and I know your throat is parched. Your eyes are swollen from weeping, waiting for my help. I will be your refuge and strength and your very present help in times of trouble."

*Based on Psalm 69:3 and Psalm 46:1*

# 61. Receiving Support

*Everyone needs that support—even if at first you don't*
*think you do. Look around. See who's on your side and*
*in your corner. You don't have to go it alone.*

Louis Zamperini

When Jason was arrested for murder, the thought of telling my parents broke my heart. I desperately needed their love and compassion, but it was hard to envision their grief at realizing that this young man they loved so much—their firstborn grandchild—had committed a heinous crime.

Instead of calling my parents ourselves, we asked some close relatives to deliver the news in person. We knew how shocking it would be, and we didn't want them to be alone. Little did we know how supportive they would be!

Mom and Dad lived far away from us, so we maintained contact through regular calls. They prayed with us over the phone, often sensing when we were hanging by a thread in our ability to survive the sorrow. Then, as Jason's conviction and sentencing took place, my parents reminded us that God was not surprised by what happened, nor was He incapable of meeting all of us—including Jason—in the midst of our gut-wrenching grief.

My mom and dad continued to show their support by traveling to Florida once or twice a year to visit Jason. As time went by, health problems and aging made it more difficult for them to make the trip. During one of their visits in their late eighties, I noticed how hard it was for them to say good-bye to Jason. We all knew it might be the last time they would see him.

As he exited the prison, my father was wiping tears. "I wish I could trade places with Jason," Dad said. "I'm old and he's young. I would love to give him a chance to return to his family and to live in freedom outside of this harsh environment." Then Dad paused, smiled, and spoke with hope in his voice: "But that young man isn't just surviving—he's *thriving.*" I knew Dad was referring to the spiritual growth in Jason's life and the way he was helping and encouraging other inmates.

Later that year, at age eighty-nine, Daddy went home to be with Jesus. During the next couple months, as my sister helped Mom clean out Dad's desk, she found a letter that Jason had written to his grandpa a few months earlier:

Dear Grandpa,

Last Sunday I had the most intense dream and I just had to share it with you. I was visiting with family in the visitation room at the prison and out of the back of the room you came walking out with a huge smile on your face and a gleam in your eyes. You gave me a hug and when I released, you continued to hug me even more tightly and smiled even more brightly.

I found that from your smile and from your hug came a contagious joy that filled me so much that I got a huge grin on my face—and then I woke up. It was so short, but oh, so special. I think it was a little window into the joy of the reunion that awaits all of us in eternity. I look forward to it with you.

I love you, Grandpa,

J. P. (Jason Paul)

That letter was a reminder to me that embracing the comfort and support of my parents was not only a major encouragement to us, but a huge help to Jason as well. Sometimes, because we don't want others to endure the pain we are experiencing, we push people away emotionally. But waiting *together* is the most important thing we can do.

———

Waiting alone is the hardest work there is. Why is it so hard for us to admit that we really *need* other people to help us carry this difficult load? For me, it boils down to pride. I've gotten used to taking care of things myself, to not wanting to be a burden to anyone else, to having a secret desire that nobody know how terribly needy I really am. I tend to quietly carry the weight of the world on my shoulders.

For many of us, family members and friends are willing to help if we would just allow them to come alongside us on this uncharted path of incarceration. As I realized how my father had encouraged my son and—through his letter—how my son had blessed his grandfather, I was reminded that the Bible tells us not to try to make it through life alone. First Thessalonians 5:11 says, "Therefore encourage one another and build each other up, just as in fact you are doing."

Do you know someone who will wait with you? Do you have a family member or friend who will help you carry the load? Reach out to that person today.

## HIS WORDS OVER YOU

"Wait for me and put your hope in my Word. The load is too heavy for you; you cannot carry it alone. My unfailing love will be your comfort. As a mother consoles her child, I will comfort you."

*Based on Psalm 130:5, Exodus 18:18, Psalm 119:76, and Isaiah 66:13*

# 62. In Need of a Miracle

*Don't give up before the miracle happens.*

FANNY FLAGG

When we faced the harsh reality of separation from our two step-granddaughters, Gene and I had a hard time emotionally. Our daughter-in-law had told us she was leaving the state with the girls and would no longer be in touch with us. We ached with sadness. There was deep grief for our son's loss of regular visits from his wife and stepdaughters. There was a different kind of sorrow over our own loss. We had been very close to Jason's wife and stepdaughters, now thirteen and ten, for over six and a half years. The prospect of not having them in our lives was unthinkable.

But, at the same time, we knew how desperately all three of them needed the freedom to go on with their lives. We knew the journey had been publicly embarrassing, financially devastating, emotionally debilitating . . . and painfully long. Families who have not experienced the incarceration of a loved one have no idea how awkward life is for the spouse and children of the inmate. Imagine the questions that are posed: *What does your daddy do? Is your husband in the military? When will he be coming home? Was that your husband I read about in the paper?*

During the next six years we had a postal address for our daughter-in-law, and we sent birthday and Christmas gifts, occasional money, and encouragement notes. The girls loved pretty things and I took special delight in wrapping presents in colorful paper and fun bows. But we did not have any communication in return. The gifts never came back, but we didn't know for sure that they had been received.

My prayer life intensified during this time. I prayed that my step-granddaughters would make good friends, do well in school, and grow in their faith. I also prayed for my daughter-in-law, knowing how difficult it must have been to function as a single parent.

In August 2011, I was in Dallas attending a conference with a friend. I told Kendra about sending gifts for several years without a response, and said, "The girls are now nineteen and sixteen years old. They are becoming adults. How long should we keep sending cards and packages? We don't want to be 'stalker grandparents' if they don't want us in their lives."

Kendra looked at me and said without hesitation, "Carol, don't *ever* stop. As long as those gifts are not returned, those girls will know how much you love them."

One month later, Gene and I were traveling after a speaking engagement in Ohio. On a layover at the Atlanta airport, we had lunch together and then separated—Gene was going on home to our place in Florida while I was planning to visit some friends for a couple days. A half hour after we'd parted, Gene called me—and he was breathless.

"Carol, I just got off the phone with our girl," he told me. "She said, 'Grampy, it's me. I'm nineteen years old and I'm a freshman at Middle Tennessee State University and I miss my family.'" Our step-granddaughter ultimately came to our home for Thanksgiving weekend and returned for a month following the first semester. That was followed by a ten-day visit during spring break.

In May of that year, our sixteen-year-old step-granddaughter graduated early from high school and asked if she could join her sister in Florida with us for the summer. They both attended MTSU the following year, but at the end of the school year they wanted to move in with us on a more permanent basis. As I write this, one is a university senior majoring in English and the other is in veterinary technician school. Both are thriving.[32]

———

Incarceration complicates the family dynamics of people we love. Gene and I longed for everything to be "fine" between Jason and his wife and her daughters. But the bottom line is that nothing is easy about this process. Sometimes, as parents, we gave opinions when they weren't requested or wanted—we were just so hopeful for a reconciliation and healing for the people we loved so much. You've probably had similar experiences.

Having our granddaughters return to our lives following a six-and-a-half-year absence was nothing short of a miracle. We didn't think it would happen, and we were close to giving up hope. If you're stuck waiting for something you long for, my best advice is to use that time to get to know God and delight in Him. Verbalize your belief that He is working on your behalf, even when you can't see the big picture. I took comfort in Psalm 37:4 (ESV): "Delight yourself in the LORD, and he will give you the desires of your heart."

32. Adapted from Carol Kent, *Unquenchable* (Grand Rapids: Zondervan, 2014), 119–20.

"I am the God who performs miracles, but be patient. Remember that my thoughts are not your thoughts and my ways are not your ways. I make the steps of those who delight in me firm."

*Based on Psalm 77:14, Isaiah 55:8, and Psalm 37:23*

# 63. The Reward for Patience

*A waiting person is a patient person. The word patience means the willingness to stay where we are and live the situation out to the full in the belief that something hidden there will manifest itself to us.*

HENRI NOUWEN

Waiting is difficult, but waiting with *patience* is even more challenging. I've received many letters from people who have family members behind bars and some of their comments are reminders of how hard this process is:

- Betty wrote: "My daughter's trial has been postponed five times and we are worn out with waiting for resolution."
- Jennifer said: "My husband was found innocent of fraud, but we have been waiting for almost nine months for his job to be reinstated. This is so unfair!"
- Jim wrote: "My son made some bad choices as a young adult and he got caught up in drug trafficking. His prison sentence will end in six months, but I'm still waiting for my wife to say whether or not she will allow our son to live at home during his probation."
- Angie said: "I used to go to church and I would call myself a person of faith. I prayed a long time for leniency as we went through my husband's trial, conviction, and sentencing, but the judge threw the book at him—and my husband was given the longest sentence allowable by law. This much waiting and praying with no apparent intervention from God makes me question my faith. We have four young children and we need my husband at home."

By definition, *patience* means "the ability to wait, or to continue doing something despite difficulties, or to suffer without complaining or becoming annoyed."[33] *That* is hard to do! I'm learning that patience isn't just about waiting for something to happen, it's far more about *how* we wait—the attitude we have while waiting.

Seeing our step-granddaughters come back into our lives was a reminder that patience is more important than we ever imagined. Since we never heard from them during their six-and-a-half-year absence, it took a staunch commitment to continue sending them notes of encouragement

---

33. Cambridge Dictionaries Online. "patience." http://dictionary.cambridge.org /dictionary/british/patience.

along with birthday and Christmas gifts. On the surface, it appeared that they had no interest in a relationship . . . or love for us.

Without reciprocal communication, it's hard to know what people are thinking. It wasn't until the girls returned to us as young adults that we knew how much our gifts meant to them. We found that they had greatly looked forward to our notes and packages, even though they weren't allowed to contact us. Eventually, our patience was rewarded and our prayers were answered beyond anything we could have anticipated when the girls—now young women—asked if they could live with us.

I knew we were experiencing the truth of Lamentations 3:25 (ESV): "The LORD is good to those who wait for him, to the soul who seeks him."

———

By controlling our emotions and proceeding calmly amid the challenges of our loved ones' incarceration, we demonstrate patience. The benefits are many. We have less stress and we're better decision-makers. We slowly (and more wisely) process what we're going through and learn to overcome obstacles. We're more relaxed, and demonstrate a calm demeanor and peaceful countenance to our family members. We think before we speak, rather than blurting out judgment, disappointment, anger, fear, and hurt.

Patience is not an absence of action. Rather, it allows us to wait for the right time to act, and to take action for the right reasons. Waiting with patience is harder than restless activity or yelling about injustices, but the reward is great.

For me, that reward is a heart at rest because I have released my anxiety to God. That's how the Bible character Micah dealt with his worries in a world that seemed strongly opposed to him: "But as for me, I will look to the LORD; I will wait for the God of my salvation; my God will hear me" (Micah 7:7 ESV).

When we demonstrate patience, waiting on God for His timing and wisdom, we will know what to do—at the right time and for the right reasons.

### HIS WORDS OVER YOU

"I long to show you my love and compassion. I am a faithful God and you will be blessed if you wait for my timing. Ask for my help and I will respond to the sound of your cries."

*Based on Isaiah 30:18–19*

# 64. This Is My Life

*Acceptance of one's life has nothing to do with resignation; it
does not mean running away from the struggle. On the contrary,
it means accepting it as it comes, with all the handicaps of
heredity, of suffering, of psychological complexes and injustices.*

PAUL TOURNIER

Susan had worked for me for over five years. In her midthirties, she was attractive, intelligent, creative, fun loving, and a gifted administrative assistant. Over time, we became good friends.

One day she told me, "I've been living my entire adult life with the thought that I'm getting ready to get married and my 'real' life will begin then. I've purchased secondhand furniture that doesn't quite match my décor and I've waited to make decisions about buying a more reliable car. Recently it hit me that I'm living as if everything about what I'm doing now is temporary, while I'm waiting for my dream of having my own family and decorating a home with my spouse to come true." She paused and then continued. "I just realized that I am in my thirties. I haven't been asked out on a date in over a year, and apart from a drastic change that I can't currently see, *this is my life!*"

As Susan accepted the fact that she might remain single and would likely never become a mother, I enjoyed watching the decisions she started to make. She had been saving money for her dream wedding, but I now saw her purchase a set of dinnerware she wanted. Next, she bought some much-needed new furniture, window coverings, and accent pieces that were perfectly suited to her taste. Then she began inviting friends over for meals in her redecorated apartment. Six months later she took her first cruise and enjoyed every minute of the trip.

"The best decision I made during the past year is to accept that the life I'm living right now *is* my life!" she told me one day. "It was way past time for me to quit fantasizing about a relationship with a husband who didn't exist, or to keep longing for a house with a white picket fence around it, with three young children filling my home with laughter. Making the decision to accept my current life situation with all of its flaws and opportunities has given me a new purpose and a whole lot more joy!" Susan began living out the truth of God's direction in Psalm 32:8 (NLT): "I will guide you along the best pathway for your life. I will advise you and watch over you."

Susan's comments are a great reminder to us about the decisions we all face. Will we live in limbo, or will we take action? The choice is ours. We can hide from the world, hoping no one finds out that we have a loved one in prison, simply waiting for an end-of-sentence date when we can try to forget that our family was ever in such a controversial, messy, complicated situation. The other option is to accept what's happened, and intentionally look for opportunities to make a difference—in our own loved one's life and in the lives of other inmates and their families.

Accepting what's happened doesn't mean we shrug our shoulders, sigh, and say, "Oh, well." It has everything to do with our attitude about not wasting our experience. It doesn't mean we have to like our situation, enjoy hanging out at jails and prisons, or condone the criminal actions of our family member. It simply means we embrace the chance we now have to do something positive in this once unimaginable situation. It is saying to ourselves and to everyone else—*this is my life!*

---

So what are these new opportunities? What should we do first? As Gene and I began our "new normal," we didn't immediately think we would use our son's crime as a springboard to helping other people make better choices or to improving the criminal justice system. Here is an outline of how we progressed—we hope it will be of help to you:

- Before you look for opportunities to help others, give yourself time to grieve. I identify with what David wrote in Psalm 31:9: "I am in distress; my eyes grow weak with sorrow, my soul and body with grief."
- Accept compassion in any form—physical gifts or emotional support—from the people around you who want to help.
- As the "crisis mode" gives way to the reality of the sentence, take notes on physical needs within the prison or on issues that need to be addressed.
- Brainstorm with your incarcerated loved one about how people on the "outside" can help inmates and their families.
- Pick one project and work on a creative solution for meeting needs. If possible, involve organizations, churches, or other families. Working together is always more enjoyable than working alone.

The following chapters will give you details of what others have done, and you will no doubt come up with many of your own proposals too. No one can do everything, but each of us can do something—even if you have only enough time and energy to advocate for your own family member. That's a great way to begin!

## HIS WORDS OVER YOU

"If you know me, you are the light of the world. You are like a lamp placed on a stand that gives light to everyone around you. Your good deeds shine out for all to see."

*Based on Matthew 5:14–16*

# 65. Please Call Me

*Act as if what you do makes a difference. It does.*
WILLIAM JAMES

The phone bill arrived and the amount due was staggering!

Our son had been incarcerated at the jail in Orange County, Florida, for a little over a month. Gene and I were in Michigan. We soon realized that with all the out-of-state taxes and fees that were added to the basic phone rate, Jason's fifteen-minute collect calls to us cost almost twenty-two dollars. We immediately thought, *How is that possible? Shouldn't that be called "gouging the families of inmates"? Who is making the money off these calls? Is there any way to get around these gigantic fees and still have telephone communication with our son?*

Gene and I sprang into action. To that point, we would never have called ourselves "advocates"—but when we have a family member behind bars, we soon discover that if *we* won't ask the questions and take the actions that lead to positive change, no one else will. The sad fact is that if unfairness doesn't affect their own family, most people just don't care.

We called the jail to ask why the phone costs were so high. The person who answered said, "Well, that's not really my area of expertise. I guess it's because it just costs a lot more to make out-of-state calls." That response sounded ridiculous—on the "outside," we could call anyone else long distance for a fraction of the cost. In fact, all over the country, fees for long distance calls were declining, to a level far less than they had been a couple of decades earlier.

The word "racket" came to mind, especially when no one was able to give us a good reason for the outrageous rates. We didn't know where else to go with our questions.

I continued to tell Jason to call us because we desperately needed to know he was okay, and he needed the support from our encouragement. Gene and I put up with these exorbitant fees for almost six years before we moved to Florida to be closer to our son. The rates for in-state calls were considerably less expensive.

Then in 2010, a thirty-six-year-old mother of two began advocating the reform of the prison phone system. Bethany was from Maryland, and her husband had begun a ten-year sentence for a drunk-driving-related death. Their household income had been cut in half because of his absence, so she downsized and relocated in order to communicate more regularly. "Just hearing his voice is critical for my kids, to know they *do* have a dad," she said. "He was a very involved father and wants to be involved now."

In August 2013, Bethany traveled to Washington, DC, to testify at a Federal Communications Commission hearing on the skyrocketing cost of interstate phone calls from prisons and jails. She said, "Choosing between essential needs and keeping kids connected to their parents is a choice no family should have to make." The FCC heard and responded, issuing an important ruling in favor of inmates and their families. Going forward, interstate phone rates would be capped—at about a fifth of what we had paid for our calls with Jason.[34]

———

Unaffordable phone calls put additional pressure on families that were already struggling with transportation costs to visit their loved ones. Many families were unable to come up with the money to purchase food and beverages out of the vending machines or the canteen window during visits . . . or even to feed their kids at home.

State prison systems and the telephone companies both profited from those exorbitant rates. The battle for reform went on for a decade before there was a decision that helped the incarcerated and their families.

What made a difference? It was the family members of inmates who stepped up to initiate change and then follow through, speaking up for those who were hurt the most. What Bethany and others did reminds me of a verse in the Bible: "Defend the weak and the fatherless; uphold the cause of the poor and the oppressed" (Psalm 82:3).

Has your family encountered injustices important enough to make you willing to speak out? What specific actions can you take to inform the authorities about what's happening? Are you willing to stand in the gap for your incarcerated loved one?

### HIS WORDS OVER YOU

"Dear ones, as much as you are able, encourage the disheartened, help the weak, and be patient with everyone. I have set this example for you and you will be blessed if you do these things."

*Based on 1 Thessalonians 5:14 and John 13:16–17*

---

34. Rolling Stone. "Prison Reform Advocates Speak Up for the Voiceless" by Andrea Jones, August 19, 2013. http://www.rollingstone.com/politics/news/prison-reform-advocates -speak-up-for-the-voiceless-20130819.

# 66. Can't Somebody Do Something?

*When you do nothing, you feel overwhelmed and powerless. But when you get involved, you feel the sense of hope and accomplishment that comes from knowing you are working to make things better.*

Pauline R. Kezer

Earlier in this book, you read how our son was attacked in the Orange County Jail by ten inmates who kicked him repeatedly in the head. As devastating as that beating was, all of his wounds eventually healed. However, we still had a problem: Jason's two front teeth had been broken off, and he was facing a trial for first-degree murder. One day I said to Gene, "Some jurors will take one look at him with those jagged front teeth and believe that he's a rough, mean guy who gets into a lot of fights." We determined we should do everything possible to get those teeth fixed.

Gene called the jail to ask about the process of getting a dental appointment for an inmate. The woman at the desk said, "Oh, I'm sorry, sir, but prisoners never get dental repairs at the jail. After their trial, once they get to prison, their teeth will be cleaned and checked once every other year."

Gene was insistent. "Our son was beaten up at the jail and urgently needs to get his two front teeth replaced before his trial," he said. "Please put me through to someone who can give my son permission to get a dental appointment."

"Maybe my boss can give you more information about this, but today is his day off," the woman answered. "You can call back another day."

Then Gene called our attorney, asking him if he could request a dental appointment. The response was discouraging: "Jason is a maximum-security inmate and I am sure there is no way they will allow him to be taken off the compound for a dental appointment. It just isn't done."

Next we called Jason's pediatric dentist back in Michigan. Dr. Baribeau's daughter had been in the same high school graduating class as Jason, and we had all remained friends. Gene explained that there was an urgent need to fix Jason's teeth before his trial, and asked Dr. Baribeau if he knew any dentists in the Orlando area, where Jason was incarcerated, who would be willing and able to help. Dr. Baribeau said he had a friend, a dental school classmate, in the area. He would make a call and get back to us.

In less than twenty-four hours, Dr. Baribeau called to say his friend had the expertise necessary to repair Jason's teeth and would be happy to take him on as a patient. This dentist just asked that the authorities at the jail would transport Jason to the dental office where the needed equipment was located.

We had now secured a dentist who practiced near the jail, but we still needed a prison official to give permission for Jason to make the trip. Gene called again and got through to a supervisor, but was told, "This kind of appointment is not allowed." For the next two weeks we prayed for an open door. Gene called during different shifts and always asked for the highest authority on duty. The answer was always no.

On the thirteenth day of this mission, Gene got through to a new officer. "My son is facing a first-degree murder charge," Gene told the man. "He was beaten by inmates in the jail and his two front teeth were broken off. If he were your son, how would you go about getting permission for a dental appointment so those teeth could be repaired?"

There was a sound of compassion in this man's voice. "I will secure that approval for you," he said. "Get the date for the appointment and I'll have his transportation arranged." That was it! Within a week, two guards transported Jason to the dental office.

Jason wore handcuffs, a waist chain, ankle cuffs, and a chain between his legs at the dentist's office, but he was there—and his teeth were fixed perfectly. We knew God had answered our prayer and we believed we were experiencing what the Bible says in Isaiah 42:16 (ESV): "I will guide them. I will turn the darkness before them into light, the rough places into level ground. These are the things I do, and I do not forsake them."

———

It was a new experience for us, stepping into the advocates' role. We became the principle promoters of a cause we believed in—getting our son's teeth repaired. You have perhaps already discovered that there are times when your own determination, as a family member of a prisoner, will accomplish more than the request of an attorney or the permission of a jail or prison official. We advocate for those we love until a bright light shines and we get results.

As you travel this uncertain road, be a "squeaky wheel" to make sure your loved one is receiving appropriate care. Rather than shouting about rights, be gracious and kind, follow proper protocol, have your facts summarized and in order, offer a solution to the problem, and thank the people who help you reach your goals. Always remember this great proverb: "A gentle answer turns away wrath, but a harsh word stirs up anger" (Proverbs 15:1).

## HIS WORDS OVER YOU

"You are tired of so much trouble. Always remember that you are blessed when you're at the end of your rope. With less of you, there is more of me. You're blessed when you feel you've lost what is most dear to you. That's when you'll feel the closeness of my embrace."

*Based on Matthew 11:28 and Matthew 5:3–4*

# 67. The Dress Code

*Remember there's no such thing as a small act of kindness.*
*Every act creates a ripple with no logical end.*
Scott Adams

It was laundry day. I pulled the dark clothes out of the dryer and moved them to my kitchen island for folding. Later, I moved the clean piles of clothing to our closet. It seemed odd that Gene's stack of black T-shirts was getting shorter. I was sure he had just purchased more of them.

When Gene returned home, I asked him about the missing T-shirts. He flashed me a mysterious smile. "You'll figure it out soon," he said. It was impossible to drag any more information out of him.

After five years of living in Florida, Gene and I were now in a rhythm—we were going to the prison for visitation almost every Saturday and Sunday when we were not away for speaking engagements. Visits are always a challenge. It often takes two tedious hours to get through security, and we've learned that the clothing guidelines change frequently. They can even vary from week to week, depending upon which corrections officer is interpreting the rules.

In the prison we visit, clothing guidelines include: (1) no white T-shirts or tops; (2) no camouflage, even on babies or young children; (3) no sleeveless tops; (4) no slacks or jeans with spandex—pants must be baggy. Frustration comes when the officers who check in visitors are inconsistent with what they allow.

One day as we were waiting in the prison's security line, a woman came out of the building entrance, sobbing. She was wearing a sleeveless blouse, and I overheard her saying to another visitor, "I'm so frustrated I could scream! I drove five and a half hours to visit my son and I've been up most of the night, but the prison rules have changed. I'm not allowed to wear this sleeveless blouse into the visitation area—and it's all I have. I've waited in this line for two hours, and the nearest Walmart is twenty minutes away!"

As I watched this woman, I didn't even notice that Gene had slipped out of the line and walked back to our car. Moments later I saw him approaching the woman with a black T-shirt in his hand. "Ma'am," he said, "I have an extra shirt with me. It's my gift to you today. Go to the front of the line and have a great visit with your son!" Thanking him profusely, she pulled on the shirt and headed back into the building.

Gene was grinning sheepishly as he returned to the line. I was chuckling as I hugged him and whispered, "How long have you been giving clothing to strangers?"

"Quite a while," he said quietly. "It's my T-shirt ministry."

I once shared the story of the disappearing T-shirts at a women's conference. A few weeks later we received a large box of black T-shirts from one of the attendees. She wrote:

> Dear Carol . . . I attended the event in Wisconsin. After hearing about your husband's T-shirt ministry, I wanted to help out. . . . I work for a sportswear company, so I am able to purchase T-shirts at a good price. . . . What an amazing story! Please use this gift toward your husband's T-shirt ministry through his trunk distribution program. . . . Who could have imagined the Lord would use your son's circumstances to help you reach out to women in all stages of their walk with God.[35]

—

All of us who wait in visitation lines meet people we might never have met under normal circumstances. I remember noticing how friendly other adults were, and how bored and restless the children were. I remember the heart-crushing sadness of seeing women, who thought they were going to visit their son or husband, turned away because of a minor clothing infraction.

Gene and I realized we couldn't personally help everybody, but we could help one person at a time. And the ripple effect was huge. I saw the joy this T-shirt project brought to my husband. The woman who heard our story and contributed shirts was happy to share kindness with people she didn't know and would probably never meet. Even the prison guards started asking Gene for T-shirts when visitors needed them.

The Bible says that one of the fruits of the Spirit is kindness (Galatians 5:22). When we surprise someone with an act of kindness, we experience joy.

## HIS WORDS OVER YOU

"I have loved you with an everlasting love; I have drawn you with unfailing kindness. When you help others, you reveal my character and love to them. The key is to treat others as you would have them treat you."

*Based on Jeremiah 31:3 and Luke 6:31*

---

35. Adapted from Carol Kent, *Between a Rock and a Grace Place* (Grand Rapids: Zondervan, 2010), 107–8.

# 68. Can You Help Me, Sir?

*I spent much of my prison time reading. . . . As long as I was
engrossed in a book, I was not in prison. Reading was my escape.*

FRAZIER GLENN MILLER

In the prison visitation area, Gene approached the food window and
noticed an inmate straining to read the list of sandwiches, snacks, and
drinks for sale. The man gave Gene a side look, peered again at the sign,
and asked, "Can you help me, sir?"

Gene instinctively realized that the inmate couldn't read, and
quickly explained the choices to him. Later, when we researched prison
statistics, we discovered that *half* of all inmates in the state of Florida
are illiterate—a shockingly high percentage.

We have been involved with the prison system long enough to know
that educational opportunities vary from institution to institution and
state to state. Most prisons offer programs for inmates who want to get
their high school equivalency diploma. But it is very embarrassing for a
prisoner to admit to fellow inmates that he can't read.

A month after Gene's experience with that inmate, we were in Illinois dining with a newly retired couple. Frank had been a high school
English teacher and he spoke openly of how difficult it was for him
to leave a profession that had brought him so much satisfaction and
enjoyment. It had been a mandatory retirement, and he missed his students. Gene asked, "Have you ever thought of volunteering to teach at
the men's prison in your area?" Frank looked startled by the thought.
"I can honestly say that thought has never crossed my mind," he said.

We discussed Jason's situation, and how much he enjoyed reading to
pass the time in prison. Then Gene shared the story of the man at the
canteen window. When Frank heard the man's request, "Can you help
me, sir?" he was visibly moved. "I think I'll check on the possibility of
teaching reading and writing skills at a prison," he said. "I know there
are a lot of hoops to jump through to get the proper security clearances,
but I can see the effort would be well worth the investment of time—
and right now I have plenty of time." The evening ended and we said
our good-byes.

Three years later, we had another event scheduled in this same area.
Frank and Barb contacted us to ask if we would once again share a meal
with them. We set a time and a place to meet.

As Frank walked into the restaurant, he looked relaxed and happy.

Barb told us, "You may never know how much our time together three years ago has impacted our lives."

Frank said, "I contacted the program director at an area prison and said I was very interested in teaching reading and writing skills to inmates at the prison. It took a few months for me to follow all the guidelines necessary to get my educational proposal accepted, but I currently have fifteen students. Barb comes in with me and helps with tutoring."

Then he pulled a folded piece of paper out of his jacket. "I thought you might appreciate this letter," he said, and read out loud,

> Thank you for coming to the prison and for teaching me to read and write. Nobody ever cared about me like you have. Because you taught me these skills, I write letters to my son and daughter every week and they have started writing back to me. You changed my whole life for the better. I love you, man!

Gene and I were both wiping away tears as Frank and Barb spoke of their fulfillment as they invest in educating inmates. Instead of being bored in retirement, they are using their time in more productive ways than they ever imagined. I am convinced that most people would do something to help inmates if they just had an idea of *what* to do.

How can we help people on the outside to bless those inside? Earlier in this book I wrote about the importance of vulnerability as we talk with others. Neither you nor I have the life we wanted—living through the incarceration of a loved one was never on our goal chart. However, it *is* the life we are living now, so when we speak openly with others about our challenges and opportunities, we encourage them to consider using their resources, education, and special skills for the benefit of inmates.

Hebrews 10:24 tells us to "consider how we may spur one another on toward love and good deeds." Would you consider praying about this verse today? You and your loved one are in the middle of a long, painful waiting period. But you might use this time to "spur others" to make a difference in a jail or prison. When we do that, everybody wins.

### HIS WORDS OVER YOU

"As you look at the needs, be alert. Whatever your hand finds to do, do it with all your might. I can do far more than you could ever imagine or guess or request. I don't do this in a pushy way, but by working deeply and gently within you."

*Based on Ecclesiastes 9:10 and Ephesians 3:20*

# 69. Read Me a Story

*After listening to a recording of her incarcerated mother
reading her a story, nine-year-old Monica said: "It makes
me smile and it makes me cry. I miss my mommy!"*

JEFFREY ZASLOW

Gene and I kept asking each other what we could do to help inmate families build a better bond and stay together. Each week, standing in line next to children wanting to visit an incarcerated parent, we saw how desperate the needs were. We checked online and found the following statistics:

- 2.7 million children in the United States have an incarcerated parent (that's one in every 28 kids).
- One in five of these children have depression, anxiety, or withdrawal.
- One in three of these children have aggression, attention problems, or disruptive behavior.
- Many children believe they are at fault for their parent's incarceration.
- Children of the incarcerated are often teased, rejected, or taunted at school.[36]

Our hearts ached for these children, some of whom we were meeting on a regular basis.

We had heard some success stories of a few organizations that were videotaping an inmate reading to his or her child, and then sending the book and the recording to the child. We prayed carefully over the opportunity and its challenges—especially of the need to raise funds to launch the program—and then made "Read Me a Story" our next focus.

Over the next few months, a couple of generous donors covered the cost of the equipment we needed. Then individuals and organizations purchased books that would be appropriate for inmates to read to their children. And then we hit a wall of resistance. I tried to contact wardens, assistant wardens, chaplains, or program directors in three different prisons in central Florida. Day after day my e-mails got no response and my calls were not returned.

Finally, I got through to the chaplain at the largest women's prison

---

36. Prison Fellowship. "FAQs about Children of Prisoners." http://www.prisonfellowship
.org/resources/training-resources/family/ministry-basics/faqs-about-children-of-prisoners/.

in central Florida. Immediately, I knew I had connected with a prison employee who saw his job as not only employment but as his opportunity to bring life, hope, faith, and encouragement to the inmates in his facility. "We are so grateful for this program," he said. "Our only problem is that there isn't an incarcerated mom on this compound who wouldn't *love* to read a story to her child. It will be hard to decide which ones get this opportunity."

Arrangements were made and on the appointed day the chaplain met us in the parking lot and quickly led us through the security process. Then the designated inmates started arriving. Once everyone was in the room, we offered a welcome, introduction, and prayer. We had placed books on a table and asked the moms to select one that would best suit their child. Women who wanted to practice reading their book before taping could do so with a volunteer. Then the taping began.

One by one the inmates sat in front of the camera. We had cue cards with some important reminders: (1) greet your child and tell them how much you miss them; (2) share a special memory you made with your child; (3) tell your child you picked this book just for them; (4) show the cover and read the book to your child; (5) if you'd like, say a prayer over your child, or sing them a favorite song; (6) thank the caregiver of your child; (7) give them a virtual hug and send kisses as you say good-bye.

A woman I'll call Janice was our first volunteer. Her face radiated love as she greeted her child and read her story. Tears filled many eyes, as we all realized that Janice was physically separated from her daughter— and this caused her great pain. I was reminded of a Bible character named Job who went through severe losses, including the deaths of his children. At one point he said, "Where then is my hope? Can anyone find it?" (Job 17:15 NLT). After the taping, we knew we had helped these inmates to find hope.

---

When you and I first discover a new way to help the families of inmates, we are very motivated and excited. We see the need. We think we can help to meet the need. And then we face challenges. In our case, we had to raise the necessary funds. Then it was hard to reach the prison official who could approve our program and volunteers.

If we're going to make a difference, we need to form a plan of action: (1) decide on a specific way you can help; (2) make a list of the supplies needed; (3) find volunteers and donors; (4) pray for the success of your project (of course, this advice goes with every step of the action plan!);

(5) implement the plan—and don't be discouraged if you face a few interruptions on your way to the finish line.

We believe this door opened because of prayer. The results reminded us of the truth of Proverbs 16:3 (NLT): "Commit your actions to the LORD, and your plans will succeed."

## HIS WORDS OVER YOU

"I love to give you the desire of your heart and help you accomplish your plans. I understand what opposition feels like. Don't grow weary and lose your focus."

*Based on Psalm 20:4 and Hebrews 12:3*

# 70. Inmate Involvement

*Our character is determined not by our circumstances
but by our reaction to those circumstances.*

CHARLES COLSON

I was near the end of the long line of people waiting to exit the prison's visitation room. Next to me stood one of Jason's best friends, a classmate from the United States Naval Academy. I'll call him David. We had enjoyed a great visit. It had been a delight for me to listen to their banter about the military schools they had attended. Now I sensed it was hard for David to leave.

He was tenderhearted as he watched Jason and me say our final good-byes with "I love you" in sign language. There were tears in my eyes as I watched my son line up on the other side of the room. I knew Jason would soon have to remove all his clothing for a mandatory security inspection before returning to his cell.

Jason smiled and waved and then turned to go back through security on his side of the room. David was choking up. "How do you do this every week?" he asked. "I can't bear to see him going back through those doors, knowing he will never walk in freedom for the rest of his life."

"It's the hardest thing I do, but I know it's even harder for him," I answered. Then I thanked David for his loyal friendship to Jason. At great expense, he flew in from out of state for these visits—and he had done so on numerous occasions since Jason's arrest. "When you visit," I told David, "you give Jason a mental break."

I continued. "It also helps me to see the purposeful way Jason uses his training and even his survival instincts to help other inmates. Almost every time we visit him, and sometimes when we talk on the phone, he mentions plans he has to do something proactive on the compound.

"I know he has discouraging days too," I told David. "But overall, I think he's been able to take on new opportunities because he's determined to maintain a positive attitude and become productive in this harsh environment."

After saying good-bye to David, I thought about two very important things we can do as the family members of inmates. We can encourage our loved ones to receive positive input from other visitors, and we can encourage them to do meaningful work behind prison walls. Because Jason has faith in God, I know he sees his unpaid work as a service to his heavenly Father. He has been living out the challenge in Colossians

3:23 (NLT): "Work willingly at whatever you do, as though you were working for the Lord rather than for people."

———

Not every prisoner will want to pursue wholesome opportunities behind the razor wire. Some inmates are too depressed to get involved. Others are sleeping as much as possible, hoping the time will go faster that way. But as family members, we can support our loved ones by gently and persistently urging them to find meaningful friendship and activity throughout their sentences. Here are some ideas:

- Help to arrange meetings between your inmate and friends or relatives who aren't currently visiting. Often, people would visit if they just understood the system, and you can help make connections between the classification officer and new visitors.
- Encourage your loved one to join prison sports teams.
- Introduce yourself to the chaplain and find out what classes and programs are available at the prison. Talk about these options with your inmate.
- If your loved one has special skills or educational qualifications, find out if he or she can use this expertise to facilitate classes for other inmates at the prison. Obviously, an inmate needs self-motivation to follow through with this, but you can gather information and make appropriate suggestions.
- As much as is possible, send books to your inmate to give him or her an opportunity to escape the monotony through reading.
- If you are a person of faith, ask for God's direction and wisdom as you look for ways to bring meaning and productivity into your inmate's life. Ecclesiastes 4:12 describes a "triangle of faith" involving you, your loved one, and God: "Though one may be overpowered, two can defend themselves. And a cord of three strands is not quickly broken."

Sometimes just a little effort will help our inmates discover new opportunities that bring meaning and fulfillment to their lives.

### HIS WORDS OVER YOU

"I work all things for good for those who love me. I long to say to you, 'Well done! You have been a good worker! Since you have been faithful with a few things, I will put you in charge of many things.'"

*Based on Romans 8:28 and Matthew 25:21*

# 71. Acknowledge the Truth

*It takes strength and courage to admit the truth.*

RICK RIORDAN

When my son was arrested, one of the toughest things to deal with was the fact that he had pulled the trigger. A man was dead. My son had committed a murder.

Following the initial, paralyzing grief, I found myself wanting to explain that there were reasons that Jason had committed such a horrible crime. I had a whole list to share.

Never was I more aware of this instinct to protect my son's reputation than when I was called for jury duty. Ten years had passed since I sat through my son's weeklong trial, but my emotions went out of control when I read:

> By order of the Circuit and County Court of Polk County, Florida, you are hereby summoned to appear for jury service. Any person who is summoned to attend as a juror in any court and who fails to attend without any sufficient excuse shall pay a fine. . . . Report to the Jury Assembly Room . . . on 2/20/12 at 8:05 a.m.

I immediately searched the document to find out how I could decline. Surely the court would not expect me to serve on a jury deciding someone's guilt or innocence after I'd lived through my son's murder trial! But none of the reasons for excusal applied to me.

On the assigned date, I drove to the courthouse where I was given a group number. At eleven o'clock, my group was taken up an elevator to the top floor of the courthouse. Our guide said, "This is the floor where the really bad cases get tried."

Panic and nausea swept over me. In the courtroom, the judge greeted us and introduced us to the attorneys for a pending trial. They began asking questions. One of them looked at me and said, "I see, on the form you filled out, that you and your family have had an experience in the courtroom. Do you think that would in any way influence your ability to evaluate a case fairly?"

I flushed and burst into a lengthy, unneeded explanation that described how my son was a U.S. Naval Academy graduate who had married a previously-married woman with two children and killed their father because he believed he was protecting the girls from potential abuse. (Yes, it was one long, disjointed, run-on sentence.) Instead of stating a simple yes or no, I was a fire hose of unnecessary information. I finally ended by saying, "That experience would definitely influence how I process information during a trial." From that moment on, I felt like I had a sign on my forehead that said, "Mother of a Murderer." The day was emotionally exhausting and publicly humiliating.

In the end, I didn't have to serve anyway. Our group was dismissed because the case we were assigned to was resolved with a plea bargain.

———

All the way home, I rehearsed my ridiculous, unexpected response. Why was I trying to justify my son's horrific crime—even in front of total strangers? Wasn't I responsible enough to admit that what he did was wrong, no matter what "extenuating circumstances" I might want to suggest? I wasn't living out a Bible verse I had memorized as a child: "An honest witness tells the truth" (Proverbs 12:17). I had thought I was an honest person, but when it came to being completely candid about the worst parts of what had happened, I was defensive rather than forthright.

Not only does the person who committed a crime need to accept responsibility, but we as family members of the prisoner need to acknowledge and articulate that what was done was wrong. A crime has been committed—we need to admit that to ourselves and to others.

Obviously, when a court case is pending, we need to speak carefully, taking the wise counsel of our attorney on when it's appropriate to say certain things. But eventually there comes a time for acknowledging the truth. That doesn't mean *we* are responsible for the crime; it does mean that we own the fact that our loved one is guilty.

Some family members of inmates are sick and tired of the repeated criminal behavior of their loved one. Others know that what happened was a onetime aberration that does not represent the true character of their relative. Either way, we need to acknowledge the ugliness of what happened.

Perhaps like me, you have come to recognize that your loved one's crime hurt the victim and caused great pain to the victim's family—and that there is absolutely no justification for what has been done. I still struggle with this, but I'm working on being more transparent and straightforward. I believe the words Jesus spoke of himself in John 8:32 can also apply to the way we approach our loved ones' crimes: "You will know the truth, and the truth will set you free."

"I will teach you to speak truth and to share honest reports. Move forward with confidence and victory as you stand for the causes of justice, humility, and honesty."

*Based on Proverbs 22:21 and Psalm 45:4*

# 72. Wait for Words of Remorse

*Remorse [is] the pain of sin.*

THEODORE PARKER

How does an inmate move forward with life, knowing his or her crime produced pain, loss, hurt, destruction, chaos, and irreparable damage to a victim and the victim's loved ones?

It can be difficult. Every crime is life altering, to some extent, both for victims and their families as well as the offenders and their loved ones. Everyone involved has been thrust into an unexpected, life-changing situation.

I wept as I read a letter from my son, acknowledging that he understood the horrific impact of his actions on his victim, his victim's family, and his own family.

Dear Mom and Dad,

. . . After my arrest I felt numb, almost like I was in a dream. I was left in an interrogation cell for several hours and then transported to the county jail where I was fingerprinted and stripped. My head was shaved, and I was confined. . . .

As I slowly reconnected with reality, the immensity of it all—including the harm I had inadvertently done to those I had sought to protect—began to sink in. I was completely empty, exhausted, depressed, and felt like a failure as a man, as a husband, as a father, as a son, and as a Christian. I considered the massive shame for you, Mom and Dad, as I destroyed our family name, and I envisioned the horror that you, along with my wife and stepdaughters, would experience as you were dragged with me through the trial. . . . And I certainly had not considered the huge loss and sorrow of my victim's family. . . . I can only imagine the pain I have caused the father of the man I killed. I have stolen from him his relationship with his son.

Only in retrospect can I recognize how arrogant, self-righteous, and self-reliant I became in the weeks leading up to the murder as my fears and worries consumed me. My lack of trust in God to intervene on behalf of my family left me feeling like I was the only one who could rescue them. . . . I relied on my efforts, my skills, my weakened and worry-filled mind to get me and my family through. . . . I had experienced a crisis of faith, and I did not behave as a strong Christian man in the face of it. Instead, my actions reaped death, devastation, grief, and destruction of everything my life previously represented.[37]

———

I've come to realize that those arrested often don't process the full impact of their crimes until some time has passed. When the arrest occurs, our family members may be in shock over what they did. Then there are court proceedings and meetings with attorneys. Very soon, survival instincts are tested among fellow inmates at the jail. There is a surreal, "this isn't really happening" feel to the entire process.

Then time does its work and reality sets in. The passion, fear, anger, vindictiveness, and myriad other emotional and psychological factors become less intense—and our loved ones understand the devastation their unlawful action produced.

Your incarcerated loved one may not yet be able to say, "I was wrong." You may wait a long time to hear those words of remorse, which can be so important for *you* to make a new beginning and move into a productive life. But don't give up on your inmate.

Patience—your ability to wait to hear your family member's remorse—is an important tool for survival. Be prepared: sometimes it takes a while before our loved ones reach the emotional and spiritual point where they can say, "God, make a fresh start in me, shape a Genesis week from the chaos of my life. Don't throw me out with the trash, or fail to breathe holiness in me. Bring me back from gray exile, put a fresh wind in my sails!" (Psalm 51:10–12 MSG).

## HIS WORDS OVER YOU

"Continue waiting with hope. I will guide you and satisfy your needs in a hard place. My strong arm will strengthen you and I will meet your needs. You can count on me to be your helper."

*Based on Psalm 33:20 and Psalm 89:21*

---

37. Adapted from Carol Kent, *Between a Rock and a Grace Place* (Grand Rapids: Zondervan, 2010), 28–29.

# 73. Understand the Slow Process
# of Forgiveness

*Unforgiveness denies the victim the possibility of parole and leaves them stuck in the prison of what was, incarcerating them in their trauma and relinquishing the chance to escape beyond the pain.*

T. D. JAKES

One weekend I was speaking in an Atlanta suburb, and shared the story of our journey with our son. The following week an e-mail arrived from a woman named Tammy. She said:

> Carol, I needed to hear your message. . . . On December 9, 1995, my mom was shot and killed by a young man named Matthew Ben Rodriguez during the robbery of a pharmacy in St. Petersburg, Florida. . . . I looked your son up on the Internet and discovered that Matthew is serving his life sentence in the same prison where Jason is incarcerated.

Several communications passed between Tammy and me. Her mother's death was a devastating loss to her, to her sister, and to her brother, who was still in high school at the time. "For the past several years I have been praying that someone would share the gospel with Matthew," Tammy said. "Do you think that Jason would try to meet Matt and share his faith with him?"

I am not allowed to initiate calls to my son, so I immediately printed Tammy's letter and mailed it to him. A few days later, while at prison visitation, I asked, "Jason, do you know Matt Rodriguez?"

He smiled. "Mom, he's one of my best friends," Jason said. "We don't live in the same quad, but he's in my biblical counseling class and he's a dynamic Christian. After our class I said, 'Matt, is your middle name Ben?' He told me it was and I said, 'Then I have a letter for you.'"

Jason went on to describe what happened next. As Matt read this note from the daughter of the woman he had murdered in a botched robbery more than thirteen years earlier, he wept.

Then my son said, "Mom, you're going to meet Matt today. His sister is coming to see him, and he'll be here in the visitation room."

A half hour later, Matthew came out and greeted his sister, then walked over to our table. He knelt and had tears streaming down his cheeks. "Mrs. Kent," he said, "thank you for sending Tammy's letter. I had already written a five-page letter asking Tammy and her family for their forgiveness for taking the life of their precious mother. It was an accident. The gun misfired—but I was holding the weapon and I alone am responsible for her death. I've had no address to send the letter to. Will you ask Tammy if she's willing to receive my letter?"

I said, "I certainly will, Matt." As soon as I got home, I e-mailed Tammy, asking if she was willing to let Matt send her his letter. She sent this note in response:

> Dear Carol . . . I am thrilled beyond words to hear that Jason and Matt know each other. It has been my prayer for years that Matt would find peace. If Matt would like to send me a letter, that is fine. I am a little nervous just because of the situation, but I think this is a "God thing." . . . Thank you for letting me know that Matt is a Christian and is growing in his relationship with God. . . . I know God is at work even now, and though I am anxious, I know He is working all of this out for His glory. I pray that this will be an opportunity to grow and heal just a little more.[38]

Tammy's response demonstrates what author Johann Christoph Arnold writes: "Forgiveness is power. It frees us from every constraint of the past, and helps us overcome every obstacle. It can heal both the forgiver and the forgiven. In fact, it could change the world if we allowed it to."[39]

———

Forgiveness—both the giving and the receiving—is one of the most difficult and complicated issues we face as the family members of the incarcerated. We long to have our loved one request forgiveness . . . and our hope and prayer is that the victim or victim's family members, like Tammy, will see the sincerity of our inmate's heart and verbalize forgiveness. Of course, forgiveness does not negate the wrong done or take away the devastation and pain of the losses involved in a crime. It does, however, set the offended person free from bitterness and resentment and bring a greater peace to the prisoner.

There is important instruction in Matthew 5:23–24 (MSG): "This is how I want you to conduct yourself in these matters. If you enter your place of worship and, about to make an offering, you suddenly

38. Adapted from Carol Kent, *Between a Rock and a Grace Place* (Grand Rapids: Zondervan, 2010), 164–66.

39. Johann Christoph Arnold, *Why Forgive?* (Farmington, PA: Plough Publishing House, 2000), 158.

remember a grudge a friend has against you, abandon your offering, leave immediately, go to this friend and make things right. Then and only then, come back and work things out with God." These Bible verses remind me that if we hold unforgiveness in our heart, it will interfere with our relationship with God.

Forgiveness doesn't mean that a sentence will be lessened or that the victim (or the victim's family) will necessarily become friends with the criminal. But forgiveness is always a worthy goal. As family members, we should do everything we can to help our loved ones pursue forgiveness with their victims.

### HIS WORDS OVER YOU

"I am a compassionate and gracious God, slow to anger, abounding in love and faithfulness. I am the God of redemption and forgiveness. I will meet you more than halfway."

*Based on Psalm 86:15, Colossians 1:14, and Psalm 34:4*

# 74. Experience Forgiveness

*Forgiving does not erase the bitter past. A healed memory
is not a deleted memory. Instead, forgiving what we
cannot forget creates a new way to remember. We change
the memory of our past into a hope for our future.*

LEWIS B. SMEDES

Over the past few years many people have written to me asking for help
on the topic of forgiving their incarcerated loved one. Here are some of
their questions:

- Our daughter was recently arrested and is very remorseful for the
  pain she caused another individual due to a robbery. We've always
  taken care of her financial needs and I'm struggling to understand
  why she committed this crime. It's difficult to forgive her.
- My husband has destroyed the happiness we once enjoyed as a
  family—by committing a white-collar crime, that means he will
  be incarcerated throughout the rest of the growing-up years of
  our children. He has never asked for forgiveness from me or from
  our children. Should I point this omission out to him?
- My son was found guilty of molesting a young boy when he was
  a counselor at a summer camp. The innocence of that child can
  never be restored and the parents are angry. I'm angry with my
  son too! We raised him to know right from wrong.
- Even though I put money in the account of my daughter and visit
  her regularly, I am filled with anger when I realized she has never
  asked her father or me for forgiveness for what she did to *our* lives
  when she committed her crime. Should we bring this issue up?
- Am I crazy? Sometimes I think I need to ask my incarcerated husband to forgive me for having such a long-term negative, unfor-
  giving attitude toward him for messing up my life. I love him,
  but I can't seem to forgive him.

Are there any absolute answers to those difficult questions? The
Lord's Prayer includes these words: "And forgive us our sins, as we have
forgiven those who sin against us" (Matthew 6:12 NLT). But what does
that look like when we want to forgive our loved ones for what they did
while simultaneously wanting them to know how much they've hurt the
victim, the victim's family, and our own family?

Surviving the incarceration of a loved one definitely involves learning how to forgive those family members who have caused us great emotional pain by their unlawful behavior. An important principle I've learned is that forgiveness isn't usually a moment in time—it often takes a while. Author and radio host Elisa Morgan says, "Forgiveness usually isn't a onetime experience. It's an ongoing process. You have to work at it."[40] There are no easy answers to the questions you read above. It takes prayer, wisdom, and courage to forgive.

The best tools I've discovered that lead to forgiving your incarcerated loved one are:

1. Letting go of anger—it is more destructive than prison walls and razor wire.
2. Allowing time to give you and your loved one enough "margin" to mentally, emotionally, and spiritually work through the wrong choice, the remorse, the punishment, and the pain.
3. Studying what the Bible says about forgiveness. "What happiness for those whose guilt has been forgiven! What joys when sins are covered over! What relief for those who have confessed their sins and God has cleared their record" (Psalm 32:1–2 TLB). We long to see our loved ones experiencing that kind of joy after seeking forgiveness from the victim, the victim's family, and our own family—but we can't force them to make that decision.
4. Having reasonable expectations. The crime and punishment our family members have experienced have thrust them into great loss—loss of freedom, loss of reputation, loss of employment, and loss of intimate family relationships. They may not ever be able to fully comprehend what they did to us and offer the response we desire.
5. Focusing on the future. If our loved ones never seem to "get" how much hurt and pain we have endured as a result of their crime, let go of resentment and focus on doing the next right thing.

---

40. Elisa Morgan, quoted by *Today's Christian Woman* magazine in *Closer to God* (Wheaton, IL: Tyndale House Publishers, Inc., 1996), 134.

## HIS WORDS OVER YOU

"When you seek answers to tough questions, remember that when you pray, there is a connection between what I do and what you do. As you forgive others, you, in turn, receive forgiveness from me. Seek me while I'm here to be found and pray to me. You will discover that I am merciful and lavish with forgiveness."

*Based on Matthew 6:15 and Isaiah 55:6–7*

# 75. Take Care of Yourself

*Taking care of yourself is the most powerful*
*way to begin to take care of others.*

Bryant McGill

The letter was hard to read. A woman I'll call Betty wrote:

> Dear Carol,
> My son was arrested for armed robbery five months ago. He had sole custody of two children—a four-year-old boy and a two-year-old daughter. His drug addicted wife left him more than a year ago. I am now the sole caregiver of the children and I am sixty-four years old. I love these children and they need me, but they are very active and I am nearing the end of my ability to cope.
> Every weekend I take the children to the jail to visit their father and during the week I'm juggling childcare, babysitters, doing part-time work as a housekeeper to pay for the additional expenses, and trying to take care of the needs of my husband who is recovering from a stroke. I am burned out, discouraged, and exhausted. I feel guilty even thinking about my own needs, but I don't know how much longer I can go on.

This mother of an inmate describes what many parents of prisoners go through—having long-term responsibilities thrust upon them as they deal with all the other matters of life. In this case, she is caring for a husband recovering from a health crisis, managing her regular work duties, and carrying the extra weight—of physical care and finances—related to the children of her loved one. Add in regular visitation at the jail or prison, where it's hard to entertain those kids for any length of time, and the whole situation spells B-U-R-N-O-U-T.

When my son was first arrested, the grief was overwhelming. That was followed by a lot of waiting, with all the uncertainty about when the trial would take place. It was an emotional roller coaster—there were times of hope followed by seasons of great discouragement. Then came the trial and the devastating "life without possibility of parole" sentence. As I worked full-time to help pay legal fees, handled questions from friends and relatives who wanted to know about Jason, and scheduled as many visits with my son as possible, there were times when I felt detached, even cynical. At my most exhausted, I had feelings of ineffectiveness and failure, followed by guilt for allowing myself to feel overwhelmed.

———

Family members of prisoners often juggle harder and faster and more intensely, thinking that *somebody* has to keep all the balls in the air for the family during the incarceration of a loved one. We sometimes feel that everything will fall apart if we don't run faster than a gerbil on a wheel. People of faith may be tempted to think that's the spiritually correct thing to do. Wrong!

How can we care for ourselves when there are so many other demands? Here are some things that have helped me get my life in balance:

- Exercise regularly. Walking three to four miles a day gives me one hour of time to breathe fresh air and get my blood flowing. It's a time when I can think without interruptions.
- Eat a healthy diet. When I'm under pressure, I love to snack on all the wrong, sugary items. Sometimes, after spending hours at the prison and feeling sad, I feel like I deserve to reward myself with food. Resist the urge to do this. Healthy food renews your strength in ways that junk food never will.
- Sleep seven to eight hours a night. When it's time for bed, turn off the television and stop using electronic devices. Texting, surfing the web, and keeping up with social media will all wait until tomorrow. Have a cup of hot, decaffeinated tea and do some light reading to wind down. Before you know it, you'll be asleep.
- Do the important first, not the urgent. There are always unrealistic demands in our lives—and some of those come from our own inmate. Each morning, make a list of specific things that need to be accomplished. Then mark the items that must be done that day. Leave the rest for another day.
- Relax without guilt. This may be the toughest, because there is always something we think we should be doing. But stop. Take a nap. Read a book. Watch a movie. Call a friend. After a short break, the work will still be there—but you'll have more energy for tackling your "to do" list.

In the Bible we see Jesus' instruction to the disciples who were traveling with him: "Come with me by yourselves to a quiet place and get some rest" (Mark 6:31). When you and I walk the tightrope, balancing the needs of our inmate with taking care of ourselves, we, too, need a quiet place to rest!

### HIS WORDS OVER YOU

"Come to me if you are weary and tired of carrying heavy burdens. I will give you what you need. Allow me to teach you to find rest for your soul. Spend time with me and you'll learn how to live freely and lightly."

*Based on Matthew 11:28–30*

# 76. Learn to Laugh Again

*I have always felt that laughter in the face of reality is
probably the finest sound there is. . . . In this world,
a good time to laugh is any time you can.*

LINDA ELLERBEE

The man was angry. He was responding to a picture on Facebook, a
recent photo of us with our son at the prison. Gene and I had our arms
around Jason, and all three of us were smiling. A private message came
to my in-box:

> I find it disgusting that you, your husband, and especially your son
> can stand in front of a camera and smile—as if you want the whole
> world to know you are happily spending time together and laugh-
> ing out loud. Your son killed a man. His family will never have an
> opportunity to laugh together again. They will never stand in front
> of a camera and take a photograph that depicts the fun you appear
> to be having with your son. Their son is dead and your flippant
> attitude, as depicted in the picture you posted, makes me sick!

The letter was unsigned. I was noticeably upset as I read the note to
my husband. "Carol," Gene said to me, "there is one thing you should
always do with unsigned letters—delete them or toss them into the
wastebasket."

I knew he was right, but the letter still hurt—a lot! Part of the sting
was the accusation that we didn't care—the truth is that we have great
compassion for the family of the deceased. We would never want to do
anything that would increase their pain or cause additional hurt. Still,
the letter made me ask myself some questions:

- If a life has been taken or a serious crime has caused a victim
  and/or a victim's family to endure great loss, does that mean the
  criminal and his or her family should never laugh again?
- Does a smile indicate that a prisoner is not remorseful?
- Does it show disrespect to smile and to offer hope to other families of inmates?

In my heart I already knew the answers to those questions—*of
course not!* Without in any way diminishing the severe impact of what
our incarcerated loved one did, we must acknowledge that our lives

continue—and we must move forward in the best, most appropriate way we can.

So why laugh again? The Bible says, "A cheerful heart is good medicine, but a crushed spirit dries up the bones" (Proverbs 17:22). I think we can all agree that we desperately need "medicine" that will point us in the direction of hope and healing.

—

In numerous studies doctors have determined that laughter is good for our physical health. It boosts our immunity, lowers stress hormones, decreases pain, relaxes muscles, and prevents heart disease. And there are additional emotional benefits that are especially helpful to families of the incarcerated:

- Laughter helps us to recharge. Because it reduces stress and increases energy, laughter enables us to stay focused and to get more accomplished.
- Laughter dissolves negative emotions. It's impossible to feel anxious, mad, or sad when you're laughing.
- Humor shifts our perspective. When we're laughing, we see our challenging situations in a more realistic and less threatening light. We feel less overwhelmed.

When we laugh, our bodies release endorphins that aid in the healing process and function as natural pain relievers. Laughing does not lessen the seriousness of your loved one's crime, and it doesn't mean you're disrespecting the victim and their family. Laughter means you have faced the reality of your circumstances and you are working at surviving a great sadness. It means you are moving forward.

As you and I intentionally add humor to our lives, we'll have a more positive outlook, cope with the stresses of our situation more effectively, and solve our problems more effectively. Learning to laugh again restores a certain sense of normality to our lives.

### HIS WORDS OVER YOU

"I will give strength to you when you're tired and worn out. Wait on me and you'll be able to run without growing weary. I will guide you continually and water your life when you're dry, keeping you healthy. You will be like a well-watered garden and an ever-flowing spring."

*Based on Isaiah 40:29–30 and Isaiah 58:11*

# 77. Embrace Your Reality

*Someone's opinion of you does not have to become your reality.*

LES BROWN

The woman in the department store stared at me as I was making my purchase. "Have we met before?" she asked.

Nothing about her looked familiar. "I don't think so," I responded. She continued to concentrate on my face and then loudly exclaimed, "I *do* know you! I saw you on *Dateline NBC*. Your son committed a murder and you and your husband were interviewed." By this time a few curious bystanders were tuning in to this unexpected conversation. Now all of them were staring at me, waiting for a response.

"Yes, that was our family on the program," I admitted.

She continued. "I saw another program and the father of the deceased was being interviewed and he said he had forgiven your son."

I mumbled a few words as I completed my purchase and awkwardly left the mall to find my car. My mind raced: *Why did I allow myself to feel so humiliated in that store? Why wasn't I confident enough to have a real conversation with a woman who was actually very happy to meet me? How many years will it take before I can feel comfortable when someone surprises me in this way?*

Honestly, many years into this process, I am still dealing with the harsh truth of my son's crime and conviction. I am still learning to embrace my own reality. As I do, it's been helpful for me to list the changes that have transpired in the fifteen years since Jason's arrest:

- We moved from Michigan to Florida to be closer to our son.
- I had opportunities to write about our journey in *When I Lay My Isaac Down*, *A New Kind of Normal*, and *Between a Rock and a Grace Place*. (And I wonder why it was easier for me to write about what happened in the solitude of my own home rather than talking to people about the details in a department store.)
- Our step-granddaughters lived with us for two and a half years.
- Gene and I have gotten to know many families of inmates, and we have felt a mutual support from those relationships.
- As news of what happened spread, opportunities to speak about finding hope and faith multiplied. (Hmmm . . . I wonder why it was easier to speak to hundreds of people from a platform than to face individuals who wanted to talk.)

- We began the nonprofit organization Speak Up for Hope, offering tangible help to inmates and their families. (That would not have happened apart from our son being incarcerated. We wouldn't have known about the needs and we probably wouldn't have taken the time to learn more about prisoners and their families.)
- The "Stretcher Bearers," friends and family members who encouraged us, provided examples of how to reach out to the families of inmates in compassionate, helpful ways. Because I wrote about what the Stretcher Bearers did, readers began letting us know that *they* were helping others too. (That was encouraging!)

———

I soon realized that many good changes had taken place in my life during my unwanted foray into the world of jails and prisons. Being caught off guard in a department store by someone who saw us on television wasn't my true reality. For you and me, there is a *new* reality—what will we do now, with this life we have, with all of its imperfections, embarrassment, and sadness?

Our survival tools are very simple:

1. Accept the reality that your loved one is in prison—and use your knowledge of that system and the legal process to help others.
2. Maintain relationships with friends and family members, even when you're busy dealing with your incarcerated loved one. (One of my greatest joys is to stay in touch with my nieces and nephews and their new spouses. We celebrate the births of their babies and keep them updated on Jason.)
3. Make plans for birthday celebrations, family reunions, and vacations, special things that take you away from the demands of incarceration.
4. Discard guilt! Acknowledge that a meaningful life needs to be a permanent part of your reality.

It might help you to do what I did: list what has happened in your life since your journey began—both the good and the bad. Then, for each entry, write what you've learned along the way.

One day as I was reading the Bible, I came across this verse: "You gave me life and showed me kindness, and in your providence watched over my spirit" (Job 10:12). That's a reminder to embrace the life we have!

## HIS WORDS OVER YOU

"Look to me and I will do immeasurably more than you ask or imagine. Allow my power to be at work in you. Live wisely and make the most of every opportunity. Let your conversation be gracious; you will have the right response for everyone."

*Based on Ephesians 3:20 and Colossians 4:5–6*

# 78. How Can I Find Faith?

*You'll get through this. It won't be painless. It won't
be quick. But God will use this mess for good. In the
meantime don't be foolish or naïve. But don't despair
either. With God's help you will get through this.*

MAX LUCADO

The e-mail was intense. A woman wrote:

Dear Carol,

My brother is ruining his life, and in the process, he is totally
wrecking any hope for a happy life for me and for my parents.
As a teenager he got hooked on marijuana, and the older he got,
the more his appetite for illegal drugs increased. After high school
graduation he went to a local junior college, but lived at home. My
mom started to notice that money was missing from her purse.
Then dad discovered that his coin collection was gone. At first they
didn't want to believe it was Matt doing the stealing, but when he
came home high on drugs, the truth was obvious.

For the next two years mom and dad sent him to rehabilitation
programs, including an expensive month-long detoxification and
counseling center. That time he stayed clean about a month before
he went back to his old friends and to his old habits. Then he was
arrested, not just for possession, but for selling drugs to a minor too.
My parents had no savings left, so they withdrew their retirement
funds and paid for an expensive attorney. Matt was found guilty and
was sentenced to five years in prison. But that's not the end. When he
got out, he violated his probation and was arrested again. Our family
is sick of his cycle of bad choices and incarceration. He is a cancer in
our lives, robbing us of money, reputation, peace, and joy.

I used to think that God was real and loved people, but I no
longer feel like I can trust Him. Why would God allow my parents
to lose all of their security for a loser like my brother? I feel hopeless
and discouraged and I really want to find faith, but I don't know
where to look and I doubt that I could make myself believe in God.
If He exists, I feel like He doesn't care about our family.

———

Sadly, stories like this are repeated again and again. They often include
different crimes, but have the recurring theme of family members breaking

the law, getting arrested and convicted, going to prison, getting out, and making the same bad choices again. Have you experienced this, or feared it could happen? Where is God in all of this? Is faith worth the risk? The Bible describes what faith is: "It is the confident assurance that something we want is going to happen. It is the certainty that what we hope for is waiting for us, even though we cannot see it up ahead" (Hebrew 11:1 TLB). This kind of faith must be placed in something real, and there's nothing more real than Jesus. But we often want to have "faith" to believe that God will change our loved one's heart and make him or her into a law-abiding citizen. Whenever I wondered where God was in my situation, it helped me to remember that God is not a dictator—He always allows people to make their own choices. If our faith hangs on our family member leading a crime-free life, we'll be miserable if they find themselves in trouble again.

Real faith, though, is in God—and it's personal. Your decision to follow Him will not change your incarcerated loved one, but it will help *you* to make right choices. Your faith will help you to have endurance for the long road ahead.

You may feel it's too hard even to take a first step toward faith. But there's a great Bible verse in which Jesus says, "Truly I tell you, if you have faith as small as a mustard seed, you can say to this mountain, 'Move from here to there,' and it will move. Nothing will be impossible for you" (Matthew 17:20).

Faith begins with a personal relationship with Jesus. If you are willing to invite Him into your life, look back at chapter 23, page 60, and you'll find a prayer that will help you begin. Praying a prayer will not take you out of a messy life situation—but having faith in Jesus means God is *with* you and He is *for* you. He's on your team!

Start reading the Bible's book of John, and look for a good church or Bible study to attend. You'll discover that, as you wait for progress in the life of your inmate, there will be other people of faith waiting with you and praying for you. You will not endure the pain alone. You *will* get through this.

### HIS WORDS OVER YOU

"I loved the people in the world so much that I gave my one and only Son to die on the cross to pay the price for everyone's wrongdoing. This is why: so that no one needs to be destroyed. By having faith in Jesus, you can have a whole and lasting life."

*Based on John 3:16*

# 79. Raising Children Alone

*There will be so many times when you feel like you've failed, but in the eyes, heart, and mind of your child, you are Super Mom.*

STEPHANIE PRECOURT

I met Emily at a women's conference. She had e-mailed ahead of time, saying she would appreciate an opportunity to talk to me during the event. As she introduced herself, I was struck by what an attractive, confident, and articulate young woman she was.

Following the usual pleasantries, she said, "I've read your books, so I feel like you're a safe person to talk to. My husband is incarcerated and his sentence is ten years. I'm thirty-two years old and our children are eight, five, and three years old. He had a great job, working as an accountant for a respected firm, but he got caught embezzling funds. The news was all over the papers and on local TV. It's been humiliating and devastating."

I put my arms around Emily and wept with her. She went on. "I was a stay-at-home mom, but I had to find work to support our family. My salary is less than half of what my husband made. It's a stretch for me to cover the basic bills, buy groceries, pay for childcare, and put money in my husband's inmate account. We're losing our home and next week we're moving into a small rental unit. My parents are furious with me for staying with my husband after what he's done, but I still love him."

Once again, Emily's tears were flowing. "A friend paid my way to come to this conference," she said, "but I'm missing a visitation day with my husband to be here and that makes me feel guilty. I'm careful about what I say to my children about what their father did because I don't want them to lose respect for him. They're very young now, but my oldest son will be in his senior year of high school when his dad is released. When I get home from work, the kids need me, but I'm exhausted and I know they deserve more attention than I can give them. I feel overwhelmed and fearful. I come from a strong Christian background, but right now it's hard to see how God could possibly be at work in the middle of so many challenges. I am having a hard time thinking about living through the next decade of my life while raising three children alone."

Emily is one of many inmate wives I've spoken to. They tell me they don't know if they can function as a single parent while also meeting the needs and demands of an incarcerated spouse. Is God *really* in the middle of their mess?

Emily said she was from a Christian background, so I reminded her that while her husband is away, *God* will be a helper to her children: "But you, God, see the trouble of the afflicted; you consider their grief and take it in hand. The victims commit themselves to you; you are the helper of the fatherless" (Psalm 10:14). Sometimes we think of the victims of crime as only those who were hurt or wronged by an illegal action—but the family members of the prisoner are victims as well. They are living through the same sentence as their convicted family member, only outside the prison walls.

We talked about practical steps Emily could take. If the following ideas don't apply directly to your situation, you might be able to share them with others. For a parent raising children alone while a spouse is incarcerated, I would say:

- Get involved in your local church. You may feel embarrassed at first, but in the end, you will find support and encouragement from caring people.
- Talk to your spouse about a reasonable visitation schedule. You can't work full-time, care for children, *and* attend prison visitation every week. Perhaps visiting every two weeks or once a month will allow you to balance other responsibilities more easily and give you time to attend events and activities with your children.
- Trade childcare responsibilities with a single parent who also needs assistance. That eliminates a large weekly bill.
- Nurture friendships that build you up—especially with people who love your children too. Plan picnics and outings with other families, so your kids can enjoy the fun and interaction and be a part of a group.
- Connect with your spouse on a spiritual level by selecting a Bible study to do together. Study chapters on your own time, then discuss them together at visitation or over the phone on weeks when you're not at the prison. Pray together for your children. As you grow spiritually as a couple, you'll rediscover God in the middle of your messy life situation.

We know God cares deeply about children. In Matthew 19:14 (NLT) Jesus said, "Let the children come to me. Don't stop them! For the Kingdom of Heaven belongs to those who are like these children."

Try not to look at all the years of incarceration your spouse faces. Live one day at a time, and you'll discover—as I did—just enough of what you need to make it through. Yes, you'll be tired. Yes, you'll feel like there's never enough money. Yes, you will mourn your losses. Yes, you'll feel like all of the weight of parenting is on you. But God is in the middle of your mess. He loves you and He provides.

### HIS WORDS OVER YOU

"Don't be afraid. I will continue to take care of you and your children. My goodness and unfailing love will follow you all the days of your life."

*Based on Psalm 103:17 and Psalm 23:6*

# 80. Can My Marriage Last?

*In a word, live together in the forgiveness of your sins, for without it no human fellowship, least of all a marriage, can survive. Don't insist on your rights, don't blame each other, don't judge or condemn each other, don't find fault with each other, but accept each other as you are, and forgive each other every day from the bottom of your hearts.*

DIETRICH BONHOEFFER

According to studies quoted by Prison Fellowship, 85 percent of marriages collapse when one spouse goes to prison—even for a short stay. Under the combined weight of financial hardship, distance, misunderstanding, shame, and stress, it's more than challenging to keep a marriage intact.

I met Stephanie one weekend when I was speaking at an event in her church. She asked if we could talk privately, and we arranged to meet for coffee after the conference ended. "I don't usually tell my story to people I've never met," she told me, "but I know your son is incarcerated, so I'm hoping you can give me some advice. My husband and I have been married for fifteen years. We have two sons who are eleven and thirteen. I was stunned when my husband was arrested for purchasing child pornography on the Internet. He served on the board of our church, taught an adult Bible class, and together we led a small group of several couples who are part of the class he taught."

Stephanie was doing a good job holding herself together emotionally until she talked about her kids. "After his arrest I had to tell my sons why their father was arrested," she said. "It was all over our local newspapers and I knew it would be easier for them to hear it from me rather than getting the news through snide remarks from their classmates." By this time her tears were flowing. "Jerry has been a good husband, a wonderful provider, and an incredible father. I'm shocked, humiliated, and deeply hurt by his actions. What has happened has rocked my faith and made me question what it is about *me* that made him look for fulfillment in such a horrible place. I don't know whether or not I should divorce him. He's apologized and asked for forgiveness. He's begging me to stay in the marriage, but I don't know if I can ever trust him again."

That afternoon Stephanie and I had a long talk about how she and Jerry met and about their hopes and dreams for the future—which certainly didn't include incarceration. I could tell she loved her husband very much, even though she was angry with him. He had told her a friend at work introduced him to the website that had now cost him his job, his reputation, and the freedom to live with his family. Stephanie said Jerry seemed genuinely remorseful, and that he had apologized and begged for her forgiveness. I sensed that Stephanie believed he was repentant, but determining whether or not to stay in her marriage was a heavy decision for her.

———

Hundreds of women have contacted me about the challenge in marriage following the incarceration of their spouses. In Stephanie's case, she already had a well-paying job and is able to stay in her home. But she is trying to determine if she should leave her marriage or give her husband a second chance to be the man she thought she married. Stephanie is blessed to have a strong support system in her family and in church.

Here are some helpful tips for a person whose spouse is in jail or prison:

- Communicate honestly. Speak truthfully about the depth of your hurt and of the way you and your children have been ripped apart by your spouse's crime and incarceration.
- Have friends care for your children during some visitation times, so you can talk as a couple without distraction.
- Make a list of the important things you need to cover in phone calls. Calls may come unexpectedly, and it's easy to run out of time before you can address the things you most need to discuss.
- Decide together how many calls your spouse should make from prison each week. Calls are expensive, and this decision will help you to stay within your budget and avoid additional financial challenges.
- Pray together during your phone calls and visits. James 5:16 (NLT) says, "Confess your sins to each other and pray for each other so that you may be healed. The earnest prayer of a righteous person has great power and produces wonderful results." Praying together can be a glue that strengthens your marriage.
- Study the Bible together. Read the same chapters in the Bible, and discuss what you're learning. Psalm 119:105 (NLT) reveals the benefit: "Your word is a lamp to guide my feet and a light for my path." That means that, as you and your spouse study God's Word and ask Him for direction, He will give you wisdom for your important decisions.

Encourage your spouse to open up emotionally. Talk about your fears, your challenges with the children, the pressures you've encountered, and the opportunities you've had to help others in similar circumstances. Be sure to express your love for each other and your desire to keep God at the center of your marriage.

There will still be conflicts—that's to be expected. But if you work at communicating honestly, clearly, and respectfully, with a constant focus on God and His Word, you will have a much better chance of maintaining your marriage through an incarceration.

### HIS WORDS OVER YOU

"Honor your marriage and guard the sacredness of your union. Most importantly, continue to show deep love for each other, for love covers a multitude of sins."

*Based on Hebrews 13:4 and 1 Peter 4:8*

# 81. God Must Love You More Than Me

*If you're struggling with questions or uncomfortable feelings about faith and God, tell Him. He already knows. When you are willing to reveal yourself completely to God, He reveals himself to you.*

JENNIFER ROTHSCHILD

A letter was forwarded to me from the SpeakUpforHope.org website. A woman I'll call Amelia wrote that a friend had given her my book *When I Lay My Isaac Down* because she was going through a similar trial. Reading the book was bringing her no comfort, Amelia said, and was even making her more depressed. "I thought, selfishly," she wrote, *"How nice that your life had been almost perfect and well blessed [to the point of Jason's arrest]. What's it like to have a taste of the good life?"*

The remainder of Amelia's letter was heart-wrenching:

> When my son took another man's life twenty months ago, my own life was already in crisis. I'd had surgery two weeks before to repair a cracked wrist bone and torn tendon. Since my son's arrest, escalating pain continues to ravage me. . . . I haven't received yellow roses or anything depicting sunshine or hope or peace. My family hasn't rallied around me. Instead, it's splintered, and I've been left alone—with the exception of my supportive and loving husband who betrayed me six months after the arrest.
>
> The downpour of terrible circumstances has been relentless, including living in a twenty-three-year-old RV with less than three hundred square feet after being only days away from closing on our dream house of three thousand square feet. It would have housed my mother permanently and my grown children for visits for the first time ever. I've prayed to God not to see the sun rise again. Twice in the last eight months, I've made halfhearted attempts to take my life. Instead, I constantly awaken to more burdens.
>
> No one has offered to establish a network of support. In fact, I've received a total of fifty dollars cash and your book from family and friends. Except for a smattering of Christian gestures from well-meaning folks who feel sorry for us, we've been abandoned. No one's dropping off a casserole to make sure we have something to eat!
>
> I've prayed to God around the clock for a reprieve from the pain. At one point, I decided that I must be dead, that life on earth

couldn't possibly be so hellish. Even my loving, devoted Christian mother won't see my son. *Who does that?* I don't know why God has blessed you and left me floundering. I am utterly exhausted and beyond the point of giving up. I'm so broken that I don't think anything will help at this point.

———

You may have had similar thoughts while reading this book: *Carol Kent had encouraging support, and our family had almost no help.* I can only imagine your frustration. It was hard for me to read Amelia's letter. No matter how much pain my family has endured, she has gone through so much more—because she's had no one to wait with her. Why would God allow this woman to live in such a mess of physical, emotional, mental, and spiritual turmoil? Nothing about it is fair!

Amelia's situation reminds me of a story in the Bible. Some of Jesus' disciples came to Him with a man who had been born blind. The disciples asked, "Why was this man born blind? Was it because of his own sins or his parents' sins?" (John 9:2 NLT). I *hate* Jesus' answer: "It was not because of his sins or his parents' sins. . . . This happened so the power of God could be seen in him" (John 9:3 NLT). That explanation feels like there's *no* answer. Why are some families chosen to bring God glory by enduring unthinkable suffering? Why do some people dealing with incarcerated family members have no support at all?

I don't have "a poem and a prayer" to neatly wrap up this article. All I can tell you is what I know to be true about God, what my own life experience as a Christian has taught me: if we know Jesus and we go through fiery, messy, painful experiences, we do not walk through the fire alone. If you feel like you're without support or hope today, cling to Him and claim Isaiah 43:2: "When you pass through the waters, I will be with you; and when you pass through the rivers, they will not sweep over you. When you walk through the fire, you will not be burned; the flames will not set you ablaze."

Today's pain is not the end of your story. God is in the middle of your mess, and He will not leave you.

## HIS WORDS OVER YOU

"I have seen your misery. I have heard your crying, and I'm concerned about your suffering. I will not leave you comfortless. I will come to you. You will not be abandoned. I'm coming back."

*Based on Exodus 3:7 and John 14:18–20*

# 82. Does God Answer Prayer?

*God will answer your prayers better than you think. Of course, one will not always get exactly what he has asked for. . . . We all have sorrows and disappointments, but . . . His own solution is far better than any we could conceive.*

FANNY CROSBY

During the past few years, many people have asked me questions about prayer. Their inquiries are often similar because they all want to know if God really hears and answers. At some point, as we walk with our loved one through their trial and sentencing, we all think: *Do my prayers matter?* The following notes indicate people are definitely asking that question:

- My husband was sentenced to eight years in prison and all three of our children will graduate from high school while he is incarcerated. I begged God for a shorter sentence so my husband could be at home while the kids need him most. Why didn't He answer my prayer?
- I used to think that God heard my prayers, but I'm not sure anymore. My wife and I tried to raise our son to uphold the law, but he got in with the wrong crowd in high school and became drug addicted. He's been clean for up to three months at a time, but always returns to his addiction. He can't keep a job and has been arrested three times—this time for armed robbery. We've prayed for him night and day, but it doesn't seem to help.
- Our beautiful eighteen-year-old daughter went to a party with her boyfriend and a group of friends after the final football game of the season. All of them drank too much. Our daughter tried to drive home and hit another car head on. There were three fatalities and she is facing a fifteen-year sentence for vehicular manslaughter. She's an honor student, has never been in trouble before, and has a strong faith in God. We prayed for a shorter sentence that would allow her to have some of her young adult life back, but God didn't come through for us.

Early in my marriage, I thought I knew how to pray. I had heard it was important to have a specific place to pray, and I assumed my prayers were more likely to be answered if I was on my knees, humble before God. But after my son was arrested, my prayer life became very different. I prayed anywhere, mostly out of desperation. Sometimes I yelled my prayers, but more often I *groaned* them. Occasionally, I would ask for specific things, but more often I would just say, "Jesus." I didn't even know what to pray for, but I hoped He was listening.

———

Somehow, deep in my soul, I knew that I needed to pray. And if I needed to pray, that must mean that God hears and answers. But *how* should I pray? The following thoughts have been helpful to me, and I hope you'll find them useful too.

1. Confess your own sins to God before you pray for your family member. Psalm 66:18 (NLT) says, "If I had not confessed the sin in my heart, the Lord would not have listened." Even if your sin seems unimportant compared to the sin of your loved one, confess to God everything you have done wrong. It's important to allow Him to clean your heart of impurity before you go further in prayer.
2. Faith is required. The Bible states: "And it is impossible to please God without faith. Anyone who wants to come to him must believe that God exists and that he rewards those who sincerely seek him" (Hebrews 11:6 NLT).
3. What we ask must align with what God wants, as He has explained it in the Bible. First John 5:14 states: "This is the confidence we have in approaching God: that if we ask anything according to his will, he hears us."
4. We must be willing to wait. This entire book has emphasized the importance of waiting together in the middle of our messy, unwanted situations. Psalm 27:14 tells us: "Wait for the LORD; be strong and take heart and wait for the LORD." Realize that God may have reasons for our waiting, even when His timing makes little sense to us. Believe that God's purposes are much better for our incarcerated loved one and for us.
5. Thank God for working on your behalf, even when you don't yet have an answer. We know He is a God of mercy, even toward our loved ones who have broken the law. First Thessalonians 5:18 (KJV) says, "In every thing give thanks: for this is the will of God in Christ Jesus concerning you."

Through all my years of praying for Jason, I haven't seen God answer my prayers for leniency by the court or an eventual end-of-sentence date. Instead, God has chosen to use Jason right where he is to help other inmates and to encourage them spiritually. God *has* answered my prayers for a purposeful life for my son—and He has answered my prayers for a more compassionate heart in me.

Even when it seems, on the surface, that God is not answering our prayers, He is actually answering—just in a far different way than we were anticipating. Yes, our prayers matter to God!

## HIS WORDS OVER YOU

"Pray always and give thanks in every circumstance. Pray often for each other and remember that the prayers of a righteous person are powerful and effective."

*Based on 1 Thessalonians 5:17 and James 5:16*

# 83. Redefining Joy

*I've survived because I've discovered a new and different kind*
*of joy that I never knew existed—a joy that can coexist with*
*uncertainty and doubt, pain, confusion, and ambiguity.*

Tim Hansel

Exhausted, I dropped into a large chair in my hotel room and kicked off my shoes. It had been a long day. After an early flight to the Northwest, I arrived at the conference center and spoke during the first session of a weekend women's conference. My mind was still whirling from the busyness of the day when the phone rang. It was the front desk clerk, who said a sobbing woman was asking for me. I agreed to talk to her.

I met Charlotte in the lobby and we found a quiet place talk. She was visibly shaken. "Forgive me for bothering you at this late hour," she said, "but I don't know where else to turn. I drove three hours to hear you speak and I feel like you're the only person who can really understand what I'm going through."

She spoke of her growing-up years, filled with abuse at the hands of her alcoholic father. Her mother pretended not to see what was going on. Charlotte went on to tell me that, when she was sixteen, a friend had explained how she could have a personal, faith relationship with Jesus Christ—and her decision to believe in Jesus had brought her hope and real joy. When she was twenty-two, she married a man who made her laugh, encouraged her, and provided for her, and they had a happy life together. They enjoyed enough income for a lovely home, restaurant meals on the weekends, and vacations. Their three children were a delight. But then the bottom dropped out of Charlotte's life.

"One day the police showed up at our front door," she said, wiping away tears. "They put my husband in handcuffs and told him he was under arrest for owning and operating a prostitution ring. The media created a frenzy over what happened, and there was no mercy shown during my husband's trial, conviction, and sentencing."

Then Charlotte's story got even worse. "I discovered I'd contracted multiple sexually transmitted diseases from my husband's intimate encounters with the women he employed," she told me. "My children have been humiliated at school. We have lost everything—our home, our reputation, our closeness as a family, our hopes for the future, and most definitely our joy. How could I go from having so much happiness to weeping day and night over these severe losses?"

She went on. "I am in the middle of a divorce from the scumbag I married and I'm trying to help my children find some normalcy in their lives. I think I'm really asking you: *Where is God in the middle of this awful mess? Can I ever get my joy back?*"

———

The dictionary defines *joy* as "the emotion evoked by well-being, success, or good fortune or by the prospect of possessing what one desires."[41] It can also mean a feeling of great happiness or success in doing, finding, or getting something.

All of us remember times, before incarceration touched our family, when we experienced these feelings of success and good fortune. We recall birthdays, graduations, weddings, awards, promotions, spiritual milestones, and family reunions with great joy. But after a family member is arrested, we often doubt if we will ever experience joy again. Joy not only seems illusive—it has disappeared completely!

You and I can rediscover joy by pursuing it in a new way: by inviting God into the mess of our lives. Well-known pastor and author Rick Warren says, "Joy is the settled assurance that God is in control of all the details of my life, the quiet confidence that ultimately everything is going to be alright, and the determined choice to praise God in every situation."[42] If that sounds good to you, here are some practical ideas to help you rediscover and cultivate your joy:

1. Read Psalm 103. Then write down reasons you find for trusting God.
2. Make a list of everything that brings you joy—things your children say, unexpected kindnesses from friends, a great cup of coffee, a funny movie, or a specific Bible verse.
3. Surround yourself with joyful people—because joy is contagious.
4. Fill your mind with uplifting music, especially praise and worship music. That will draw you closer to God and to His Word.
5. Read Scriptures that remind you of the source of true joy: "You make known to me the path of life; you will fill me with joy in your presence, with eternal pleasures at your right hand" (Psalm 16:11).
6. Believe that God has a better future for you. "Weeping may stay for the night, but rejoicing comes in the morning" (Psalm 30:5).
7. Thank God for everything in 1 through 6!

---

41. Merriam-Webster.com. "joy." http://www.merriam-webster.com/dictionary/joy.
42. Daily Hope with Rick Warren. "The Definition of Joy," May 21, 2014. http://rickwarren.org/devotional/english/the-definition-of-joy.

Following ten years in prison, my son sent me his own definition of joy: "Joy, for me, is knowing as concretely as I know my name and my birthday that God is real and He loves me personally, that I'm never alone, and that He can be trusted with my heart."

Can you and I get our joy back? Yes, it's possible! But it will be a process, not just a moment in time. And it will be a different kind of joy, one that isn't based on the things and events of our lives, but that points us deeper into the experience of God's love throughout our messy journey.

## HIS WORDS OVER YOU

"If you call out to me, I will restore the joy of your faith in me. I began a good work in you and I will carry it to completion. Allow my joy to be your strength."

*Based on Psalm 51:12, Philippians 1:6, and Nehemiah 8:10*

# 84. Waiting for God to Work

*Waiting for God is not the abandonment of effort. Waiting for God means, first, activity under command; second, readiness for any new command that may come; third, the ability to do nothing until the command is given.*

G. CAMPBELL MORGAN

Waiting is one of my least favorite activities. It feels like wasted time, or even a bit of an insult—at the doctor's office, for example, it feels like my time isn't being respected if I arrive at the appointed hour but I'm not immediately called into the examination room. It's irritating—and there's absolutely nothing I can do about it.

The unexpected incarceration of a loved one can stop your life in its tracks. Those of us who have lived through this have learned a lot about waiting. Sam contacted us via e-mail, describing what his family is experiencing:

> Our son has been in a maximum-security prison for the past eight years. He has a twenty-five-year sentence, so my wife and I are very concerned about the quality of life inside the prison. The new warden has instituted restrictive changes to the usual way programs and schedules have been run. He dramatically reduced the number of faith-based and educational programs that have had long-standing success on the compound. All evening chapel services have been canceled and new chapel programs have been greatly restricted. He has also instituted severe cuts on how much yard time the inmates get. The inmates used to be given a couple of hours in the morning and a couple of hours in the afternoon for recreation outside, but now they are only allowed out once or twice a week to participate in sports or exercise on the yard—all in the name of keeping the prison more safe. These changes seem irrational.

> Our son has told us that there is much more violence on the compound because of keeping the men locked in their cells for long periods, and the morale of the inmates is at an all-time low. There have been two murders (prisoner-to-prisoner violence) in the past six months, and the tense atmosphere is a direct result of these senseless new restrictions. We have prayed hard, made calls, written letters of inquiry to the Department of Corrections, and waited for months for positive change—and *nothing* happens. Our son

is discouraged and feels like there's no hope for positive change. I know God could do something about this. What's He waiting for?

—

If we're honest, we believe God should handle problems much more quickly—especially those problems that hurt us and cause stress to our inmate. We wish He would make all prison officials act responsibly. We know He could speed up the visitation lines. And couldn't He get some momentum going to resolve our family issues following the arrest of our loved one?

Since we know He is God, we simply expect Him to work faster on our behalf. He *is* aware of the mess we're in, right? Perhaps you, too, have prayed, "I am worn out waiting for your rescue" (Psalm 119:81 NLT). But there's a second part to that verse: if you look it up, you'll find that the psalm writer also said, "I have put my hope in your word."

After several years of impatience, I now understand that there are benefits to waiting for God to work:

1. We grow in character. We become aware of our weaknesses and place our trust in God's timing. "But they that wait upon the LORD shall renew their strength; they shall mount up with wings as eagles; they shall run, and not be weary; and they shall walk, and not faint" (Isaiah 40:31 KJV).
2. We grow spiritually during the wait. What benefits us most is not what's happening *to* us, but *in* us. "Wait for the LORD and keep his way, and he will exalt you" (Psalm 37:34 ESV).
3. We see God at work in the life of our incarcerated loved one. I am consistently amazed as I see the creativity of inmates who are under duress due to harsh restrictions. They bond over Bible studies that they lead themselves when volunteers can't get in. They depend upon God completely because they have nowhere else to turn. They remind us that waiting is the highest form of trusting God—and we realize He is at work in all the messy situations of our lives.

### HIS WORDS OVER YOU

"You waited patiently for me and I heard your cry. You are blessed when you listen to me, and when you watch daily for me to act. I will be your help and shield as you wait in hope for me."

*Based on Psalm 40:1, Proverbs 8:34, and Psalm 33:20*

# 85. Freedom on the Inside

*Freedom is an inside job.*

Sam Keen

Sitting at the kitchen table, with my computer in front of me and a coffee cup in hand, I feel like I'm beginning to say good-bye. It's a difficult task—you have become my close friends, my fellow sojourners on our difficult path that features unexpected detours, formidable obstacles, and an uncertain destination.

No matter what encouragement you may have found in this book, you will no doubt face other issues that haven't been addressed. There will be a day when you feel like throwing your hands in the air because nobody "gets" what you are experiencing.

I've had enough of those days myself. But I've learned that, no matter how dark the situation gets, the sun always rises the next day. With that sun comes fresh ideas, new insights, a call from an old friend, or a Bible verse that leaps off the page and grabs my heart. And somehow I make it to the next day.

We really are in this together. One afternoon I received a beautiful, handmade card in my mailbox with this note inside:

Dear Carol,

You haven't met me, but I feel like I know you after watching your interview on *Dateline NBC*. It was obvious that you and your husband are Christians. I saw in your responses something I am trying to live out in my own life as the mother of a daughter who has a lengthy prison sentence—freedom on the inside.

It's a bit of a mystery that both of us have children behind the razor wire, but in a very real way, you and I face our own prisons. We have a totally altered lifestyle, with going to visitation on the weekends instead of taking our families to the beach or using that time to catch up on household tasks. We anxiously await calls from our children—and when they don't call, we wonder if they are in lockdown or if they have been transferred to a different facility.

We worry about prison health care and fights on the compound, knowing that when our inmates stick up for the underdogs, they may cause themselves a lot of trouble—from both the inmates and the guards. Most often we are caught in a prison of anxiety, because of the "not knowing" that accompanies every day.

As I completed Megan's letter, I decided to list things that inmates and their loved ones need in order to be set free from the "inner bondage" of incarceration. Use the following as a checklist to see where you are in this process:

1. Know Jesus as your personal Lord and Savior. This may sound "churchy" if you are still investigating whether to say yes to this step of faith—but it is the first and best choice that brings inner freedom. John 8:36 says, "If the Son sets you free, you will be free indeed."

2. Choose liberty of the heart. Freedom is something most of us take for granted. We decide on our own daily activities and we move around at will. But inner freedom involves being at peace in the midst of circumstances that, humanly speaking, make us feel confined or without control. This inner freedom is only possible by nurturing the spiritual dimension of our lives. Second Corinthians 3:17 (NASB) says, "Now the Lord is the Spirit, and where the Spirit of the Lord is, *there* is liberty."

3. Give and receive forgiveness. I know, that *forgiveness* word is starting to sound like a broken record—but it is essential to this process of freedom. Forgiveness is a two-way street: when the hearts of those on both sides of a crime are liberated by forgiveness, grace pours in from a supernatural source. The result can be mental, emotional, and spiritual freedom that is surprising, humbling, and inspiring. This is true of criminals and their victims, but it is equally true of prisoners and their family members. "Blessed is the one whose transgressions are forgiven, whose sins are covered" (Psalm 32:1).

As you seek to find peace and inner freedom for the remainder of your journey, write out your own definition of forgiveness. Have you ever spoken forgiveness to your inmate for what he or she did to *your* life as a result of the crime and incarceration? If not, fill in these blanks and turn your words into a prayer:

Lord, I need to forgive _____. My emotions of [anger, fear, resentment, etc.] _____ have kept me in a prison of my own making. I confess to you all wrongdoing and wrong thinking on my part, and I ask for your wisdom about what steps to take next. Please move me in the direction of restoration, redemption, and true liberty of the heart. Amen.

"Dear ones, I am here to bind up the brokenhearted and to proclaim liberty to captives and freedom to prisoners. I will forgive your wrongdoing and I'll remember it no more. When I set you free, you are free indeed!"

*Based on Isaiah 61:1, Jeremiah 31:34, and John 8:36*

# 86. Visitation Matters

*Can you imagine what it is like to be in prison*
*waiting for a visit that does not come?*

JACK MILES

I was sitting in the visitation room, picking at the broken tabletop as I talked to my son. At that time, we were approaching sixteen years of visiting Jason, both in jail and multiple prisons. I asked him, "What is the single most important thing—besides Jesus—that helps you keep your sanity in this place?"

Before he could answer, my finger dislodged a piece of someone's dried-out, leftover food from the tabletop. "This is so disgusting!" I blurted out, referring to the crud on the table. Then I realized it was even more revolting that I was picking at it with my own fingers!

I laughed out loud as I realized how it would have bothered me to be assigned a seat at *that* table in my B.P. (Before Prison) years. Now, A.P., I'm more focused on the person I'm visiting, rather than the furniture or décor in the room.

To answer my question, Jason said, *"Visits* are one of the most important things anyone can do for an inmate." I asked him if he would write out some insights on the importance of visitation so I could share them with you. He mailed me handwritten notes that read:

> Visitation is the only time when a prisoner can count on getting to physically touch (albeit very briefly) those he loves. Our visitors are also our connection to the outside world with its life, freedom, taste of fresh air, and hope. Getting to talk face-to-face, share a meal together, and simply hold hands means more than I can say.
>
> Prison is a very lonely place and it's inherently alienating from the life we all previously knew. Any connection through letters, phone calls, and visits shared together is a deep encouragement and reconnects us to those we love. Friends who come remind us that we aren't forgotten and they're comforting to the soul.
>
> People on both sides of the fence desperately need that contact. You realize in here how very important relationships are and how much you miss everyone that you may have previously taken for granted.
>
> Visits can also be emotionally charged and stressful—but what is the alternative? We can either choose a slow loss of connection

and experience broken relationships, or embrace the risk and the opportunity of seeing each other regularly—even with the myriad of restrictions, personal misunderstandings, and hurdles of prison rules.

I encourage everyone to take a chance and visit those they care about behind prison walls. Letters and phone calls are valuable, but an actual visit in the flesh is truly priceless. It makes us know you care.

———

In one facility where I volunteered, I chatted with a prisoner. He said, "One of the saddest things I've seen is when an inmate who had not gotten a visit for two years got word that his sister was coming on the weekend. He shaved, showered, and dressed in his 'best' prison uniform and waited for the call telling him to come to the visitation room. But that didn't happen. He waited for five hours before he finally collapsed into tears, realizing that no one was coming."

As you and I get into the rhythm of our new normal, we may think that our visits don't really mean that much. And let's face it—those visits are inconvenient and expensive. We have much to do and our weekends are already short. And it's not cheap to buy gasoline to get to the prison or to purchase breakfast and lunch to feed your inmate and any family members who are with you. There are lots of reasons not to go.

Here are some reasons we *should* go:

- God tells us that when we visit someone in prison, it is as if we are visiting Him (see Matthew 25:34–40).
- Several hours visiting your incarcerated family member gives you a chance to know him or her more personally than you might ever have before. When all you can do is talk, you may discuss some important things. You can also resolve weightier family issues more easily than in a fifteen-minute phone call with an automatic cutoff.
- Visitation provides an opportunity for you to meet other prisoners' family members, both adults and children. Waiting in long lines together gives you a chance to brainstorm ideas for helping each other and advocating for your inmate loved ones.
- By caring for our loved one, we follow God's example . . . because He doesn't forget us. "See," He says, "I have written your name on the palms of my hands" (Isaiah 49:16 NLT).

Visiting your inmate regularly can bring joy and healing, even laughter into a very dark environment. Jason and I find comfort in discussing creative ways to show compassion to inmates and their families, followed by sharing prayer needs and praying out loud for each other. Philippians 2:3–4 says, "In humility value others above yourselves, not looking to your own interests but each of you to the interest of others." As you keep moving in a forward direction, remember how important visits are.

## HIS WORDS OVER YOU

"I hear the voices of those in need. Remember those who are in prison as if you were there with them. Overflow more and more with love for each other and keep growing in spiritual knowledge and insight."

*Based on Psalm 69:33, Hebrews 13:3, and Philippians 1:9*

# 87. Drenched in Grace

*Grace comes after you. It rewires you. From insecure to*
*God secure. From regret-riddled to better-because-of-it.*
*From afraid-to-die to ready-to-fly. Grace is the voice that*
*calls us to change and gives us the power to pull it off.*

MAX LUCADO

Once when Jason was five years old, we were getting ready for a Sunday evening service at church. I had bathed and dressed him in a crisp, clean shirt that matched his jeans. I then secured his brand-new white tennis shoes with their distinctive Velcro fasteners. There were some unruly hairs in a cowlick, so I carefully sprayed them down until they submitted to my authority. The kid looked "picture perfect."

I needed about five more minutes before I could declare myself ready to leave, so I gave Jason permission to go outside, with these instructions: "You can walk around the backyard while Mama gets ready for church, but don't go near the creek!" (In truth, it was a drainage ditch. We called it a creek, hoping that description would increase our property value.)

Hurriedly, I ran a brush through my hair and touched up my makeup. Minutes later I headed for the door—but the sight before my eyes was unnerving. There stood Jason, with the obvious marks of dis-obedience. He was wet and covered in green slime, his tennis shoes were muddy, he had a bloody scratch from a tree limb, and all three hairs were standing straight up in defiance along the cowlick!

My blood was boiling. I was prepared to blurt out an angry lecture, and needed no rehearsal for this speech! As I drew a deep breath to sustain the volume and intensity my emotion required, I heard a small, repentant voice say, "Soakers again, Mom! I just don't understand it. My feet just won't do what my mind says it wants to."

I wanted to be stern, but I burst out laughing. Jason was misera-ble, and he had learned his lesson. That day he experienced grace—but he grew to understand a much deeper meaning of grace after his incarceration.

---

I'm still trying to understand what grace is. Perhaps the best defi-nition is that it is the undeserved favor of God when we really deserve disapproval and condemnation. Grace is God looking at us—in the middle of the blame we've placed on ourselves for our wrong choices, and our false guilt over the choices of our incarcerated loved one—and saying, "Let it go. I've got that covered. Shame off you. Grace on you." Jason was drenched in grace when he humbly arrived at the place where he could say, "I began to make an idol out of my ability to protect my stepdaughters, instead of trusting in God alone." In one of his letters he wrote:

I was wrong. My arrogant pride and self-righteousness allowed me to embrace Christ for eternity in heaven, but I had little trust in Him for the here and now. I now know to my core that I not only can't make it into heaven without Him; I can't make it tomorrow or the next day or even the next five minutes. I thought I was protecting my stepdaughters, but in reality I trusted and counted on myself—and the result was devastation and death. My sins made me in dire need of a Savior. I don't ever need less grace than anyone else. I prayed, "God forgive me for taking the life of the father of my girls. I'm appalled by what I did. I'm beaten down, hurting, and sick of trying to make it on my own. I need you. God, I'm crawling back to you."

My son is still living with the harsh reality of the punishment for his actions. But he has been thoroughly and completely covered by the grace of God. It's evident in the letters he writes, the way he interacts with visitors, the proactive way he encourages other inmates, and the way he lives his Christian life.

Throughout this book, I've discussed the sorrow, shame, fear, pain, exhaustion, and never-ending emotional journey of being the family member of an incarcerated person. I pray that one of your takeaways is this: *let go of shame, take hold of grace.* God has said, "My grace is sufficient for you, for my power is made perfect in weakness" (2 Corinthians 12:9). That's why Paul, the man who recorded those words in the Bible, could say, "Therefore I will boast all the more gladly about my weaknesses, so that Christ's power may rest on me."

The next time you blow it—when you have to go to God and say, "Soakers again, God, my feet just won't do what my mind says it wants to"—know that He will still have enough grace for you.

## HIS WORDS OVER YOU

"Dear friends, I declare that my grace, freely given to you, makes you whole and complete. This was accomplished when my Son died on the cross to free you from the penalty of your sins. I am giving you grace and peace."

*Based on Romans 3:23–25 and John 14:27*

# 88. Tell Your Own Story

*God is able to take the mess of our past and turn it into a message.*
*He takes the trials and tests and turns them into a testimony.*
CHRISTINE CAINE

Once we get through the shocking reality of the arrest, conviction, and sentencing of our loved one, we have a big decision to make. Will we hide as much of the story as possible, hoping no one in our work, church, and social circles will hear about it? Or will we bring up the subject honestly, admitting the truth of what happened and discussing what we've learned in the process of this unwanted, and in most cases, unexpected, situation?

Over the past few years, I've received many comments and questions on this issue:

- "You were already a public speaker before your son was arrested, so it's easier for you to speak up about your story."
- "I'm afraid my neighbors wouldn't allow their children to play with my kids if they knew my oldest son is in prison for molesting a child."
- "I hate being judged, and I think most people would shun me if they knew I was a convicted felon."
- "Hearing you tell your story helped me to move forward, but I'm too afraid to tell mine. I live in a constant state of anxiety, wondering if people in my building have heard rumors about my wife's incarceration for fraud."
- "I actually moved my family to a different state, hoping to start over in a place where no one had heard about my husband's arrest for armed robbery."

We have many more reasons for keeping the truth about our journey hush-hush. Most of our reasons revolve around fear: What will the repercussions be if we "go public" with our story? But that's a scary way to live our lives, never knowing when the truth will be revealed, destroying that invisible protective bubble we've tried to place around ourselves.

---

I've discovered the benefits of telling our story far outweigh the liabilities, if we can just find the courage to move forward. You may not tell your story from a public platform like I do, but you'll have many opportunities to speak to individuals or small groups in an open and honest way. Here are some practical ideas for preparing your story for others to hear:

1. Pray first. Ask God for the courage to proceed and for wisdom about what to include.
2. Determine your aim. What is your goal in telling your story? If you're a Christian, it will no doubt be to give other people hope—the hope that God will also work in the midst of their hard circumstances too. Part of your goal might be to lead people to the point of choosing to follow Jesus.
3. Be alert to the right timing. Before my son's trial, I needed to be very careful about saying anything publicly that could affect the legal process. One-on-one or in small groups I would say, "We are in the middle of a gigantic family crisis. I'm not free to share the details at this time, but I would appreciate your prayers." That way, people who had heard rumors about our son's arrest knew I was honestly addressing the fact that something bad had happened. I wasn't hiding it.
4. Talk about your life before the arrest of your loved one.
5. Explain what landed your loved one in jail, and the emotional, spiritual, financial, and physical challenges you've experienced as a result of your inmate's actions. Be as concise as possible. When our emotions are connected to our stories, we can be long-winded.
6. Speak about what you've learned as a result of this life detour. What unexpected benefits have you discovered? What Bible verses helped you hold on to hope?
7. Decide what action step you want your listeners to take. For them to share their own hard stories, or to choose faith instead of fear, or to be intentional about showing compassion to others, or to lead them in a prayer to accept Jesus? Be specific. People usually follow through when they know what to do.
8. Finish with a hope-filled thought, challenge, or quotation. I like to highlight what Pastor Max Lucado has said: "The past does not have to be your prison. You have a voice in your destiny. You have a say in your life. You have a choice in the path you take."

So how will you begin? It's best to work on the introduction of your story after you know what your complete presentation will be. Often, my introduction is this: "How many of you have had your life turn out differently from what you were expecting?" Almost 100 percent of the hands go up.

If you speak to a world in pain, you will always have an audience. When we share our stories, we give people around us an opportunity to speak of their own unexpected challenges. We develop a bond with others and a risk-free environment for people to say, "This is what happened to me." And God can use these times to bring about much good. The Bible character, Paul, wrote this while he was in prison: "I want you to know, my dear brothers and sisters, that everything that has happened to me here has helped to spread the Good News" (Philippians 1:12 NLT).

You may think you could never speak about your family's experience, but perhaps you can use these suggestions and *write* about it. If you'd like training in either case, consider attending the Speak Up Conference. Annually, I host an event that will help you to put your story into spoken or written form. You'll find additional information at www.SpeakUpConference.com.

Will telling your story be easy? No. Will you sometimes be anxious, fearful of what people might think? Probably. Is it worth it? Absolutely! I find great encouragement from God's words in Isaiah 41:10: "So do not fear, for I am with you; do not be dismayed, for I am your God. I will strengthen you and help you; I will uphold you with my righteous right hand."

## HIS WORDS OVER YOU

"When it comes to presenting a message of hope to others, you may feel like the least qualified, but I will see to it that you are equipped. Lean on me and I will do more through your story than you could ever imagine or request in your wildest dreams. I do this not by pushing you around, but by working within you, deeply and gently, by my Spirit."

*Based on Ephesians 3:7–8, 20–21*

# 89. Join the Adventure

*The only way to live in this adventure—with all its
danger and unpredictability and immensely high stakes—
is an ongoing, intimate relationship with God.*

JOHN ELDREDGE

When Gene and I got married, I thought I loved adventure—but by the time Jason was in his preteen years, watching the way my husband and son engaged in new experiences, I realized I had a lot to learn. We lived near Lake Huron, and my guys greatly enjoyed our secondhand Sunfish sailboat—falling off, getting up again, trying over and over to stay atop the rough waves. They loved hiking in Canadian provincial parks and running or taking long bike rides together.

One summer our family made a trip out west to Yosemite National Park. We rented a cabin and got settled before our explorations would begin the next day. Gene and Jason laid out our gear—caps, sunglasses, snacks, water, sunscreen, and insect repellent—so we could get an early start. The next morning, following a pancake breakfast, we were off to climb to the top of Lower Yosemite Falls. The weather was perfect and the path was level and easy for the first mile; however, the second mile was exhausting—all uphill. But we were psyched for the trip, and every so often we heard Jason yelling, "Hey, Mom and Dad, come and look at the view. This is awesome!"

We finally reached the summit and saw a panorama of breathtaking beauty. It was invigorating to feel the spray from the Lower Falls and hear the distant roar of the Upper Falls. Jason was energized, and Gene said, "It's only two more miles to the top of the Upper Falls. Can we do it?" We agreed to try.

Two miles of switchbacks made this trail much more grueling. The sun was hot and we were sweating profusely. It took three more hours to reach our new destination, where we heard the deafening sound of the Upper Falls. We were surprised to learn that the edge of the falls wasn't fenced off and walking to that point was not forbidden. Gene and Jason discovered pipes embedded in the rock, allowing hikers to hold on, lean over the falls, and take in the view—about a half mile above the valley floor! (I didn't join them for that part of the adventure.)

There was a pool near the edge of the falls just before the water plunged over the cliff. As we relaxed nearby, I noticed a sign that said, "If You Swim in These Waters, You Will Die!" We laughed about the bluntness of the warning. That would be more adventure than we cared to pursue. [43]

———

*Adventure* is a unique word. It means "an undertaking usually involving danger and unknown risks."[44] It can also refer to an exciting or remarkable experience. You and I have certainly experienced the "exciting or remarkable" adventures—some have included personal successes, proud family moments, and dreams for the future. However, our experience with the incarceration of a family member has often felt like a frightening foray into dangerous, risky places. There have been times when I cried out the Bible verse, "Rise up and help us; rescue us" (Psalm 44:26).

Like it or not, we're on a journey that will only end in God's good time. So how can we put the dangerous and frightening part of this adventure behind us, and move into the exciting and remarkable part of our journey with God?

- Get to know Him more personally by studying the Bible. "I gain understanding from your precepts" (Psalm 119:104).
- Follow His guidelines for living a life that matters. "I will instruct you and teach you in the way you should go" (Psalm 32:8).
- Look for ways you can assist others and your loved one. Expect the result to be joy. "I have told you this so that my joy may be in you and that your joy may be complete" (John 15:11).

Our personal and spiritual adventures often take us down unanticipated paths, and we find obstacles that seem to stand in the way of our happiness. However, when we look back in the rearview mirror of time, we realize that each barrier simply challenged us to get to know God more intimately. We've seen Him dispelling our fears and pushing us toward a different adventure than we first anticipated.

## HIS WORDS OVER YOU

"When you join my adventure and listen to my voice, I will be the One who rescues you. Allow me to be your rock of refuge and your fortress. Don't be afraid or discouraged. Be strong and courageous. I will be with you wherever you go."

*Based on Psalm 31:2 and Joshua 1:9*

---

43. Adapted from Carol Kent, *Between a Rock and a Grace Place* (Grand Rapids: Zondervan, 2010), 171–72.

44. Merriam-Webster.com. "adventure." http://www.merriam-webster.com/dictionary /adventure.

# 90. Together Forever

*Something more is coming. . . . Everything in Scripture points to Eternity, and everything within us cries out for it. [God's] work with us is not finished in this life.*

RAY STEDMAN

Through these devotionals, we've had daily contact for the past three months. Although we haven't met in person, I feel like I know your concerns, your stresses, your broken places, and your fears about what the future holds for you and your loved one. I hope you've found it encouraging to endure hard things with someone who understands what you're going through.

By now you know my faith is extremely important to me. It has helped me through every step of the journey, and it will in years to come. My son is still incarcerated for the rest of his life.

One day I was talking to Cheryl, the sister of a "lifer." She told me, "I had the most unusual dream. As a Christian I believe that one day Jesus will return to earth and that all of those who believe in Him will be miraculously transported to heaven." I nodded, and she went on. "In my dream I was almost at heaven's gates. I looked to my left and saw a group of inmates. They were dressed in prison jumpsuits and each of them was in handcuffs, attached to waist chains. They were also in ankle shackles. As I was watching, the gates of heaven opened and the chains fell off the inmates, and together, we walked into a place much better than this one."

I wiped away tears, and so did Cheryl. "It was a very short dream," she exclaimed, "but I feel like it was God's way of reminding me that when we have a personal faith in Jesus Christ and our incarcerated loved one knows Him, even a life sentence is not the end of the story. We'll be together forever in heaven. That thought makes it possible for me to get through my hardest days. I don't know exactly when the shackles will fall off or precisely how we'll get there, but I know one day those of us who follow Christ will live in freedom—*home at last!*"

During our time together, we looked at John 14:2–3 in the Bible. In those verses, Jesus says, "My Father's house has many rooms; if that were not so, would I have told you that I am going there to prepare a place for you? And if I go and prepare a place for you, I will come back and take you to be with me that you also may be where I am."

That day Cheryl encouraged me to look ahead to a better future.

We know life is hard—for us and for our incarcerated loved ones. We will continue to find bumps in the road with family difficulties, financial stresses, other people's criticisms, and legal issues. As we look ahead, let's quickly review some of the things we've covered:

- Accept the encouragement and compassion of others. Going through tough stuff together is always easier than facing it alone.
- Develop a heart of gratitude. Remember to thank God and those around you for all they've done. "In every thing give thanks" (1 Thessalonians 5:18 KJV).
- Prioritize your own well-being. Take breaks, without feeling guilty, when you need to recharge.
- Use visitation times to grow closer as a family. Talk about current events, family memories and milestones, and spiritual concerns.
- Advocate for your loved one. Always remember to show respect for the corrections officers and the guidelines of the jail or prison.
- Forgive and be forgiven. Don't forget that this is a process.
- Seek advice from others who have walked this path. Prayerfully decide what advice to keep and to discard.
- Allow this experience to draw you closer to God and to each other. Look forward expectantly to the freedom that awaits you and your loved one in heaven.

You and I have a decision to make. Will we wait with hope, allowing the interruption of incarceration to make us more loving, more compassionate, and more in tune with God? Or will we wait with anger, allowing resentment to fester within us? Whatever you're experiencing on your journey—no matter how difficult the challenge is today, next week, or next year—God's grace can make all the difference.

Turn to Him, draw close to Him, and allow Him to fill your life with His love, joy, and peace. Keep your eyes focused on eternity, where you'll be together forever with your loved one—in complete and perfect freedom.

### HIS WORDS OVER YOU

"You haven't met me face-to-face yet, but that doesn't make any difference. I'm on your side, right beside you. You're not in this alone. Keep looking forward with hope to the wonderful day when I'll return."

*Based on Colossians 2:1 and Titus 2:13*

# ACKNOWLEDGMENTS

From the beginning, this was a uniquely special project. The Discovery House publishing team came to me with an idea to write a devotional for the families of inmates. This devotional would describe my own journey through the arrest, trial, conviction, and sentencing of my son, Jason, while including practical and spiritual encouragement for others. We agreed that there were very few resources for people thrust into unexpected and unwanted circumstances due to the wrong choices of their loved ones.

On a beautiful July day I met with Discovery House's then publisher, Carol Holquist, executive editor, Miranda Gardner, and acquisitions editor, Andrew Rogers, in Pentwater, Michigan. Over lunch we began discussing the topics a book like this would need to address and what format would be the most helpful. Andy was tireless in his passion for this project, and together, we created a book proposal that the Discovery House publishing team warmly embraced.

I'm deeply grateful to Andy for his extraordinary direction, guidance, and creativity from the time this manuscript was in the first stages of development throughout the writing process. He researched the need and understood how underresourced most jail and prison ministries are with regard to firsthand accounts of this process: from the beginning stage "when the news is fresh," to the wait for resolution, to advocating for loved ones, to learning to nurture our own physical and spiritual lives throughout the unwanted stresses. Andy's relentless commitment to this project reminds me that when Christians see a need and say, "I will be the one to *do* something to help," ideas become realities and positive results emerge. Thanks, Andy!

My family has been a major support during this project. Thanks go to my husband, Gene, for his help with household and ministry tasks while I wrote, for supplying me with lots of coffee, for providing humor when I needed a break, and for sharing generously from his personal journals. Thanks also go to my son, Jason, for his honest responses to my questions, his firsthand insights on incarceration, and for the gut-wrenching entries from his letters. Jason, thank you for allowing other families to benefit from what we've learned throughout your incarceration—this book is powerful because of your understanding of the genuine needs of inmates and their loved ones. I am also grateful to my sisters and brother, who are an ongoing encouragement to me, and my mother, Pauline Afman, who prayed for me during every laborious day of writing.

I am deeply grateful to several inmates and to many family members of prisoners who allowed me to use excerpts from their letters and gave me permission to share their experiences. Their honesty made this book ring with authenticity.

Thanks go to Sandi Banks and Kathy Blume for their prayers, along with many other friends who also prayed for me during the long months of writing. I failed to anticipate the emotional toll of reliving such a personally devastating experience, and I felt like I was "carried" by the prayers of God's people.

Finally, thanks go to the gifted publishing team at Discovery House! Content editor Paul Muckley admits to giving me a little heartburn— but I grew to deeply appreciate how thorough his edits were. Paul dares to ask the hard questions and his relentless commitment to excellence made the finished project extraordinary. Thanks, Paul! You made me a better writer. Josh Mosey, marketing manager, is visionary in his pursuit of getting the message of this book into the hands of the intended readers. It's been a privilege to brainstorm with you, Josh!

Most of all, I say "thank you" to my Lord Jesus Christ, for walking with me through the firestorm of my son's incarceration. He has given me a message that burns in my heart, fresh energy to speak and write, a renewed hope for each day, and a joy that endures.

is a nonprofit organization that seeks
to live out the principle of Proverbs 31:8–9.

*Speak up for the people who have no voice,*
*For the rights of all the down-and-outers.*
*Speak out for justice!*
*Stand up for the poor and destitute!*

**Vision:** To help inmates and their families adjust to their *new normal.*

**Mission:** We exist to provide hope to inmates and their families through encouragement and resources.

It is the goal of Speak Up for Hope to give hope to the hopeless, encouragement and strength to the weary, reparation to marriages that have been torn apart by incarceration, and mental, spiritual, and physical stability to the children of prisoners.

We pray that people all over the world will begin speaking up for those who cannot speak up for themselves. As people become the hands and feet of Jesus to "the least of these," something miraculous happens. As we choose to get personally involved by giving, volunteering, and praying, we are transformed from the inside out as we model for others how to become hope givers.

GENE, CAROL, AND JASON KENT

For more information on the variety of ways
in which you can be involved
in Speak Up for Hope, please contact:

**Speak Up for Hope**
P.O. Box 6262
Lakeland, FL 33807-6262

Make tax-deductible contributions payable to Speak Up for Hope,
or donations can be made online at SpeakUpforHope.org.

### Resources from Carol Kent for Families of Inmates:

*When I Lay My Isaac Down* (NavPress)

*A New Kind of Normal* (Thomas Nelson)

*Between a Rock and a Grace Place* (Zondervan)

*Unquenchable: Grow a Wildfire Faith that
Will Endure Anything* (Zondervan)

All of these resources are available at CarolKent.org.

To book Carol for speaking engagements, call 586-481-7661
or request additional information at CarolKent.org.

For information on the Speak Up Conference, go to
SpeakUpConference.com.

To learn more about the nonprofit organization Gene and Carol
have launched, go to SpeakUpforHope.org.

# ABOUT THE AUTHOR

Carol Kent is a best-selling author and international speaker. With vulnerable openness, irrepressible hope, restored joy, and a sense of humor, she directs you to choices based on God's truth. Carol says, "When God writes your story, you will be in for the adventure of a lifetime!"

She is the president of Speak Up Speaker Services, a Christian speakers' bureau, and the founder and director of the Speak Up Conference, a ministry committed to helping Christians develop their speaking and writing skills. She and her husband, Gene, have founded the nonprofit organization Speak Up for Hope, which benefits inmates and their families. Carol holds a master's degree in communication arts and a bachelor's degree in speech education.

Carol has trained Christian speakers for over twenty-five years and she's been a featured speaker at Women of Faith, Extraordinary Women, and Women of Joy arena events. She is the author of over twenty books, including the bestselling *When I Lay My Isaac Down* and *Becoming a Woman of Influence*. Her newest books are titled *Unquenchable* and *Waiting Together*.

On her at-home days, Carol enjoys cooking for her grand girls, Chelsea and Hannah, sunset walks with her husband, and indulging in chocolate-covered potato chips.

# NOTE TO THE READER

The publisher invites you to share your response to the message of this book by writing Discovery House, P.O. Box 3566, Grand Rapids, MI 49501, U.S.A. For information about other Discovery House books, music, or DVDs, contact us at the same address or call 1-800-653-8333. Find us online at dhp.org or send e-mail to books@dhp.org.